Social Inclusion, Human Development
and Nation Building in Nepal

Social Inclusion, Human Development *and* Nation Building *in* NEPAL

DHRUBA KUMAR

Vajra Books
www.vajrabooks.com.np

Published & Distributed by

Vajra Books

Jyatha, Thamel, P.O. Box 21779, Kathmandu, Nepal
Tel.: 977-1-4220562, Fax: 977-1-4246536
e-mail: bidur_la@mos.com.np
www.vajrabooks.com.np

First Published 2013

ISBN 978-9937-623-08-7

Printed in Nepal

To
BHIM BAHADUR TAMANG
(1991-2069 BS)

Saluting the man and his sterling morale

Contents

List of Tables
and Figure

List of Abbreviations

ADB	Asian Development Bank
APF	Armed Police Force
BBC	British Broadcasting Corporation
CA	Constituent Assembly
CBS	Central Bureau of Statistics
CPN (UML)	Communist Party of Nepal (United Marxist-Leninist)
CPN-Maoist	Communist Party of Nepal-Maoist (Vaidya Group)
GDI	Gender Development Index
GDP	Gross Domestic Product
FIR	First Information Report
GEM	Gender Empowerment Measure
HDI	Human Development Index
HEI	Human Empowerment Index
HPI	Human Poverty Index
ICRs	Indian Currency Rupees
IGP	Inspector General of Police
IMF	International Monetary Fund
INGOs	International Non-Governmental Organizations
LDO	Local Development Officer
LIC	Low Income Country
LSGA	Local Self-Government Act

MDGs	Millennium Development Goals
MPI	Multidimensional Poverty Index
MWCSW	Ministry of Women, Children and Social Welfare
NC	Nepali Congress
NEFIN	National Federation for Indigenous Nationalities
NGOs	Non-Governmental Organizations
NIWF	Nepal Indigenous Women's Federation
NPC	National Planning Commission
PAF	Poverty Alleviation Fund
PMO	Prime Minister's Office
PRSP	Poverty Reduction Strategy Paper
ODA	Official Development Assistance
LGBT	Lesbian, gay, bisexual and transgender
Ka.	Comrade
SIRF	Social Inclusion Research Fund
SPI	Social Protection Index
SSR	Security Sector Reform
TMLP	Tarai Madhesh Loktantrik Party
UCPN (Maoist)	Unified Communist Party of Nepal (Maoist)
UN	United Nations
UNDP	United Nations Development Programme
UNMIN	United Nations Mission in Nepal
USD	United States Dollar
WB	World Bank
WOREC	Women's Rehabilitation Centre

Acknowledgements

The progenitor of this study is the report I wrote on social inclusion. That was an independent study commissioned by the EPN-II Project of ADB-Ministry of Finance, Nepal. That report was confined to the prescribed Terms of Reference (TOR). However, this publication is the thoroughly revised and updated version of my previous report without changing the original thrust. The arguments developed in this study are the result of several years of probing on the subject. I am intellectually indebted to those who had generously contributed to broadening my perspectives on the related issues.

Sincere thanks to Mr. Lal KC, the Chief of the Full Bright Consultancy for providing me with the two months (April-May 2010) contract to prepare the report; also to Shahid Parwez, Programmes/Project Implementation Officer, Nepal Resident Mission, Asian Development Bank (ADB). Team Leader: Prof. Parthiveshwor P. Timilsina, Coordinator: Prof. Dilli Ram Dahal and, Reviewer: Prof. Kailash N. Pyakuryal individually deserves my sincere gratitude. Prof. Dahal has gone through the entire raw manuscript providing valuable suggestions. Appraisal of the last three chapters is done by Col. JP Cross.

I am indebted to Prof. Pyakuryal in raising certain relevant issues in relation to the reasons of income inequality as well as facts corrupting policy incoherence. Constructive but critical comments of the reviewers during the workshops are also well taken and incorporated where appropriate. The generous help Prof. Bishwambher Pyakuryal has provided with some significant materials for the study and suggestion while revising the draft is gratefully appreciated.

Indebted to Mahendra P. Shrestha, Secretary, and Ratna Kaji Bajracharya, Joint Secretary of the Ministry of Women, Children and Social Welfare, Government of Nepal. Dipendra Pant of Full Bright Consultancy, coordinating research logistics from the Ministry of Finance, deserves thank. Two Workshops held on 27 August 2010 in Kathmandu and 22 November 2010 in Chitwan amongst the stakeholders were useful. Presentation at this Focused Group Discussions (FGD) had drawn adequate responses from the participants. Relevant comments and ideas floated in the workshops are duly incorporated in the final draft. The National Seminar was held on 29 April 2011 at Hotel Everest, Kathmandu, to wrap up the project launched as the EPN-II. Appreciate the enthusiastic participants.

This study was completed before the publication of the Preliminary Report on the National Census 2011 by the Central Bureau of Statistics, Government of Nepal. However, while revising the draft, some new census data are used in the text and the notes as well for comparison with the old data without changing the mode of overall analysis.

This study is published to encourage an open and informed debate on the issue of crucial importance to Nepali future. I am beholden by the unstinting support of my publisher Bidur Dongol of the Vajra Books for turning the crude manuscript into a readable book. The usual disclaimer, however, applies.

I
Introduction

Social inclusion has become a powerful concept for development in Nepal ever since it was formally determined that exclusion is the reason for perennial poverty and underdevelopment. Exclusion based on class, caste, ethnicity, language, gender, culture, religion and region is identified and discrimination against women, Dalits, indigenous people, ethnic, religious minorities and Madheshis recognized. Social inclusion is generally defined as a process of removing institutionalized social barriers and "the enhancement of incentives to increase the access of diverse individuals and groups to development opportunities" (World Bank/DFID2006: 9).

The Preamble of the Interim Constitution 2007 has promulgated a policy "to resolve the persistent problems related to class, caste, regional and gender for the progressive restructuring of the state" as the federal democratic republic along with provision for autonomous local self-government through elimination of the centralized and unitary state structure (Article 138 and 139). The focus of development thus has become human centric by "mainstreaming the poor and marginalized together with the ultra poor, vulnerable and deprived groups" as a crucial ingredient of poverty reduction strategy (NPC 2003: 41).

Poverty has long been problematized as inheritace of the successive generations of culturally and socially discriminated people. Social inclusion is an idea articulated for nothing except the provision of equal opportunity to the people irrespective of their caste in particular and gender based discrimination in general. Every policy document conceived on planning the future of Nepal has reiterated its firm commitment to inclusion and poverty reduction by upholding human rights as evident, for example, in the *Approach Paper for the Three Year Interim Plan* drafted by the National Planning Commission (NPC 2007: 74-93). Nepal is an unstable, low income and a high cost economy. According to the *World Development Report 2012*, it is the poorest country in Asia with an average 3.8 per cent GDP growth between 2000 and 2010 and USD 480 as per capita income (World Bank 2012).

Poverty is the consequence of 'capability deprivation' (Sen 2000a; Sen 2000b) the implication of which could be vulnerability leading to insecurity, defencelessness, and exposure to risks and shocks (Chambers 1989) affecting the notion of human security defined as 'freedom from want and freedom from fear' (Haq 1996; UNDP 1994). Vulnerability of the people to the 'risks and shocks' of challenges to their life chances can be traced in the 'post-conflict' situation facing trauma and economic hardship by the internally displaced people (IDPs) and particularly by the widows and the orphans who had lost their breadwinner to the violent conflict.[1]

The impact of the violent political upheaval has been noted by Bina Pradhan as the pulsating phenomenon of feminization of agriculture and localization of poverty with systemic increase in female labour force in family farm that is never accounted for economic activity and female-headed households exacerbated by insurgency (Pradhan 2006: 113-14). Although the social sufferings of the people from the insurgency could be understated, unacknowledged and numerically insignificant, insecurity featuring social exclusion could be an addition to the penury and misery of the people of Nepal. Social inclusion therefore has become a post-conflict recovery agenda.

Nepal has long been identified as a country with chronic poverty and underdevelopment. Poverty is obviously characterized by vulnerabilities related to life chances and physical survival of the people. With increasing socioeconomic tensions, gender discrimination and violence reflected in gang rape and child labour, human trafficking and possible AIDs spread; the appalling inequality between the rich and the poor coupled with the armed insurgency have become the poverty syndrome in Nepal. Implacable poverty and social discrimination have been defined as causes of the Maoist insurgency in Nepal. There is a persistent fear of poverty-violence and insecurity nexus leading to state collapse. Stagnant economy and increasing instances of poverty are the consequence of insurgency. Deepening dependency on foreign aid is the devastating consequence of underdeveloped economy in the country. Yet foreign aid has failed to defeat poverty, rather it has helped expanding corruption and perpetuating dependency. Foreign funds, though increased pressure for poverty alleviation, have mostly fallen in the wrong hands compromising both state autonomy and capacity to deliver. In their study, *The Tangled Web: The Poverty-Insecurity Nexus* published in 2007, Lael Brainard, Derek Chollet and Vinca LaFleur assert,

> Extreme poverty exhausts governing institutions, depletes resources, weakens leaders, and crushes hope fueling a volatile mix of desperation and instability. Poor, fragile states can explode into violence or implode into collapse, imperiling their citizens, regional neighbors, and the wider world as livelihoods are crushed, investors flee, and ungoverned territories become a spawning ground for global threats like terrorism, trafficking, environmental devastation, and disease.

Poverty leads to insecurity which cannot be generally comprehended. Induced by economic shocks – more than institutional or political causes – poverty engenders violence as poor do not have choices between economic and political rights (Brainard and Chollet 2007). Unpromising geographical situation as the landlocked country lying in the periphery of the periphery and resource lag was considered to have cast Nepal into an inescapable poverty trap.[2] It is not that people are lazy and unproductive, unable or unwilling to work, thus, they are poor. Rather it is the working people actually constituting a significant proportion of the chronically poor. The largest group of persistently poor people in Nepal are casual agricultural workers, farm labourers; either landless or near-landless, and wages dependent groups, marginalized and excluded people of low caste status or girls and women. Gender discrimination in labour wages has continued to keep the weaker sex poor. They are paid less mostly in unorganized sectors. This work force remains neglected and its contribution invisible even in industrial set up. Despite the legislations on equal opportunity and contractual obligations for women employees, a fair deal is absent at the work place. For example, child labour and women are exploited at Carpet and Garment factories with low wages and long hours of work as well.

Besides this common feature, it was also diagnosed that poverty becoming a crisis has a different dimension. This crisis has further deepened by the state policies of social deprivation leading to the struggle for basic needs of the people with the widening gap between agricultural productivity and the rate of population growth (Seddon 1987; Blaikie, Cameron and Seddon 1980). The slash and burn agriculture practices have hardly meet the sustenance need of a majority of peasants. Land was central to the common bonding among the people in the family and social cohesion despite land being the main reason for family feuds and social disruption as well. Land fragmentation has driven successive generation of population out of the farm land. As per the data, 25 per cent of Nepali people are landless (UNDP 2004:176).

Landlessness as an acute problem (Shrestha 1990) remains the undeniable sign of poverty in agrarian Nepal, which, in the words of Amartya Sen (2000: 13-14), is instrumental deprivation generating economic and social exclusion. Landlessness and poverty are the condition of human suffering as a case of social deprivation. The *Kamaiya* system prevalent in the Western Tarai till the turn of the last century was a situation caused by the landlessness that had become a living monument of human suffering. The *Kamlari* (related to women) system is yet to go. The bonding of the landless people with the land was the illustrious case of slavery in other name despite slavery was abolished early in the 20th Century Nepal. Land is privy to the few notwithstanding land reform programme was launched back in 1963 with iron-fist. Farm income is shrinking; non-farm income sources for the rural population are precariously few. The rural poor tend to depend on sale of their labour for mere survival. Thus the rural poverty is fundamentally the cause of landlessness of the majority and the absence of alternative to the farm work in the villages.

Historians have recorded the reason behind the formation of the Nepali state was the "land-military complex" (Stiller 1975; Regmi 1995). This has continued to be so after every political upheaval; land is the precious property and prized possession for political elites and commoners as well. Land grab, therefore, continues as the policy priority of the people associated with the power elites in Nepal. Dissociation from the land ownership has led to deprivation and destitution of the multitude of peasantry. In the social matrix, the status of a person, for long, has been particularly determined by the individual's relationship to the land. Migratory flow of the people too relates to their relationship with land as exemplified by cobblers leaving their villages reasonably because of "increasing loss of land to the Brahmins through mortgages or sale" in Western Nepal (Caplan 1972: 41) or the loss of *kipat* system to Brahmins through its abolition by the government in Eastern Nepal (Caplan 1970). Crucially linked to this fact of life is the prevalence of Hinduism as a religion determining the social status of people characterized by caste and race defining hierarchical mode of relationships.

Development scholars have lately recognized that the persistent poverty in Nepal cannot be understood only by unravelling economic factors. It requires a closer understanding of multiple facets of poverty by examining the social structure permeated traditionally by structural violence (Galtung 1969) caused by the exclusionary policies of the state. Acknowledged widely as the most unequal country socially, economically, and regionally Nepal remains a poverty pocket in the world. The NPC acknowledges that "persistent poverty and inequalities have provided a fertile breeding ground for the crisis" (NPC 2003: 35). This statement reflects the collective perception on poverty of national power elite enjoying influence in the national decision making process through policymaking.

Poverty is, thus, defined and explained as one of the crucial reasons for the decade-long armed violence in Nepal. Indiscriminate killings had however reverse impact on numerous rural households by robbing them from the bread earners and resulting into households headed by women. The political-economy of armed violence was also an additional burden to the people in general; extortion, taxation and fund raising by the Maoist under different pretext had adverse impact on the fixed income group as well as working class. Thus poverty, in its definitional mode, has graduated from simply an economic to a political and sociological concept and as a factor determining human relationships.

Defining poverty, however, is slippery. Poverty measures done on the basis of diverse criteria too result differently. Poverty is also defined with the adjectives such as perennial or chronic. These are the poverty characteristics. There is, thus, no safe way to conclude the absolute level of poverty. The debates on measuring poverty as absolute or relative condition are yet inconclusive. Poverty measured on multidimensional criteria in the case of Nepal, for example, has resulted into a much wider scale of people falling below poverty line than the official estimates (OPHI 2010). People, in general, do not believe what the government estimate suggests. The distrust of the government is the common problem.

The government's claim of poverty declining to the level of 25 per cent of the population is disputed by the independent study conducted by the OPHI in 2010 suggesting 65 per cent of Nepali people are below poverty line. Poverty level too varies on account of the measures applied for estimates. The World Bank USD1.25 a day makes 56 per cent and its USD 2.0 a day income makes 78 per cent of people living under poverty line in Nepal in comparison to different estimates of the MPI and the NPC. These estimates reached are based on the method adopted. The range of indicators identified by the "human development index" of the United Nations has however helped understanding poverty in comparative terms within the state.

The objective of this study is setting national priorities, for example, for meeting MDGs by integrating aspirations, goals and resources. I have used both authoritative and publicly available general material sources to argue the case; nevertheless, data from my extensive field works conducted on the related issues in the past are also liberally incorporated in sustaining the arguments.

Popular aspirations have been gathering mass and momentum that has transformed into goals in Nepal with the explicit role of government in making these goals both situational and social requisite. Goals and aspirations are set against the social milieu reflecting on the need of building human capital through social inclusion for human development and nation building. This study intends to examine the interrelationships of these three conceptual variables and explicate how these can be mutually complicit with contributing to equity and social justice through poverty reduction in Nepal. Attempting to ensure poverty reduction can be seen as an investment on human capital that will make for a more productive society with properly trained and mentally aware people to contribute to national economy.

Social inclusion, therefore, has become the anti-poverty agenda. It is at the heart of the decision for human development.

Social inclusion is primarily a process of nation building which is antithetical to state building as the latter is presumably a process of promoting the authority of establishing and maintaining the state apparatuses to regulate and control the defined order. Building up the state with well functioning public institution is the concern of the Western countries to preserve their security interests that Fukuyama has promoted classifying the weak, fragile and failed states could become a serious challenge to international stability as the 9/11 indicates. State building, as Fukuyama (2004) asserts, is the process for "the creation of new government institutions and strengthening of existing ones". Primarily based on the use of force state building is a process that consciously strives at forming a new relationship by destroying the old by centralizing power and homogenizing cultural identity. Culturocide is the concept behind state building that destroys diversity. Nation building celebrates diversity by upholding multiculturalism. Zaum (2007: 16 fn) thus says, "State building refers to the establishment of institutions of government in a society, while the term nation building implies the creation of a nation, addressing issues of identity rather than government". Social inclusion, in this respect, becomes integral to cementing social cohesion in a multicultural state.

The major contribution of this study will be the attempt to construct an interactive process for nation building through social inclusion and human development amidst the failure of assimilation and homogenization processes of state building in Nepal. The erstwhile Panchayat System had exemplified the acute failure of an endeavour for homogeneity with the slogan like "...*euitai bhakha, euitai besha*". That system controlled by monarchy had prefered selectariat rather than electorate, despite farcical elections were also held.

The campaign for state restructuring, therefore, should be understood as a consequence of the failure of state building by the monarchical regime. Though elitist approach in fostering homogenized ruling class with monopoly of power has continued unabated, democratic struggles have, however, challenged this tendency. Although the safest wayouts from the socially entangled historical issues are yet incomprehensible, the opening up of political space has definitely changed the texture of social relationships. Meanwhile, electoral politics has significantly altered the political landscape where competition matters. People are provided with honest choice; at least the rights to vote and decide. This way, the study advances beyond the grievance and victimization perspective of the research on social exclusion that, for instance, the World Bank/DFID 2006 and SIRF 2007 and 2009 had meritoriously undertaken.

Social inclusion, as a policy thrust, is fundamental to transformation of the Nepali state from a centralized and unitary structure to federalism with the objective of realizing pro-poor governance through power-sharing. Social inclusion as a concept is thus reinventing the state by broadening avenues of participation and representation of the hitherto excluded groups in the national mainstream. This political ambition requires to be situated within the socioeconomic and cultural context of the state and society. Changes in the exclusivist norms and practices to more inclusive and equitable behaviour are necessary. This could obviously lend support to concretize the objective of human development. Simply put, human development is to include 'missing people in development planning' (Haq 1996).

The 'missing people' in the Nepali context are those who were traditionally excluded in terms of gender, caste, geography and even religion by the dominant coalition of interest comprising the hill high caste groups by maintaining elite cohesion and denial of participation and representation to a large segment of society. Despite being a multicultural and multiethnic society the homogeneity in the composition of politico-bureaucratic-military and even business elites straddling different economic and social sectors has continued to dominate the national sphere. Initiatives have been taken to change this context with the introduction of the proportional representation system in Constituent Assembly (CA) elections (2008) in accordance with the provision of 'proportional inclusion' of all people in the state structure, as stipulated in the Interim Constitution 2007 (Article 33 [Gha1]). The constitutional approach enshrined in the directive principles and policies of the state would certainly be a reflection of undisputable state commitment contributing towards social inclusion imparting a sense of belonging together among hitherto excluded people. Belongingness is the sharing of the social space. And sharing signifies inclusion. Social inclusion therefore is integral to human rights; equality before the law governing the state; impartiality in social interactions inclusive of life sustaining opportunities with poverty reduction of the majority of people living on the margins.

In the post-Jana Andolan-II period, social inclusion has been a phenomenon in which democracy is rewarded with an adjective, making it inclusive democracy despite being contested as a concept. Thus *inclusive democracy* has joined the large family of more than 550 subtypes of democracy previously identified in some 150 published studies (Collier and Levitsky 1997: 430-51). For example, the classic note on democracy is the statement of the scholar Robert Dahl, who defines the government's responsiveness to the preferences of its citizens, considered as political equals with rights to inclusiveness and participation, as the key characteristic of democracy (Dahl 1971: 2). The task of achieving stability through institutionalizing democracy and overcoming hurdles of transition by legitimating authority, however, remains.

The multifaceted challenges of transition, commonly described as "the process or a period of changing from one stage or condition to another" (Oxford 2005:1631) are further complicated by the weak state structure, stunted economic growth and overwhelming dependency on external resources corresponding to the rising food and petroleum prices crippling the purchasing power of already poor and low income people. Carothers has pointed out that moving from an authoritarian to a democratic regime is one of the five core assumptions behind transition which is eventually followed by democratic consolidation. However tracking political processes is difficult in newly founded democracies as assumed perfectly under the transition paradigm (Carothers 2002: 6-8). Transition is also a period of striving for stability by legitimating the process of change by breaking with the past and building authority for the future. The transitional initiatives should not only be confined to political processes but it should also be focused on responding to the need of restructuring socioeconomic affairs of the state to cement and consolidate the process of political stability.

This study is divided into eight chapters. The introduction follows an overview of pattern and trend in poverty reduction undertaken by the government of Nepal in chapter II. Attempt is also made in this chapter to examine the correlation between poverty reduction and human development. The third chapter assesses the effect of the government policies on structural factors perceived as the prominent causes of inequality, poverty, denial and discrimination. The fourth chapter reviews the trend in budgetary allocations made by four post-Jana Andolan-II national budgets prioritizing social security and effects on target groups. The narratives, discussions and analyses that follow are data based to substantiate the arguments. The fifth chapter discusses the interrelationships between social inclusion and human development and its contribution to nation building. The sixth chapter assesses the social policies undertaken by the government in the recent past and their impact on the state and society.

Following this, the seventh chapter recounts some suggestions to the stakeholders, particularly to the government which is the driver for poverty alleviation through reducing social inequality and investing for human development. Transforming governance practice remains an imperative for nation building within the context of national reality. It points out to certain reasons why poverty persists and why is the gap widening? Why the number of poor is increasing despite the success of poverty reduction strategy? Is the government effective in reducing poverty? Central to the questions pertaining to social inclusion in promoting human development for nation building are the context and the situation facing the Nepali state, which is weak, infirm, and unstable with incompetent leadership making difficult the process of inclusive democracy.

Nation building is an indigenous process based on the creation of a new social order by integrating the multicultural and multiethnic people and transforming their status and identity to equality irrespective of sex, caste and creed. In other words, nation building is an inclusive process of restructuring the inherently exclusionary and exploitative state. Interrogating how a weak and fragile state deals with such agenda of state restructuring in the post-conflict situation, the study stresses on the necessity of social inclusion for preventing state failure. The potential output of this study would, therefore, be assessing the thrust of current policies of government in relations to the national priorities and its impact on poverty reduction and human development. The study reports how the agenda of social inclusion has influenced the development discourses questioning who really counts. Finally, this study closes with certain observation of the trends setting national polity and their likely impact on the future of nation building in Nepal.

Notes

1. Conservative estimates vary on the authenticity of the number of internally displaced people from around 60,000-70,000 to 300,000-400,000. So is the case with widows and orphans. However, the accepted figure for orphans is 8,000-10,000. The World Bank is understood to have initially provided USD50 million contribution in support of rehabilitation of the conflict affected families and other benefits to widows and families of those killed during the conflict.

2. All the *traps* defined by Collier in chapter two of his very insightful book also reflect the experience of Nepal (Collier 2007: 17-75).

II

An Overview of Poverty Pattern

Back in 1956 Nepal's first Five-Year Plan had a goal to "raise production, employment and *standards of living* ... thus opening out to the people opportunities for a richer and more satisfying life." The total financial outlay of that plan was a meager Rs. 330 million of which over 70 per cent was met by foreign aid. The main thrust behind that plan was community development conceptualized on the need of rural development where the real Nepal actually lies. That was the first exercise in the role of the state in national development process taking popular aspirations into consideration. The state capacity, however, was so limited that only Rs.215 million was spent in the entire plan period.

Decades after the first Five Year Plan was conceived and implemented with considerable expansion of the role of the state the focus of the national planning remains the same. For example, the main objective of the Tenth Plan (2002-2007) was also based on poverty reduction by "extending economic opportunities and opening new ones enlarging employment opportunities" to disadvantaged people. By recording the dwindling economic growth in the second half of the Ninth Plan (1997-2002), the Tenth Plan document had noted that the "absolute number of people living under poverty line is estimated to have increased" (NPC 2002:29) from over 38 per cent target level of the previous plan period. The performance of the Ninth Plan was considered dismal by the policymakers. "Crisis and underdevelopment" (Blaikie, Cameron and Seddon 1980) have long featured the human woes such as poverty in Nepal. Following this, a study has noted, "Poverty... has increased at an annual rate of three per cent and the number of absolute poor has almost doubled in the past 20 years" (NESAC 1998). Thus, Nepal has become a case of 'failed development' with increasing incidence of poverty along with record deaths from famine and starvation in the plan period (Panday 1999:90).

Embracing human development as an overarching goal, Nepal has aimed at a policy of social equity and equality ever since the planned development efforts were made in 1956. Rural poverty was a priori assumption made in the framework of rural development with priority given to agriculture and service sectors. Expansion of transport infrastructure was ingredients of national planning to overcome the challenges of accessibility in the mountainous country. Land reform was the *mantra* to vanish rural poverty.

The credit to initiate this programme for poverty alleviation was attributed to King Mahendra after the Royal coup in 1960, which resulted into tenants without entitlement to land, actually benefitting the landlords instead of the peasants. It perpetuated poverty as rural Nepal remains dominated by the landed gentry in alliance with the political class at the centre. Development discourses therefore ranged from "Back to Village National Campaign" (that almost coincided with the beginning of Cultural Revolution in China), "Unleash the Fountain of Development" to "Meet the Asian Standard" of living with provisions of Basic Needs coached by political overtones for social mobilization during the Panchayat decades. Despite advocacy of creating an "exploitationless society" by King Mahendra under the Panchayat system to vie with the Communist system around the world, the regime collapsed as its thrust becomes otherwise. Development aspirations, thus, were exceedingly translated into rhetoric letting national economy to plummet and stagnate.

The result was a meagre economy growing at the rate of 0.2 per cent per capita between 1960 and 1984. Though the Seventh Five Year Plan (1985-90) promised meeting of the Basic Needs to the people leading them to attend the Asian [living] Standard by the year 2000, the prospective economic future of Nepali citizens, however, was dismal. Official estimate of the per capita income of people increased by USD 60 between 1985 and 2000 reaching USD220 from the basic figure of USD 160 in 1984, the national economy was conspicuous without any encouraging signs. The average GDP growth rate of 4.2 per cent for over the past two decades since 1975 was not helpful in ameliorating poverty as population in the corresponding period grew at the rate of 2.25 per cent, thus undercutting the per capita growth. Again, the annual average growth in per capita income occurred not solely because of economic activities at home but because of remittance sent back by migrant workers along with the massive funds meted out by donors to sustain democracy in the decade of 1990s. Though the economy situation was more sluggish between 1995 and 2011 that grew on an average rate of 2.1 per cent per annum, the remittance helped the life style of the people change. Interestingly, the period almost covered the decade of the Maoist insurgency and over the half-decade of post-conflict Nepal.

Expectation of steadily rising living standard has been the built-in feature of national planning culture. Thus, the Eighth Five Year Plan (1992-97) formulated and implemented by the elected parliamentary government envisaged transforming the village into centre of development by attempting to channel a major chunk of national resources and public investment towards uplifting the state through a policy of decentralization for poverty alleviation (NPC 1992). Forming a "Poverty Alleviation Task Force" the government made combating poverty as one of the overarching objectives of the Eighth Plan. Following this, the "build your village yourself" programme targeting the village development ensued as the fundamental state policy (LDM 1995).

The Ninth Plan (1997-2002), for instance, had recognized the need to assimilate the long marginalized and downtrodden people (Janajatis and Dalits) in the national mainstream by exploring the possibility of their contribution to national development processes by utilizing their traditional artisan/ occupational skills as human capital, which may also help improve their socioeconomic condition. The Ninth Plan reinvented the potentiality of the human resources' use by upholding the 'downtrodden and oppressed community' as the 'asset of the country'. The national planners had acknowledged their 'occupational ability, knowledge and skill [as] significant resources for the country' asserting that the 'nation's overall development is possible only if their active participation is ensured' (NPC 1998: 712; UNDP 2004: 59-60).

Recognizing the 'resurgence of poverty and unemployment' commitments were thus made by the government to launch nationwide poverty reduction campaign "Bishweshwar among the poor" and rehabilitation programme like "Ganeshman Singh Peace Campaign". These initiatives taken by the government paralleled the Maoist insurgency were, in fact, the progenitor of the Poverty Alleviation Fund later established in 2003. It was a crucial departure from previous policy posturing of the government in Nepal in managing the human resources. But as development expenditure throughout the decade of 1990s increased only by 1.3 per cent in real terms and stood around 10.1 per cent declining from 13.3 per cent in 1991 to 8.4 per cent in 2000, the government under democracy had failed in sustaining 'rural self-reliance' development concept as a policy thrust in budgeting the state (Adhikari 2004: 129). The Directive Principles and Policies of the State of the Democratic Constitution 1990 had incorporated the premises of human development with sensitivities towards the creation of an equitable society where the rights of the people would be enforced as they became the ultimate source of national sovereignty.

Built on the concept of "Attacking Poverty" (World Bank 2000), the Tenth Plan made poverty reduction its central thrust adopting four pillar strategies for (a) broad based economic growth; (b) social sector development, including human development;(c) targeted programme, including social inclusion in order to bring the poor, ultra poor, vulnerable, deprived and marginalized groups into the mainstream of development; and (d) good governance. The four pillars in compact addresses a single problem – poverty defined to include 'income poverty, human poverty and exclusion' (NPC 2003: 41). The national priority therefore was clearly defined and target set making inclusive policies and resource allocation to address economic vulnerabilities of the people. Though balancing aspirations, goals and resources have always been a challenge for a developing country, democracy in Nepal however has made donors to respond favourably as poverty has become a threat and cause of insecurity in global positioning of international order. The anti-poverty agenda has become universal.

The Poverty Alleviation Fund (PAF), established in accordance with the third pillar of the Tenth Plan to reach the 'targeted groups' as the direct beneficiaries of the programme, has addressed the need of poor women, Dalits and Janajatis with formation of community organizations in which some 80 per cent of the members are chosen from the group and 50 per cent members constitute women. As claimed by the PAF, 8,423 community organizations have been formed throughout the country comprising 239,306 members of which 35 per cent are Dalits, 28 per cent Janajatis and 69 per cent are women. Among them are 69 per cent of members of 'hard core' poor who are unable to feed themselves even for three months a year (PAF 2009: xi). More than 300,000 women since 2004 have joined various community organizations under this programme constituting 74 per cent of total community members (World Bank 2012). The World Bank had initially provided with a fund of USD36 million for the programme by 31 December 2007. It has also provided a USD 100 million grant to the second phase of PAF programme covering a three year period beginning in 2008 till the end of 2009/10, in addition to the initial support (PAF 2009: xiii).

The PAF is extending its programmes to 15 more districts from FY 2010/11 in addition to the present 25 remote districts where it has already spent nearly Rs.6 billion in income generating works along with Rs.1.5 billion in infrastructure building. Satisfied with the effectiveness of the PAF, the World Bank has reportedly committed USD 200 million for three years programmes between 2012 and 2014 against the PAF's request of USD 320 million (Annapurna Post, 3 June 2010a). The PAF by now has announced a plan to issue the Poverty Identity Card to 7.2 million people (estimated 25.2 per cent of total population) living under poverty line within eight months beginning September 2012. The PAF Board has classified the poor into three categories: extremely poor, relatively poor, and generally poor and facilitate them accordingly (Kantipur, 12 September 2012a).

However, the PAF is thought as replication of other poverty related works at the highest level and utilization of resources was considered unsatisfactory. It is observed that the programme requires sensitization at the highest level and proper utilization of resources dispensed by preventing misuse and leakage (Republica 25 January 2010; Kantipur 27 January 2010). The situation, however, is grossly different. It has been reported that an intense pressure mounted by the UCPN (Maoist) to disburse the PAF budget in favour of the Maoist cadres has led to the resignation of the Vice Chairperson, former secretary of the Government of Nepal, Janak Raj Joshi, from the post (Kantipur, 28 December 2012b). It should be noted that the Chairperson of the PAF is the Maoist Vice-Chair and the caretaker Prime Minister Baburam Bhattarai, who has a very bad reputation of forsaking all the legal norms.

The livelihood and forestry programme working with the goal of reducing the vulnerability of the poor rural people and improving their livelihood condition (LFP 2005) is another important project among several other poverty alleviation programmes launched involving socially excluded groups. Central to these programmes is the participation of the target people for effective utilization of resources at disposal and mend their domestic needs. All these efforts are made for bettering the life of the common people who had endured a life with no substantial difference over the decades of development by beating poverty. Attacking poverty however requires first attacking cronyism, patrimonialism in addition to excessive corruption prevalent in the socioeconomic and political structure of the country.

Beating Poverty: Encouraging Trend

Public policies of the government have sensitized the need of poverty reduction under democracy that virtually coincided with the publication of the World Bank's two-pronged anti-poverty strategy report in 1990 (World Bank 1990). These strategies emphasized labour intensive growth along with investment in human resources tailor made for a less developed country like Nepal. They are also subsequently bolstered by the Bank's assistance strategies to reduce poverty (World Bank 1991). "Combating poverty" was the elan of the Eighth Plan (1992-97).

Based on its own assessment the government had however found deepening inequalities and widening poverty gap in the country. Measured in terms of incidence, intensity and severity, poverty expanded pervasively and the situation were further worsening in hills and mountains (NPC 2003: 26). This led to renewed efforts towards addressing the persistent human misery by designing the Poverty Reduction Strategy Paper (PRSP) under the Tenth Plan 2002-2007 for implementing programmes. Despite the absence of the local bodies and the stalling of the decentralization plan as imperative for poverty reduction programme, unfortunately, since 2002, Nepal has reportedly made a promising start in its poverty alleviation programme. With the expansion of the role of the state in financial and managerial terms, the poverty reduction programme achieved certain optimistic results. This led the National Planning Commission to claim in its MDGs assessment report that,

> Nepal has made impressive progress in reducing poverty. It [poverty] is reduced by 11 percentage point between 1996 and 2004 (from 42 to 31) and 6 percentage (from 31 to 25) point between 2005 and 2009. Despite this very positive national trend, the difference between rural and urban areas still persists. The urban poverty was only 10% while the rural one was 35% in 2004; it has come down to 8% and 22% respectively. This gap is narrower than before but it is still wide. From regional point of view Mid Western region is the poorest and the gap between better off regions like eastern region and urban center like Kathmandu shows that the gap persists. In 2004 poverty in Mid West region was 44.8% while in central region and in Kathmandu it was 27.1% and 3.3%. In 2009 these figures have come down to 37.4% in mid west and 22.3% and 1.9% in central region and Kathmandu respectively (NPC 2010a: 6).

This assessment report is exactly modeled on the *MDGs Progress Report 2002 and 2005* and based on the previously published reports of the government of Nepal on two living standard surveys. Further with the results of the Third Living Standard Survey, the government has declared a tremendous increase in the living standards of Nepali people making remarkable progress in the areas of poverty alleviation and infrastructure development between 1995/96 and 2010/11(CBS 2011). It was a remarkable progress made amid sluggish economy and persistent political instability. Thus this is presented as an instance of a commendable advancement made by the government in the recent economic history of Nepal. The official assertions seem to convey the message that Nepal is indeed beating poverty interestingly without getting people into jobs.

Table 2.1: Poverty Indicators based on Living Standards Surveys
1995/96, 2003/2004 and 2010/11

Description	Nepal Living Standards Survey (NLSS)		
	1995/1996	2003/2004	2010/2011
Nominal Average Household Income in Nominal NRs.	43,732	80,111	----
Nominal Average Per Capita Income in Nominal NRs.			
All Nepal	7,690	15,162	41,659
Poorest 20 per cent of population	2,020	4,003	15,888
Richest 20 per cent of population	19,325	40,486	94,149
Share of farm income in household income (in per cent)	61.0	47.8	28.0
Non-farm income (in per cent)	22.0	27.6	37.0
Other income, including remittance (in per cent)	16.0	24.5	35.0

Source: CBS, Nepal Living Standards Survey 2003/04: Statistical Report, Vol. 2. Kathmandu: Central Bureau of Statistics, 2004: 29 and, Nepal Living Standards Survey 2010/11, 2 vols. Kathmandu: Central Bureau of Statistics, October 2011.

According to the Second Living Standards Survey, the average household income increased by more than 80 per cent between 1995/96 and 2003/04 with nearly doubling of the per capita income from Rs.7,690 to Rs.15,162 during the same period. The growth rate for the poorest 20 per cent of the population was 98 per cent while that for the richest 20 per cent was 110 per cent. The report also noted some significant changes in farm and non-farm income of the people, suggesting the diversified sources of income of the people. Notable decrease in the percentage of people dependent on agriculture from 83 per cent in 1995/96 to 78 per cent in 2003/04 correspondingly led to a *most* significant decline in people living below poverty line from 38 per cent to 30 per cent or even less in the same period. When compared with the target set by the Poverty Reduction Strategy Paper (PRSP) – the core document of the Tenth

Five Year Plan (2002-2007) – that aimed at reducing poverty to 30 per cent by 2007, the Nepal Living Standards Survey (NLSS-II) has already documented the achievement of the target years ahead of the completion of the plan period.

Notwithstanding this fact, the Living Standards Survey 2003/04 has also reported about an ever-widening and dangerous gap of income inequality between the poorest 20 per cent and the richest 20 per cent of the people. As shown by unequal growth rate, income inequality has created social disharmony. The widening economic disparities have fed antagonistic social relationship with pernicious consequences. Rural-urban disparities are reportedly increasing though inequality remains higher in urban than rural areas; agricultural wage earners being the poorest of the poor along with large households with dependents; poverty rate among Hill and Tarai Dalits and Hill Janajati remaining high, despite considerable decline in their poverty between 1995/96 and 2003/04. The overall decline in poverty however is accompanied by glaring rise in income inequality with Gini coefficient increasing to 41.4 (0.41) from 34.2 (0.34) during the survey period (CBS et al. 2006: 12-13 and 19).

The Fourth Household Budgetary Survey conducted by the Nepal Rastra Bank (Central Bank) has also exposed the glaring income inequality between the lowest 20 per cent of population at Rs.10,751 in comparison to the highest 20 per cent earning a monthly income of Rs. 47,767 (Kathmandu Post, 20 August 2008). The finding of a recent Asian Development Bank (ADB) survey further sheds lights on income inequalities in Nepal classifying people living below USD2 (Rs.150) a day as low; people with above USD2 to USD20 income a day as middle and persons earning above USD20 a day as high class. The ADB says Nepal has 6.1 million populations as the middle class broadly defined as those earning between USD2 and USD20 a day. It includes both blue collar and white collar workers in the organized sectors. The super-rich, however, are very few in number; 100,000 out of the estimated 26.1 million population.

Table 2.2: Middle Class in Nepal
(based on2004 household survey mean)

% of Population				Total Population (million)					Annual Expenditures (billion)				
$2–$4	$4–$10	$10–$20	Total	$20+	$2–$4	$4–$10	$10–$20	Total	$20+	$2–$4	$4–$10	$10–$20	Total	$20+
16.74	5.30	0.85	22.89	0.38	4.45	1.41	0.23	6.09	0.10	4.32	2.91	1.09	8.32	2.40

Source: The Rise of Asia's Middle Class, 2010: 8 (Table 2.3 Size of Middle Class by country, in 2005 PPP$).

Box.1: Income inequality in Nepal

- Annual expenses of the middle class amounts to Rs. 6 trillion;
- An individual in the middle class category spends Rs.100,000 per annum;
- A person with daily income between Rs.150 and Rs.1,500 is a middle class;
- A person over Rs.1,500 daily income is high class;
- Annual expenses of the high class people amounts to Rs.180 billion;
- An individual in the high class category spends Rs.1.8 million per annum;
- Size of middle class people is 22.89 per cent of the total estimated population of 26.02 million in mid-2010;
- Number of people in Rs.150-300 income bracket : 4.45 million;
- Number of people in Rs.300-750 income bracket: 1.45 million;
- Number of people in Rs.750-1,500 income bracket: 230,000.

Source: The Rise of Asia's Middle Class, ADB, 2010.

Nepal has 23 per cent middle class populations in addition to 0.38 per cent affluent class people. On this account, more than 75 per cent of people in Nepal are earning below USD2 a day, which is also taken as a benchmark to poverty measure (Box I).

Notwithstanding the figure of 23 per cent middle class, Nepal is the only country in Asia that has the smallest middle class segment falling even behind Bangladesh. A comparable figure in the South Asian neighbourhood for Sri Lanka has 59 per cent middle class followed by 40 per cent in Pakistan and 25 per cent middle class population out of 1. 21 billion people in India[1] China in the north have 63 per cent of its population as middle class (ADB 2010). Within this income bracket of the middle class population in Nepal comprises both the blue collar factory workers, top white collar bureaucrats and professional and technical manpower, inclusive of small and medium sized businessmen and industrialists. The middle class therefore constitutes a versatile group of persons representing income disparities. This middle class comprising various occupational and professional groups, however, is gradually becoming influential in setting national agendas for poverty alleviation and rural development.

Concentration of wealth of the nation in the hands of a few is problematic because it further leads to disproportionate rate of returns to the already wealthy and leaving those behind to lead stressful and hazardous life. Income inequality, for instance, is a dissenting factor prevalent even in rich socialist states like Norway and Sweden. Income disparities measured on Gini coefficient show countries like South Africa remain most unequal with 0.6 Gini. The *Economist* has argued that although inequality has caused widespread social ills, "it is a much less important problem than poverty" (The Economist, 22 January 2011: 69-70). Poverty is understood as a cause notorious enough to create social inequality, which is defined as the denial of social opportunities. Disparity, discrimination and deprivation are the baggage with which poverty is identified. Nepal thus remains in the Low Income Countries' (LIC) bracket despite considerable achievement in poverty alleviation field.

The National Living Standards Survey (NLSS-III) conducted by the Central Bureau of Statistics with support of the World Bank, on the other hand, has disclosed that people in Nepal have made remarkable progress in their accessibility to basic facilities, mainly on education and health care facilities in its final report publicized on 20 October 2011. Increased investment on these social sectors by the government with donors' initiatives and individuals with remittance received has positive impact along with improvement of living standard of the people. Remittances received by 56 per cent of households of 3.1 million families in Nepal have contributed significantly to poverty reduction, however, without any spurt of economic growth. Remittance has fattened the rural economy. It has also contributed to change the life styles of the rural folks by increasing household income. These households receive a sum of Rs.80,425 on average and 79 per cent of that amount is spent on daily consumption. A meager 3.5 per cent of the remittance amount is spent on education along with 7 per cent spent on loan repayment. The NLSS-III notes a remarkable increase in the income of the poorest 20 per cent of the population jumping nearly four times between the NLSS-II and NLSS-III from Rs.4,003 to Rs.15,888 over the period of the past seven years. Comparably the income structure of the richest 20 per cent has reached Rs.94,149. This suggests the income gap between the rich and poor is decreasing. This is reflected in the narrowing down of the Gini coefficient from 0.41 in 2003/04 to 0.33 in 2009/10.

Along with this, the income structure has also changed with less reliance on agriculture as indicated by decrease in the percentage of farmer from 83 to 74 per cent between 1995/96 and 2010/11. Eventually, the number of farmers dependent on less than 0.5 ha of farm land, however, has increased from 40 to 50 per cent. The NLSS-III survey, has determined 25.2 per cent of Nepalis are living below poverty line. This makes a figure of 6.6 million people earning less than Rs.19,261 per annum. The data on poverty level indicate 15.46 per cent urban population and 27.43 per cent of rural population suffering from poverty; the lowest 8.72 per cent of poverty is in urban hills followed by 11.47 per cent of poor people living in the national capital Kathmandu. This means urban poverty is spreading with shrinking opportunities. Previously, the Mid-Western Development Region was classified as the poorest region with 44.8 per cent people below poverty line (NPC 2010). The NLSS-III, however, has classified the Far Western Development Region as the poorest of the poor with 45.61 per cent followed by 31.61 per cent in the Mid-West, 22.25 per cent in the West, 21.69 per cent in the Central and 21.44 per cent of people living below poverty line in the Eastern Development Region (CBS 2011). In total, one in every four Nepalis is still living under abject poverty, the data suggest.

Remittance has caused poverty level decrease from34.62 per cent to 27.43 per cent in the rural areas, where 81 per cent of the total population resides. Comparably, urban poverty has increased from 9.55 per cent 15.45 per cent. This is the firm indication of deepening unemployment that will be dealt appropriately below. Despite the per capita income of the people has increased to USD 742 (Rs.58,274) from USD 414 in 2007, as claimed (MoF 2012), people are facing hard choices against the hyperinflation. This situation is glaringly expressed by a study conducted by the Nepal Rastra Bank, which concludes although the economic activities of the Kathmandu Valley amounting to Rs.4.18 trillion constitute 31 per cent of the country's GDP; livelihood challenges of the people are becoming unsustainable as a consequence of uncontrollable price rise (Adhikari, 2012). This has further added to a drift of the population towards the poverty threshold line adding the number of urban poor.

Poverty Characteristics

Actually, poverty has two distinct characteristics in Nepal. First, it is widely a rural phenomenon and second, it is deeply related to caste and ethnicity followed by varied topography. As Nepal is a latecomer in development drama it was extremely characterized by illiteracy, large dependent families and resource scarcity such as land. Joblessness, single parent working families, households with elderly, disable and minor dependents are unsurprisingly making the poorest of the poor in the country where the state's response to social service is cosmetic, thus, remains grossly inadequate. Persistent feudalistic practice and the politics of exclusion, therefore, had calamitous effects on suffering of the people as well. The state's failure in nationalizing the anti-poverty agenda relative to social justice is thus obvious.

Such a difference is evident, for example, in the situation of Muslims, a religious minority comprising 4.3 per cent (4.4 per cent according to 2011 national census) of total population. They suffer from multilevel exclusion due to their religious identity, status as minority language speakers, and identity as Madheshi people. The irony is that Muslims are grouped within the Madheshi community but they are segregated by their religious beliefs within this community. Similarly, the language Muslims speak is Urdu as their mother tongue, which is different in script that segregates Muslims from Madheshis, as the latter are mostly Hindus with various dialects as their mother tongue. Muslims, therefore, claim their separate identity from the Madheshi people. Muslims are in the category of the poor and vulnerable; they are both the religious and lingual minority unlike the Dalits who fall within the category of the followers of the majority Hindu religion and languages spoken by the dominant majorities both in the Hills and Tarai.

The economic plight of the Muslims is also exacerbated by their education in a separate religious school system (*madarsa*), which is not promising to the job market. They are thus economically down trodden, discriminated and live in destitution. This is corroborated by the Nepal Living Standard Survey-II that found that the national poverty incidence dropped by an average 11 points from 1996 to 2004 – from 42 per cent to 31 per cent. Notwithstanding this, the decrease in poverty was the lowest for the Muslims: just 6 per cent compared with 42 per cent among Bahun/Chhetri, 21 per cent among Dalits and 10 per cent among Hill Janajatis.

Table 2.3: Poverty Measurement between 1995/96 and 2003/04

(in percentage)

Population below poverty line			Poverty Gap		Squared Poverty Gap	
Areas	1995/96	2003/04	1995/96	2003/04	1995/96	2003/04
Urban	21.55	9.55	6.54	2.18	2.65	0.71
Rural	43.27	34.62	12.14	8.50	4.83	3.05
Nepal	41.76	30.85	11.75	7.55	4.67	2.70

Source: Economic Survey 2006/07, 2007:73.

Though there appeared to have been considerable reduction in poverty gaps between the survey periods, inequality, however, has persisted and not narrowed as the data show. A careful reading of the data from NLSS-I and NLSS-II posit inclusive growth and equality as constant challenges because of lack of access to socioeconomic opportunities and services by the people living in different places. Spatial and regional inequalities characterized both discrimination and destitution. In addition to this, poverty is also characterized by the single (particularly male) breadwinner in the households of five or even more with dependent elderly parents. This means the income of a person is redistributed within the family making both the level of poverty and inequality grow. Further, the situation becomes complicated when the productive contribution of female in household work remains unaccounted for.

Against the NLSS-II, the recent NPC assessment report asserts about the progress made in two crucial dimensions of poverty reduction efforts. The first is the narrowing down of the inequality gap, and the second is the considerable reduction of problems related to hunger and starvation. However, the level of poverty reduction varies from the gender and regional perspectives. As the people living under a dollar a day income has declined to 22 per cent in 2008 from 24 per cent in 2005, the problems related to hunger and starvation have also been considerably reduced from the pick of 39.9 per cent in 2005 to 22 per cent in 2010, the report claims. Poverty has declined from 31 per cent in 2005 to 25 per cent in 2008 but not the incidence of poverty. Citing Central Bureau of Statistics 2009 data, the NPC report notes the wide variation of poverty incidence in geographical and social terms. Poverty incidence in rural areas is almost four times high (28.54 %) in comparison to urban areas (7.64%) as 95.5 per cent of the poor people live in rural areas. The rate of poverty reduction in rural area is also slower than the urban area (NPC 2010:17).

The NPC report has noted three factors contributing to poverty reduction policies of the government. First, the government has been spending 43.7 per cent of total annual budget directly on poverty reduction projects and 45.2 per cent indirectly on the related programmes since 2006. The total expenses so far amounts to Rs. 283.4 billion. Second, the NGOs and INGOs spend an estimated average of Rs. 10 billion annually directly and indirectly contributing to poverty reduction programmes. Third, remittance from abroad earned through hard labour has substantially added to reduce rural poverty. Recognizing money flowing through informal channels as much higher, conservative estimate had put formal remittance at USD 240 million a year, which was about 4.4 per cent of GDP (HMG 2003: 9).

As per one estimate, the annual remittance in the year 1999 was USD1billion, which was equivalent to that year's fiscal budget (Dahal et al. 2000: 30-36). By 2010 the remittance sent home has multiplied to USD 4 billion. It is assumed to have directly contributed to half of poverty reduction with contribution to GDP already estimated above 20 per cent (Khanal 2009: 2). It was estimated in 2008 that 30 per cent of the total households in Nepal had received remittances, up from 23.4 per cent in 1995/96. It has a direct relation with rural poverty reduction where over 80 per cent of people live on subsistence agriculture[2] (NPC 2010: 6; NPC 2005: 5).

When viewed in terms of budgetary allocation, the third pillar (social inclusion) of the PRSP strategies, ironically, was the least funded of the four pillars, although they are not mutually exclusive. Table2.4 below testifies this assertion.

Table 2.4: Development expenditure classified by strategic pillars of PRSP 2003/04

Strategic Pillars	Amount Rs '000	% of Total
Higher, sustained broad based economic development	17,472,450	41.76
Social sectors and rural infrastructure development	16,297,150	38.95
Targeted programmes	2,979,150	7.12
Good governance	5,096,264	12.18
Total	**41,845,000**	**100**

Source: (Annual Development Programme 2003/04, NPC, 2003) Implementation of the Tenth Plan (PRSP), Second Progress Report, June 2005: 53.

Despite the increase in budgetary appropriation actual expenditure on targeted programmes averaged approximately 76 per cent per annum in the first four years of the Tenth Plan. Inconsistency on expenditure ranged from the high 82 per cent in 2002/03 to low 66 per cent in the following year and up to 77 per cent in 2005/06. The annual budgetary allocation, however, was raised from Rs. 2.14 billion in 2002/03 to Rs. 4.50 billion in 2006/07 (MoF 2007:73). As the data below show, development expenditure also suffers from serious lapses between appropriation and expenditure. This is the case of inefficiency in managing the programmes and incapacity of the government to sustain its performance obligation by absorbing the aid amount.

Table 2:5: Development (Capital) Expenditure in Billions of Rupees

2004/05		2005/06		2006/07		2007/08		2008/09		2009/10	
Target	Exp.	Target	Exp.	Target	Exp.	Target	Exp.	Target	Exp.	Target	Exp.
31	25	36	29	45	39	55	53	96	76	106	73*

Source: Kantipur, 10 June, 2010. * Provisional. Exp.= Expenditure

Actually, only Rs. 55 billion (51.88%) out of the total allocated amount of Rs. 106 billion for development expenditure has been spent by the second week of June, a month before the FY 2009/10 ends in mid-July 2010. The anticipated expense of Rs. 73 billion by the end of the fiscal year amounts to 68 per cent of the total whereas 79 per cent of development budget was spent on the previous fiscal year. Expenditure on education and health – directly related to MDGs – suffers most due to various reasons impacting negatively on the social situation of the commoners. By contrast, the recurrent expenditure in the same period is double (Rs.113 billion) than the capital expenditure (Awasthi 2010).

The Three Year Interim Plan (2007/08-2009/10), which concludes this year, claims to have conducted some field work and public consultation with the people of 70 VDCs of 30 districts out of nearly 4,000 VDCs of 75 districts of Nepal for the first time in the history of planning by the National Planning Commission along with consultations with political parties, professional groups and civil society before drafting the plan document to genuinely reflect the popular aspirations for setting development targets (NPC 2007, Preface). Putting 'special emphasis' on 'increasing public expenditure on relief and employment' measures the plan has focused on poverty reduction and growth but stressed on the presence of state in development especially in remote areas and inclusion of socially marginalized groups. Insurgency had obviously dislocated even the symbolic presence of the state in the form of police post in remote districts and the absence of local government has constrained development activities.

Despite this, the National Planning Commission (2010) reports a significant increase in budgetary allocation in social sector in accordance with the provisions of the Three Year Plan. The post-CA government has stressed on social safety networks with tremendous budgetary commitment on social programmes with an increase by '444 per cent' to meet the requirements of the deprived and the destitutes.[3] Allocation for social safety

Figure 1: Budget Allocation on Poverty Reducing Project (2005/06-2009/10)

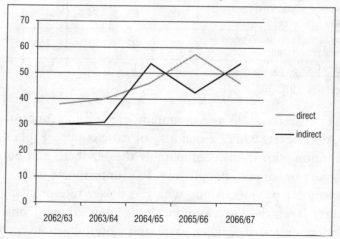

Source: NPC 2010a: 16. The fiscal year mentioned is according to Nepali Calendar.

programmes continued in the 2009/10 budget, which would be further discussed below in chapter IV, including allowance to encourage inter-caste marriages, particularly, widow marriage, which has drawn the ire of the critiques.

Buoyed by the declining poverty, the NPC 2010 report suggests about the likelihood of reducing extreme poverty by half along with potentiality in reducing extreme hunger as envisioned in the MDGs by 2015. People living below USD 1 a day was 24.1 per cent in 2005.[4] Percentage of population below national poverty line then was 31 per cent. The current Three year plan has set target to reduce it to 24 per cent. Poverty gap ratio is also narrowing down from 11.75 to 6.10 within a decade, as the table below demonstrates. Poverty reduction, as reported, has been a success story for Nepal. Within the period of two decades poverty in Nepal is down from 42 per cent in 1990 to 25 per cent in 2010. This estimated figure of poverty reduction, however, requires to be comprehended with the state of abject poverty still prevalent in the Mid-Western hills/ mountains and the Far-Western Nepal.

Table 2.6: Poverty Gap Ratio

Indicator	1990	2000	2005	2010	2015 target
Percentage of population below $1 per day (ppp value)	33.54	NA	24.1	NA	17
Percentage of population below national poverty line	42	38	31	25	21
Poverty Gap	NA	11.75	7.55	6.10	--

Source: NPC 2010: 13.

The Western hills and mountains are still the concentrated poverty pockets where a majority of caste/ethnic people share destitution with Dalits. Comparably the Madhesh and Eastern hills and mountain people are less unfortunate than their Western compatriots. Along with the slower rate of change in poverty level, the low caste and indigenous ethnic people are found poorer than higher caste and non-indigenous people.

Poverty, however, is rampant irrespective of caste and creed among the people living, particularly, in the Western hills and mountains. Thakuris, who traditionally claim their ruling class status and expect respectable treatment from others, have been found, for example, working as porters for their livelihood in Western Nepal. Monetization of economy has also led the priestly caste Brahmins to involve in several odd jobs; including tea-stall owners and cleaners to meet their family needs. Not only the low caste Dalits and Janajatis but also the high castes Chhetri-Thakuris are working as labourers and involved in menial jobs. In urban centres like Kathmandu, caste is no longer a barrier in works like vegetable vendors, and even in poultry/meat-shops, previously the specialized occupation of butchers – the untouchables.

Poverty and hunger are still the cause of suicides by the entire family and unemployed youths. The suicide rate is increasing, as the police record indicates. A total of 13,750 people had committed suicides between 2006 and 2010. Of whom the majority are male aged between 15 and 40 years. And the reasons for suicides stated mostly are poverty, unemployment and depression. The Nepal Police has disclosed that one Nepali citizen commits suicide in every two hours (Gyawali 2010; Kantipur, 7 July 2010). Food scarcity, unemployment and poverty loom large in the Far West and food crisis has become one of the grievous challenges closely related to human security. This exemplifies the poverty-insecurity nexus. The World Food Programme has estimated 3.7 million people are facing food insecurity. Some 23.9 per cent of the people in Nepal are suffering from hunger.

A total of 66 per cent of Nepali households regularly experience food deficiencies. Malnutrition is 48 per cent at the national level and 60 per cent in the hill regions. Besides 50 per cent of children below 5 years of age suffer from stunted growth due to the chronic lack of food, more than a third of 12.6 million children are living below the poverty line. Undernourishment is pervasive among the children of poor and marginalized groups (UNDP 2010). The "Children Security Grant" targeting children below 5 years of age from the extremely poor, Dalit and families from Karnali Zone beginning since the last fiscal year has continued. But the reality, as per a documentary featuring the life of the school going children of the Karnali Zone (made with special focus on the lives of the students of Dolpa district) shows, is not encouraging, notwithstanding the rhetoric of "Education for All" (Pokharel 2010). Therefore the fattened budgetary commitment to pro-poor programmes has to be qualified with actual disbursement and proper implementation, monitoring, and assessment of the impact on the targeted people. Otherwise, it would be like the case of the spending of USD 68.4 million by donor agencies, for example, on Dalits' programmes in 2003 alone, without any impact as "the Dalits have not had access to the fund as expected" (Pokharel 2004: 3).

The NLSS-III has identified three pertinent characteristics of poverty. First, widespread poverty level of 47 per cent exists in a family with more than three children below 7 years old in comparison to families without children of that age with 12 per cent poverty level. Second, households headed by women are less stricken by poverty than by the male members between 26 and 45 years of age. Poverty level of the households headed by male is 27.03 per cent whereas it is 23.69 per cent in the case of the female. The reason being so is that these households receive remittances from the male members of the family working abroad. Third, illiteracy and poverty prominently coexists. Poverty rate is the highest in the family of illiterate head with 33.5 per cent followed by 27 per cent in the family headed by the literate person. Poverty level is just 7 per cent in the families of persons with higher secondary or above level of education. These indicators typically suggest the need to invest in education by reallocating, restructuring and reforming the system making it more relevant to socioeconomic progress. The grievous reality however is that remittance directly correlates to poverty reduction.

Poverty Reduction and Human Development

The empirical method to examine the impact of poverty reduction is the human development index (HDI). Poverty reduction strategy is a policy for social inclusion promoting opportunities for empowerment of hitherto discriminated and marginalized people to sustain their life chances. HDI is three-dimensional – a healthy life, education level, and opportunity for a decent living. Poverty reduction can impact human development through enhancing capability and utilizing opportunity. Thus, poverty reduction can be correlated to human development in the context of development process in Nepal. The idea behind the concept of human development is the motive of capability expansion enabling the people to lead a sustainable and comfortable life both in social and economic spheres with their identity respected. Human development is human centric with the provisions of social opportunities of which the economic activity is a part. It is therefore asked (i) what is happening to poverty; (ii) what is happening to unemployment; and (iii) what is happening to inequality? Development therefore is defined on the basis of the progress made by a state on HDI and HEI rather than economic growth.

Nepal has produced four country specific human development reports so far. A comprehensive report on human development was first produced in 1998 (NESAC 1998). Following this, three thematic reports are published subsequently by UNDP covering (i) poverty reduction and governance, 2001; (ii) empowerment and poverty reduction, 2004; and, (iii) state transformation and development, 2009. A separate collaborative report on the assessment of poverty in Nepal has also been published.[5] These reports contain a minefield of data on incidence of poverty in relations to caste/ethnic people, severity of poverty in places and regions' like rural-urban, plains-hills/mountains, national HDI value and HDI across the five development regions and three ecological zones. Variation in HDI is widespread in which the rural-urban divide is distinct. For the purpose of this study data from the latest human development report on Nepal published in 2009 is liberally used. As the report asserts, availability of the authentic data is up to the year 2006 (UNDP/N 2009). Table 2.7 below presents a coherent picture of the state of human development in Nepal. Measured between the five years' interval the data indicate a positive trend.

Table 2.7: Change in human development index, 2001 and 2006

Region	HDI 2001 Value	Rank	HDI 2006 Value	Rank	^ HDI 06-HDI 01
NEPAL	0.471			0.509	0.038
Urban/Rural Residence					
Urban	0.581	1	0.630	1	0.049
Rural	0.452	2	0.482	2	0.030
Ecological Region					
Mountain	0.386	3	0.436	3	0.050
Hill	0.512	1	0.543	1	0.031
Tarai	0.494	2	0.494	2	0.016
Development Region					
Eastern	0.493	1	0.526	2	0.033
Central	0.490	3	0.531	1	0.041
Western	0.491	2	0.516	3	0.025
Mid-western	0.402	5	0.452	5	0.050
Far-western	0.404	4	0.461	4	0.057

Source: UNDP/N, 2009: 34.

In overall terms the data on HDI show appreciable improvement. In 1996, the adjusted HDI for Nepal was 0.403. Rural-urban gap was wide 0.384 versus 0.567 with Mid-Western (0.354) and Far-western (0.364) regions with usual disappointing HDI levels (UNDP 2004: 18). On the whole, Nepal has remained a backwater in human development in comparative terms against its South Asian neighbourhood. Nepal was ahead of Bangladesh, Bhutan and even Pakistan in HDI measures in certain years in early 1990s. But Bhutan's economic buoyancy and Nepal's embroilment in the violent internal conflict has made the former push ahead of the latter. Nepal's dependent development was further compromised by the violent insurgency as already insufficient expenditure in social sector was transferred to meet the demands of security sector. With increasing Maoists' forays the government transferred 75 per cent of funding from the local bodies to armed forces under the 'Integrated Security and Development Programme (ISDP)'. Thus, the HDI measured with diversity in mind with the end of insurgency has led Nepal to rank 0.509 in the year 2006 (UNDP/N 2009; NPC 2010).

In the regional context, spatial inequality remains a persistent problem. The Mid-West scores the lowest HDI value (0.452) and the gap between the Mid-West and the Far-West (0.461) has also increased. The central region that ranked third in 2001 has claimed the first rank in 2006 replacing the eastern region. Rural Nepal has the HDI value of 0.482 in comparison to urban areas with 0.630 HDI which is obviously higher than the national average. Hills are better placed (0.543) even in comparison to Tarai (0.494), the granary of Nepal. Ecologically, the Central hills have the highest HDI score with 0.602 followed by Western hills 0.549 and Eastern hills 0.543. The Mid-Western hills 0.448 and Far-Western hills 0.443 are less fortunate even in comparison to Eastern mountain (0.519), which is better placed than the rest of the others in that ecological zone. On the whole, the Mid-Western Development Region remains, as always, at the bottom of the HDI ladder. Though the annual rate of increase in HDI value for the country as a whole is recorded at 1.6 per cent between 2001 and 2006, the situation remains in fixed-frame in rural or urban areas or ecological zones (UNDP/N 2009:35).

The HDI value of Nepal is published in detail by another significant study in relations to various caste/ethnic and Dalits groups providing comparative perspectives on the state of human development (Lohani and Vaidya 2009). This study has identified various communities which should be made the primary target of social inclusion. Enlisting 74 caste/ethnic names inclusive of 19 others under 'other Janajatis' heading and another 5 others under 'other Dalits' heading, this study has classified poor and destitute into marginalized and extremely-marginalized category. Of all these caste/ethnic and Dalits groups the highest HDI score (0.904) is ensured by the Kayastha caste group of Tarai origin. Similarly, the Mushar (Dalits) of the Tarai origin scored the lowest HDI (0.092). Disparities between different caste/ethnic and Dalits groups at community and regional levels exist.

Among the hill ethnics, the Chepang (praja) has the lowest HDI (0.156) in comparison to the hill high caste Bahun with the HDI of 0.765. The Marwari/Jain (business community) has a better HDI (0.901) than the Newar (0.726) and Thakali (0.640) HDI, the later two ethnics also belonging traditionally to hill business communities. Of the 74 identified caste/ethnic and Dalits groups there are 30 groups with HDI above 0.400. The rest 44 groups fall below that scale. The Chepang of the hills and the Mushar of the plains are obviously the most oppressed communities in Nepal, as their low HDI evince. The study therefore has recommended for setting national priority by considering the need of providing education, health and employment opportunities to the marginalized and extremely marginalized people. These are the essential ingredients for developing an inclusive order with enhancing human capability and breaking out of the poverty trap. Steps towards social justice could be a fair initiative to bridge relative deprivation and thus minimize social alienation. Table 2.8 below describes the HDI scores of 74 caste/ethnic and Dalits groups and arrives at the average national HDI as 0.512, a figure comparable to the UNDP/N 2009 report.

A notable feature of this study is the change in the perspective on Newar as enjoying the highest HDI. In 1998, the Newar ethnic group was marked with the highest HDI (0.457) followed by hill Brahmin (0.441) and Chhetri (0.348) by NESAC report. No more is this finding true. The hill caste/ethnic groups are now overtaken by the Tarai caste groups as the Table 2.8 indicates.

A breakdown of the HDI scores into four broad clusters of caste/ethnicity shows the first cluster comprising high caste

Table 2.8: HDI of various communities in Nepal

Sr. No.	Caste/ethnic names	HDI	Sr. No.	Caste/ethnic names	HDI
1	Kayastha	0.9049	39	Kurmi	0.3601
2	Marwari/Jain	0.9018	40	Lohar	0.3566
3	Nurang	0.7680	41	Muslim	0.3553
4	Bahun (Hill)	0.7650	42	Mali	0.3466
5	Rajput	0.7331	43	Sarki	0.3461
6	Newar	0.7262	44	Danuwar	0.3378
7	Bahun(Tarai)	0.7224	45	Sunuwar	0.3347
8	Bengali	0.7015	46	Rajbanshi	0.3296
9	Thakali	0.6402	47	Hanuk	0.3294
10	Baniya	0.6344	48	Kanu	0.3279
11	Punjabi/Sikh	0.5974	49	Gangai	0.3244
12	Sudi	0.5698	50	Bote	0.3208
13	Kalwar	0.5656	51	Kumhar	0.3096
14	Chhetri	0.5492	52	Kahar	0.3070
15	Thakuri	0.5454	53	Dhobi	0.3049
16	Gurung	0.5247	54	Bhote	0.2991
17	Sanyasi	0.5231	55	Pahari	0.2929
18	Limbu	0.5033	56	Other Dalits+	0.2874
19	Haluwai	0.4968	57	Kewat	0.2823
20	Rai	0.4897	58	Majhi	0.2812
21	Gharti/Bhujel	0.5849	59	Tajpuria	0.2710
22	Teli	0.4819	60	Santhal/Satar	0.2675
23	Magar	0.4819	61	Lodha	0.2670
24	Sonar	0.4732	62	Mallah	0.2518
25	Kanu	0.4360	63	Nunia	0.2515
26	Darai	0.4143	64	Tatma	0.2420
27	Sherpa	0.4114	65	Chidimar	0.2307
28	Badhai	0.4086	66	Bhediyal&Gadheri	0.2204
29	Other Janajatis*	0.4057	67	Jhanghad	0.2097
30	Hajam/Thakur	0.4001	68	Banter	0.2081
31	Kumal	0.3904	69	Dhshad/Paswan	0.2008
32	Thami	0.3902	70	Chamar/Harijan	0.1936
33	Rajbhar	0.3898	71	Khatabei	0.1787
34	Tamang	0.3894	72	Bindarbin	0.1665
35	Yadav	0.3811	73	Chepang (Praja)	0.1567
36	Tharu	0.3793	74	Mushar	0.0927
37	Koiri	0.3788			
38	Damai	0.3622		Average HDI 0.5120	

* Includes Baramu, Byashi, Chentel, Dhimal, Bura, Hayu, Jirel, Koche, Kisan.Kusunda, Pattharkatta, Lepcha, Meche, Munda, Raji, Raute, Balung, Yakhha and Hyalmo.
+Includes Badi, Dom, Gaine, Halkhor and Kamar.

Note: Interestingly, there is no mention of Kami, the largest Hill Dalit Group in the Table and its HDI level. This omission is perhaps the glaring lapse of the report.

Source: Prakash Chandra Lohani and Bal Gopal Vaidya, "Samabeshikaran Garinuparne Samudayako Pahichan" Kantipur, 11 August 2009. Note Lohar is not treated as Dalit by the authors.

hill and high caste Tarai people fare better than the second cluster of caste/ethnic people composed only of the hill groups. The third cluster constituting Tarai/Madheshi and other caste excluding Tarai Brahmin, Rajput etc., but including Muslim is not promising either. And the HDI of the last cluster composed of Tarai/Madheshi Dalits is the lowest suggesting that the people in that category are the worst off (Lohani and Vaidya 2009). Landlessness feature both poverty and destitution of Tarai Dalits. The case study of Dhanusha district, for example, demonstrates this where 87 per cent of Dalits surveyed were landless and some 7 per cent owned less than 1 hectare of land (Dahal 2009: 147). Comparably, only 7.4 per cent of hill Dalits in Surkhet district were landless (Kumar 2009: 189). A survey conducted by the National Dalit Commission in the six Tarai

Table 2.9: HDI value of caste and ethnic groups by four broad categories

Caste/Ethnicity	HDI value
Hill Brahman Tarai/Madhesi/Brahman/Chhetri Newar	0.612 – 0.625
All Brahman/Chhetri Hill Chhetri Hill/Mountain Janajati All Janajati including Newar All Hill Janajati including Newar All Hill mountain Groups with Newar All Hill Mountain groups without Newar Other	0.507-0.559
Tarai/Madhesi other caste All Dalits Hill Dalits All Janajati Tarai Janajati Muslim All Tarai/ Madhesi Groups with Muslim All Tarai/ Madhesi Groups without Muslim	0.401-0.495
Tarai/Madhesi Dalits	0.383

Source: UNDP/N 2009: 155.

districts has found 74.14 per cent of Dalits as landless (cited in Bhattachan et al. 2008: 83).

Impact of Poverty Reduction on Socially Excluded Groups

If poverty reduction is understood as capability enhancement through social inclusion, it should be examined against women, Dalits, indigenous nationalities, Madheshis and Muslims who are gender-wise, caste-wise, ethnically, geographically and religiously recognized as excluded groups in Nepal.[6] People living in this category are commonly known as discriminated, marginalized and disadvantaged groups as a consequence of social exclusion. The policy of preventing such group of people from participation and representation in the national mainstream, though beneficial to the dominant groups comprising the elites interests, is lately thought to have harmed the economic development process as a consequence of "capability deprivation" thereby denying human resources development and human capital formation inhibiting basis needs; the idea behind the evolution of human development. Their empowerment is an imperative in realizing the socio-cultural and political potentiality of these traditionally discriminated groups. Their identity and capacity are also at the core of the state restructuring process in the aftermath of the Jana Andolan II.

Gender Status: Prevalence of the *chaupadi*[7] system in the Mid-West and Far-Western Nepal is the glaring example of inhuman treatment rendered to women first by the family and second by the society. Existence of such a tortuous ritual in the social relationship is a stab on social justice and democracy. Numerous cases of death of women caused by this customary system are reported, still the law is silent. Continuity in such cultural practice violates the norm of humanity. Till this most appalling social system persists all the efforts towards providing social justice to women would be inconsequential. Social justice can simply be understood as a system of removing inequality in human relationships. But gender discrimination is integral to Hindu religious ethos in which women are treated not only as weaker sex but also as subordinate to men as the Hindu scripture *Manusmriti* defines. In actuality, the *chaupadi* system is pure and simple customary practice of domestic violence against women towards which the machismostic society has closed its eyes. 'Girls don't count' in several districts of Mid-West and Far-Western Nepal even today (Shrestha 2008). Fortunately, Nepal has supposedly avoided gendercide,[8] which is becoming a world-wide phenomenon, as the country's sex ratio suggests. The actual national position on gender status has surfaced with the publication of the 2011 Census record.

To be born as female is to invite exclusion that begins at home as the girl child is less preferred. Deprivation is customary and systematic. Women are practically behind men in every aspect of attainment in social status; be it education, skill development, employment opportunities and decision making; not to talk about rights to inheritance and even citizenship till the recent past (HMG/NPC 2001). Women's literacy rate is low compared with their men folks. The average literacy rate of women in the country, for example, was 54.5 per cent as against 81 per cent for men. It was just 34.8 per cent for women in the disadvantaged caste groups like Dalits. The education attainment of Dalit women to secondary level was 12 per cent in comparison to 23 per cent for men. The corresponding literacy rate for hill Dalit women of 46 per cent is nearly three times of the 17 per cent for Tarai Dalit women. As the tradition suggests, women's representation in political parties, particularly, that of Dalits is not satisfactory. Dalit women's participation in the NC is 55.5 per cent followed by 45.4 per cent in the CPN (UML), 42.8 per cent in the Maoist, rare in the Madheshi parties and none in the Dalit Janajati party.[9] The need, therefore, is to sensitize the situation with free education as fundamental to Dalit female children.

The Madheshi and other caste women had lower rate of secondary level education of only 12 per cent whose literacy rate was also low at 24 per cent (Table 2.10). Muslim women attaining secondary level education is 12 per cent and their literacy rate is around 27 per cent. Perhaps the reason for this was the conservative social setting in the Tarai compared with relatively egalitarian life in the hills. But the more pervasive reason could be poverty and lack of motivation and the high rate of school drop outs of the girl child in the country. Girls everywhere in the country are used as the helping hands by their parents to look at the siblings and domestic chores. Their absence from the schools is treated as natural mostly in the rural Nepal. The change in the social norms has yet to remedy the traditional chauvinistic attitude of the patrilineal society. In the

**Table 2.10: Education attainment by gender,
caste and ethnicity (15-49 years), 2006**

Caste/Ethnicity	Literacy	Rate %	Secondary Level School or Higher Education	
	Female	Male	Female	Male
All Nepalis	54.5	81.0	29.3	53.5
All Brahmin/chhetri	68.6	92.8	44.4	75.4
Hill Brahmin	82.1	96.9	59.5	86.5
Hill Chhetri	59.4	90.0	34.0	67.1
MadhesiBrahmin/Chhetri	82.5	93.9	61.6	90.1
Madhesi Other caste	24.2	72.0	12.1	44.5
All dalits	34.8	59.9	11.8	23.2
Hill Dalits	46.3	69.0	16.0	26.4
Madheshi Dalits	17.2	48.5	05.2	19.2
Newar	74.6	93.5	46.1	70.0
All Janajatis	56.9	79.6	26.4	45.8
Hill Janajati	60.0	82.4	29.5	48.1
Tarai Janajati	51.5	75.5	20.9	42.7
Muslim	26.5	61.8	12.0	25.5
All Hill/Mountain Groups	63.4	86.9	36.1	60.5
All Tarai/Madhesi Groups	35.9	69.9	16.0	40.0
Others(unidentified)	62.3	97.4	20.8	75.8

Source: UNDP/N 2009: 47.

Note: In this educational attainment data , the literacy rate is noted from the population 6 years and above; For example, the female literacy 54.5 per cent is based on all females 6 years and above and not 15-49 years.

case of the Muslim the *madarsa* schooling system could be an impediment. Therefore, the 'education for all' policy is yet to succeed to stop illiteracy and the proportion of school drop outs.

This table reflects a contrast in the education level between Madheshi male and female, other caste and Madheshi Dalits. Evidently, the education status of Madheshi women is much lower than other groups. Muslim women are even in worst situation. Much is, thus, desirous to be done in the sphere of women's empowerment. The first necessity is the investment on education for the girl child and women. Female Dalits are amongst the largest illiterate groups whose educational attainment measured in terms of the School Leaving Certificate (SLC) – 10th grades – was below 1 per cent on the national average, as per the 2001 Census data. Dalit women's literacy rate in 2006 was 34.8 per cent; Muslim women's literacy percentage was 26.5 and Janajati women's excluding Newars' literacy figure was 56.9 per cent. A further breakdown suggests 69 per cent of Dalit women, 77.6 per cent of Muslim and 54.9 per cent of Janajati women excluding Newar were totally illiterate in 2006 (UNDP/N 2009: 167and169).

Thus, when left behind in educational attainment it automatically poses normal constraint in the competitive market for women to qualify. Sen's 'capability deprivation' thesis comes into full play in unraveling gender inequality as an impediment for human development. Looked at the status of women from the GDI and GEM perspectives that measure inequality between women and men the mountain and Mid-Western development regions indicate about the low human development of women. Gender empowerment is measured on three criteria: participation, decision making, and power over economic resources[10] (Pradhan 2006:118). The objective of microfinance projects established by the ADB in 1998 has been women's empowerment along with reducing rural poverty. Between 2000 and 2006, disbursement of Rs. 982 million to about 370,000 clients (women) was made following the Grameen Bank model (Majorano 2007; Takahatake and Maharjan 2002).

However, the situation of women is worst at the sub-regional level covering mountains and hills of all except the Eastern Development Region. There is regional as well as rural-urban disparity in GDI scores. The GDI in rural area of 0.471 is considerably low in comparison to 0.618 of urban area. The GDI in hills (0.534) is followed by plains (0.482) and then mountains (0.23). It is claimed that the ratio of GDI to HDI shows improving trend for the status of women. However, it is also suggested that this short-term improvement should be cautiously taken as the percentage of shortfall of GDI over HDI between 2001 and 2006 was considerable. The GEM indicates the share of women remains just 33 per cent of the earned income of men, notwithstanding their increased participation in the political processes that is also one third of the total 601 seats in the CA (UNDP/N 2009: 37-38). Their place in decision making circle is still nominal as indicated by their representation in the cabinet, central committees of political parties or in the Government of Nepal with only two woman secretary (special class officials). The National Planning Commission, an influential advisory organ of government decision making, is void of women's representation even after appointment of more than stipulated persons as its members. Regional disparities in GEM are usual as in the GDI or in HDI. It varies from 0.391 in Western plains to a high of 0.538 in the Eastern mountain sub-region.

The stark reality today is that both participation and representation of women have increased through the constitutional measure that has made it mandatory to adopt an inclusive policy by the state. Affirmative action and reservation policies for women have indeed made entry-points for them in shouldering responsibilities incurred by participation and representation. Initiatives towards meaningful participation of women in "every step" of decision making for peace building has been taken through an Action Plan 2010 conforming to the

UN Security Council Resolution 2000 by ensuring their equal participation. This initiative is taken in view of the women in most of the cases are not empowered, they are just presented decoratively. Their presence in public domain has remained cosmetic in actual practice. Even in the CA they are mostly used as cheerleaders. The reason lies both in aptitude and attitude.

Women's representation in the CA is so far the most satisfactory in terms of its composition of caste, ethnic and geographical dimensions and the age group as well. Of the 197 women represented through direct and proportional electoral processes, the majority is composed of Janajati groups numbering 70 in total followed by 36 Madheshi caste groups, including Tarai Dalits a 5 Muslims along with 24 Hill Dalits. Besides this, Hill Brahmins, Chhetris and others constitute the rest comprising 33 per cent of the CA representation.

However the women's caucus has emerged in the CA and subsequently in the legislative-parliament as interest group in asserting women's rights. Women activists have formed different NGOs to raise their respective voices. A few among them like the Dalit Women's NGO; Indigenous/Janajati Women's NGO, Madheshi Women's NGO and Muslim Women's NGO are prominently working to facilitate rights and benefits to their respective communities. The function of *Aama Samuha* (mother's group) in the public domain as pressure group is also influencing social actions and interactions to certain extent through mobilizing women at the grassroots level. Despite family obstructions in villages, the *Aama Samuha* has become effective in social and economic activities creating conditions for saving, welfare, and credit cooperatives for their independence to change the norms of conservative society. These trends are somehow forcing the patriarchic society to rethink over the long neglected status of women in Nepali society.

Dalits Status: Dalits, defined as a category of people, who by virtue of caste based discrimination, tradition of untouchability and backwardness, are considered impure, thus, denied of human dignity and social justice. Yet Dalits as a whole are not homogenous group. Dalits in Nepal are categorized into three distinct groups: Newar Dalits, Hill Dalits and Tarai Dalits. They are the artisan class of people, followers of Hindu religion, constitute 13.6 per cent of the total population. Nearly 65 per cent of them live in the hills of Nepal (Dahal 2009: 138; Gurung 2003:12; Dahal et al. 2002). They are the most deprived of the lots and languishing under poverty and destitution. Their socioeconomic and political situation varies considerably; a majority of them are landless; involve in customarily determined unclean manual works and mostly are seasonal labourers and daily wage earners.

The status of Dalits literacy rate is presented in Table 2.10. Their literacy status was 34 per cent as a whole; 20 per cent lower than the national average of 54.1 per cent, according to 2001 census. In comparative terms, the literacy rate between the hill Dalits and Tarai Dalits is also distinctly different. On the top of it, the literacy of Tarai Dalit women at 17 per cent and their secondary level schooling at 0.05 per cent is indeed pathetic. Literacy rate of the Tarai Dalits men is also the lowest and their education at school and above at 19 per cent is also at the worst level. Above all, the situation of the Dalits women is disgraceful (Bishankhe 2007).They have therefore become the 'wretched of the earth'.

On the whole, the lowest representation of the Dalits in the Gazetted class government service (Table 2.11) also indicates about the situation of untouchables in Nepal. Dalits are continued to be discriminated and excluded. This phenomenon has led Bhattachan et al. (2003) to list the prevalence of 205 types of caste based discrimination practiced in Nepal. The Dalit movement that begun in 1946 has yet to realise its minimum goals against the caste based discrimination. Though Dalits are the victims of caste based discrimination and the traditional system of untouchability becoming cultural practice (abolished in 1963 by Naya Muluki Ain), they also, ironically, follow the same despicable system in intra-Dalits relations.

In terms of HDI and HEI, Dalits are in the lowest rung. Though Dalits in general have 0.424 HDI, the Tarai Dalits have the lowest HDI value of 0.383. As pointed out in the Table 2.7, the Tarai Dalits are the least educated and mostly illiterate, thus denied opportunities for their empowerment in general. Thus, Mushar, whose HDI remains 0.92, are condemned to inhuman existence. Given the HDI of the Dalits and the prevalent social relations no substantial change in Dalits' status has occurred, as a study based on field survey shows (Dahal and Kumar 2009). This can be corroborated by their representation in the civil service with just 0.4 per cent constituting 33 persons of a total of 9,044 Gazetted class personnel (Nijamati Kitabkhana record; Subba 2008:28). Despite 8 per cent of Dalits' representation in the CA, their voices remain subjugated to the party interests as the majority of them belong to the CPN (Maoist).

Table 2.11: Caste/ethnic representation in civil service
(Gazetted 3rd class and above ranking officers)

Caste/ethnic	1990/1991 No. of officers	Percentage	Caste/ethnic	2006/2007 No. of officers	Percentage
Hill Brahmin	2,330	47.67	Hill Brahmin	4,721	58.3
Hill Chhetri	0,735	15.03	Hill Chhetri	1,080	13.3
Newar	1,277	26.13	Newar	1,152	14.2
Sherpa	0,003	00.06	Janajati	0,264	03.3
Magar	0,016	00.32	Dalit	0,074	00.9
Tamang	0,010	00.20	Madhesi	0,805	09.9
Rai	0,031	00.63			
Limbu	0,007	00.14			
Gurung	0,016	00.32			
Thakali	0,010	00.20			
Unknown	0,066	01.35			
Muslim	0,028	00.57			
Madhesi Brahmin	0,065	01.33			
Madhesi Chhetri	0,038	00.77			
Kayastha	0,055	01.12			
Yadav	0,047	00.96			
Tharu Chaudhari	0,026	00.53			
Unknown	0,127	02.59			
	4,887	99.92		17,096	99.90

Source: Tiwari 2009: 27.

Assertions of the Dalits' rights and their ingenuity thus have become critical in shaping of the new constitution while deliberating on the issue at the Constitutional Committee of the CA. The Constitutional Committee deliberations are heating up as the Dalits and Muslim members of the CA have continued to assert the rights of the Dalits, Muslims, along with other disadvantaged and marginalized people demanding their place in the state restructuring process by drawing public attention on the serious national agenda (Miya 2011). Though the Brahmnic precept and influence are thought to have been apparently weakened by the secularist agenda and social movements in national politics, the realities evidently prove otherwise as even the leaders of the communist parties practice religious rites and seek the advice of fortune tellers.

Janajati Status: Though Nepal is a microcosm of over 103 caste/ethnic and 92 linguistic and 9 religious groups (CBS 2002), Janajatis comprising 8.4 million (36.31%) of the total population of the country are discriminated on the cultural basis (Gurung 2003: 11). A majority of Janajatis, recognized as 59 (now 81) indigenous nationalities by the government, is of mongoloid stock, speakers of Tibeto-Burman dialect and followers of Buddhist sect, Kirati, and Animist religious practices along with Hinduism. Of them 18 groups are spread in the mountains, 24 in the hills, 7 in inner Tarai and 10 in Tarai region. However, the identity politics has placed Janajatis in the centre of national policymaking structure.

The CA is composed of 31 per cent of Janajati representation. Language has become the distinct feature of identity of the person living within the national community in the case of Janajatis. Following this, as they profess different religion they have found the state supported Hindu religion oppressive to their religious and cultural practice as well. Hence, the advocacy for a secular state has become pivotal to ethnopolitics. In addition to this, demands for inclusion, protection of minority rights, social justice, autonomy and even self-determination have become the undercurrents of ethnic assertion (Subba 2008; Lawoti 2005; Pradhan and Shrestha 2005; Gurung et al. 2004).

The government has conceded to ethnic demands for the equity, protect and promote their culture heritage and rights to participation and representation in the national mainstream. By broadening the dimension of social inclusion through rights based approach, recognizing multiculturalism and guaranteeing their distinct identity through linguistic and socio-cultural development within the PRSP framework (Bhattachan and Webster 2005: 25), the government has tried to ameliorate the ethnic contention.

Among the Janajatis, the HDI of Newars (hill group) and Thakalis (mountain group) are distinctly different from rest of the 57 other Janajati groups. As the Table 2.8 shows, Newars have the HDI of 0.726[11] and Thakalis 0.640 whereas the HDI of Tamangs, among the most populous of Janajatis, is only 0.389. Better off are Gurungs with 0. 524, Limbus 0.503, Rai 0.489 and Magars 0.481 (Table 2.7). But this does not mean that all are well off in the ethnic groups mentioned. One crucial factor making the higher HDI among the Gurung, Limbu, Rai and Magar groups is their profession of soldiering in the British and Indian armies. Their life as pensioners therefore differs sharply from others in their own communities. Their HDI supersede even that of Brahmin and Chhetri living in same locality.

Comparably, the HDI score of Janajatis, other than Newar, of the Eastern region is higher than Brahmin and Chhetri of the Mid-Western and Far Western development regions. Again, Newars who have the highest HDI due to being urbanite and opportunity holders, have also people in their community living in penury. For example, a study, though dated, has found that Newars residing in the sub-metropolitan city of Lalitpur (south west of Kathmandu) had higher levels of poverty in comparison to Brahmins and Chhetris and other hill ethnic groups residing in the same locality (cited in Pradhan and Shrestha 2005: 10). The HDR 2009 has recorded the HDI score for 'all Janajatis except Newar' as 0.494. Comparably, the HDI for 'all Brahman/ Chhetri' is put at 0.552 (UNDP/N 2009:44).

Newars, traditionally being the member of business community and Thakalis as traders along with Gurung, Magar, Rai and Limbu as pensioners, have comparably sound economy facilitating their children to attain good schooling to improve their HEI and HDI as well. The hill Janajati female has 60 per cent and male has 82 per cent literacy rate. Likewise, the secondary level schooling of female Janajati is 30 per cent and the male who has attained secondary and higher education is 48 per cent. The education level of Tarai Janajati is however correspondingly low (Table 2.10).

As most of the hill Janajatis preferred joining army their share in national bureaucracy is not promising. Table 2.11 indicates the representation of Janajatis excluding Newar is 3.3 per cent. Newars' representation in national bureaucracy has come down to 14.2 per cent in the fiscal year 2006/07 from 26.13 per cent in 1990/91. The data for the year 2008 are further disappointing recording the representation of the hill Janajatis excluding Newar in the civil service coming down to 1.8 per cent; Newar 13.0 per cent; Tarai Janajati 1.7 in comparison to 71.5 per cent of hill high caste altogether making a total of 75.5 per cent representation (Nijamati Kitabkhana record; Subba 2008: 28).

It has been noticed that representation of Brahmin in civil service is gradually increasing with the advent of democracy. They constitute a group in the top decision making position of bureaucratic hierarchy. A majority of Hill Brahmin civil servants reach the apex position of government secretary who work closely with the ministers of different political parties mostly dominated by the top Brahmin leaders. This situation is factored by their educational level, competitive intent and favoured by linguistic competency as the civil service examinations are conducted in vernacular Nepali. The language barrier is highly discouraging for the non-Nepali mother tongue people to compete in public service examination.

Madheshi Status: Madheshi known as the people of Tarai origin and largely followers of the Hindu religion constitutes 32.0 per cent of the total population of the country (Shah 2006: 1). But their share in the national power matrix remains negligible (Shah 2006; Yadav 2005; Neupane 2000; Gaige 1975). Their representation in national bureaucracy in 2008 was 5.1 per cent besides 4.2 per cent of high caste Madheshis (Brahmin, Rajput etc.). Representation of Tarai indigenous people in bureaucracy was 1.7 per cent. Tarai Dalits are nowhere to be found. Madheshi are the distinct group segregated from the hill people by geography, cultural as well as linguistic practices, although they are not also homogeneous (Dahal 2002 and 2005).

Poverty situation is reportedly most awful in the Tarai where 45 per cent of people have worst poverty ranking; the Madheshis majority districts are the poorest of the poor with 90 per cent of people deprived of education facilities and economic opportunities. According to poverty and deprivation index, Sarlahi[12] ranks 57, Mahottari 61 and Rautahat 68 out of 75 districts. Dhanusha, the hub of Mithila culture and historical city of Janakpur, ranks 46 in the poverty and deprivation index (ICIMOD et al. 2003). Unemployment is rampant as public sectors are mostly the privy of the hill people filling the slots of administrative personnel; police forces are crowed by the hill people and soldiering is not the preferred occupation of the Madheshis despite of their demand for a place in the national army. Their representation in the officers' class of the civil service was 9.9 per cent in 2006/07 in total.

A breakdown figure suggests the civil service is composed of 4.2 per cent of the high caste Madheshis, 5.1 per cent of Madheshi middle caste group, 1.7 per cent of Tarai indigenous people and zero per cent of the Tarai Dalits (Nijamati Kitabkhana, Subba 2008: 28). The hierarchical control of the hill people has forced the Madheshis to live with persecution psyche. The Madheshis living with the widespread feeling of "internal colonization" therefore is not unnatural. The mentality of being the "others" runs deep in the Madheshi phyche. Gaige (1975) and then Shah (2006) have thus noted that the Madheshi community has never been integrated into socio-cultural, economic and political mainstream of Nepali state actually founded in the hill psyche. The hill psyche treats Madheshis as settlers and therefore considered alien. The Madheshi identity was not generally recognized as they are geographically discriminated and marginalized (Gurung 2003).

The most crucial problem facing the Madheshi people has been the denial of citizenship that is somehow resolved with the distribution of over 2.6 million citizenship certificates in anticipation of the Constituent Assembly elections (GON 2007:1-2). But a widely held view in the country is that the genuine Madheshi people were not the beneficiaries of the state act as a large number of eligible Nepalis are still stateless. The types of social suffering the disfranchised Nepalis have to undergo cannot be described but felt as the torture of being treated as alien in their own motherland could turn the people to anything but normal.

Perhaps the reason why the issues of regional autonomy, federalism, and proportional representation were vigorously raised during the Madheshis movement earlier in the post-Jana Andolan-II period is attributed to such discrimination. This assertion and aspiration have resulted into an increased level of Madheshis representation in the CA to 34 per cent. Yet Madhesh remains disengaged from the national mainstream except for those Madheshi people who form and chair the factional political parties and participate as coalition partners of different awkward governments formed after the CA elections.Though the Madheshi movement has successfully achieved certain political goals, particularly, in the formation of various political parties and bettering the position of political activists and their representation through the CA, the common aspiration of the majority of the Madheshi people, however, has not changed. This is reflected in the controversies over the citizenship issue in the Tarai.

The Madheshi community itself represents a cluster of social inequality. For example, in one estimate the HDI value of Madheshi Brahmin/Chhetri is 0.625 (UNDP/N 2009: 44). However, in another estimate the HDI of the Kayastha is 0.904, Rajput 0.733 and Tarai Brahmin 0.722 (Lohani and Vaidya 2009). According to the UNDP/N estimate, the HDI value of 'Madhesi Other Castes' is 0.450; for 'all Tarai/Madhesi groups' the HDI value is put at 0.448 (UNDP/N 2009: 44). Perhaps the literacy and education level in the Tarai is one crucial aspect that continues to divide the Brahmin/Chhetri caste people with rest of the others. The literacy rate of this caste group, irrespective of male/female, is commendable. Their education level with school attainment for female is around 62 per cent and male is over 90 per cent, which constitutes the highest level even in comparison to hill Brahmin/ Chhetri and Newar in Nepal. By contrast the 'Madheshi Other Castes' female has 12 per cent and male has 45 per cent secondary level or higher level education attainment (Table 2.10). Such a situation has compromised their capability as well as prospect in the competitive market place.

Muslim Status: Muslims are supposedly religious bigot and therefore fundamentally outcast. Till very recent past they were treated by conservative Hindus as par with the untouchables. Thus they were naturally excluded, therefore, disadvantaged. Muslims, comprising 4.3 per cent (4.4 per cent by 2011 national census) of the total population of Nepal, are the migrants and minority group and most of them (95%) are settled in the Tarai regions; a few are in the hills, popularly known as *churoutee* – the bangle sellers. Muslims' settlement in Kathmandu has several centuries old history as symbolized by two mosques standing right in the heart of the city in front of the Narayanhiti Royal Palace, now converted into a national museum. The *Raki* Bazaar situated right in front of Indra Chowk at the heart of Kathmandu city is said to have been named after the Muslims trading bangles and other accessories from Iraq and later settled in Nepal. *Raki* is said to be a distorted form for Iraqi in pronunciation. The majority of Muslims are, however, settled mostly in the five Tarai districts of Banke, Bara, Parsa, Rautahat and Kapilbastu – none of the districts is with high HDI value. [13]

Muslims are not only segregated linguistically, religiously and culturally but also educationally reflecting on their poor capability enhancement for commencing economic activities. They are therefore vulnerable and the marginalized lots; linguistically as well as religiously a minority. Urdu as their mother tongue and the system of *madarsa* schooling limits their chances to create opportunities in the market place for their economic enhancement. There are 1,163 *madarsas* spread all over Nepal. Muslim children educated and graduated from these *madarsas* are not recognized in the job market, though *madarsa* education system is recognised. However those educated in the general public schools are the potential candidates for employment in government and other service sectors. Illiteracy, which is over 40 per cent among the Muslim children, denies them the chances of employment. This makes their poverty situation worst. Muslims living below poverty line is 41 per cent as compared with 31 per cent of national average. However, there is no detail on their poverty situation even though the national poverty level has officially declined from 31 to 25 per cent recently (NPC 2010). Muslims have HDI value of 0.401 which is lower than that of the Dalits as a whole but higher than the Tarai Dalits (UNDP/N 2009: 44).

There were very few Muslims in the civil administration rising up to the secretary level; they constitute 0.2 per cent of the total in the Gazetted 3rd class officers in the government (cited in Subba 2008:29). Some others were appointed ministers both during the panchayat regime, and party men elected to the parliament to become cabinet ministers under democracy. Despite being in minority, the level of their political participation has been considerable in comparison to Dalits. They had 1.8 per cent representation in the 1959 parliamentary elections; 1.6 per cent during the panchayat system (1960-90); 2.3 per cent during the 1990s democratic polity, and presently 2.8 per cent in the post-CA transition to federal democratic republic (UNDP/N 2009; World Bank/DFID 2006).

Presently there are 17 Muslim people representing as members of the Constituent Assembly. Besides this, there are Muslims appointed to ambassadorial posts abroad in keeping faith with minority representation. Despite this, Muslims are socially disaffected. They, therefore, persist on their demands for equity, inclusion in decision making processes, provisions for citizenship and proportional representation at all levels (Haug et al. 2009: 115-116). In addition to ensuring their distinct Muslim identity to be enlisted in the Constitution, the *National Muslim Struggle Alliance* has struck an 11-point deal with the Government for forming a Muslim Constitutional Commission, ensuring Muslim Family Law system and mainstreaming the *madarsa* schooling by establishing an educational board (Ansari 2012). However, keeping faith with the Islamic religious culture it would be difficult for Muslims to abnegate their exclusive identity and assimilate into the dominant Hindu cultural ethos of the country despite secularism is the new *dharma* of the Nepali state.

Notes

1. India however has its own estimate of population living below poverty line (BPL). The Indian National Planning Commission under its Deputy Chairman Montek Singh Ahluwalia has announced a person with ICRs.32.00 spending capacity a day is no longer poor. He was persuaded to revise the earlier estimate of ICRs.20.00 a day-to-day living as 'not poor' by the Supreme Court that ridiculed his guesstimate. The revised estimate suggests ICRs.32.00 for urban living per person per day and ICRs.26.00 for a person a day in the rural areas. Thus, according to Jug Suraiya, the Planning Commission poverty threshold is ICRs.965 a month for a person in urban India (less than USD20) and IC Rs.781 (less than USD16) a month in rural India (Jug Suraiya, "Juggle-Bandhi," Times of India, 27 September 2011). The international benchmark set by the World Bank is USD 1.25 a day. In the Nepali case it is less than NRs.52 per day per person which is nearly equal to ICRs. 32 per person a day @ICRs.1=

NRs.1.60 paisa exchange rate. As per the current market price and inflationary trend in Nepal, it is, indeed a great joke on poverty estimate.

2. Besides remittance received by the families back home, there are thousands of ex-Gorkha soldiers settled back home in rural Nepal as pensioners who receive regular pensions from the British and Indian Army Pension Camps. The British Gurkha pensioners are relatively rich who usually live in Kathmandu and semi-urban settlements. With the British government's liberal visa permit for its ex-Gurkhas many had left Nepal to live in Britain. This has led to a cut down in the 'remittance' earning of Nepal.

3. In the Fiscal Year 2008/09 budget, the coalition government led by the CPN (Maoist) had increased the social security allocation by 440 per cent amounting to Rs. 4.41 billion for the year in actuality. The government has increased monthly social security support to single women, senior citizens reducing eligibility age to 60 years from 75, physically disables as well as to the people belonging to fast disappearing ethnic groups ranging from Rs. 300 to partially handicapped, Rs. 1,000 to handicapped and at the rate of Rs.500 for other categories for month. Along with this, approximately Rs 1 billion was raised to constitute 'Local Literacy Volunteers' in each ward of nearly 4,000 VDCs with recruitment of some 35,000 youths for the training purpose. Likewise, the budget speech stipulated to create a fund of Rs.500 million to promoted self-employment among youths and made arrangement for providing Rs.200,000 non-collateral loans for that purpose (GON 2008). For creating the latter fund, salary of a day was deducted from all the employees of the government and University services through a notice circulation. How had all these commitment been used and whether the funds disbursed appropriately and reached the target properly is not publicly disclosed.

4. Nepal is not only in the bracket of low-income countries but also falls in the region of extreme poverty where more than 25 per cent of population lives below $1 a day. If expanded to the World Bank's benchmark for poverty estimate at $1.25 a day the poverty threshold level would certainly increase. Poverty is in itself a trap with low human and depleting natural capital forcing utterly destitute struggling to survive (Sachs 2006: 56).

5. This collaborative report prepared by the CBS, The World Bank, DFID and ADB covers the period between the NLSS-I and the

NLSS-II (1995/96 – 2003/04) indicating importance experience in improvements in economic and human development amidst violent conflict (CBS 2006).

6. Women, Janajati, Dalit and Madhesi are the four social groups recommended for critical appraisal and research on social inclusion in a concept paper by the Chairperson of the Interim Steering Committee at the Social Inclusion Research Fund (Gurung 2006).

7. *Chaupadi* is a customary system prevalent in hills/mountain district of western Nepal according to which girls after puberty and women have to spend at least a week outside their home either in a cowshed or in a leaky thatched hut during their menstruation period or child birth when they are considered impure even by their own family members and treated like untouchables. Besides women, 19 per cent of girls aged between 15 and 19 were observing *chaupadi*, discloses the preliminary report of *The Nepal Multiple Indicator Cluster Survey* (NMICS) conducted by the Central Bureau of Statistics in 2010. No legal remedy on such inhuman treatment of women is available. Similarly, widows are maltreated in the society and sometimes victimized accusing them of witchcraft and treated inhumanly. The dowry system prevalent in the Madhes (Tarai) is another social curse incongruous to civilized cultural practice that reinforces inequality and worst the dowry deaths of brides. Domestic violence against women is pervasive. The recent disclosure of the cases of women in Dang district where more than 227 women had to leave their home due to excessive violence committed by their men/husband etc., are denied justice to reconcile with their plight (KC 2010). These social anomalies have superseded laws as caused by laxity in enforcement. Preference for sons over daughter is a case in this point. The movements for violence against women are advertizing the cause by spreading social awareness; yet has failed to make any serious dent on discouraging it.

8. General preference for sons over daughters has led to girl child killings at birth is termed as gendercide questioning 'what happened to 100 million baby girls?' in the world (The Economist, 6-12 March 2010: 65-68).

9. Political Parties' Central Office Data, 2011.

10. Besides some hill ethnic groups who practice egalitarianism to some extent and provide greater equality between men and

women, the high caste Hindu groups are found more conservative and inflexible in their customary practice in relations to women. Among the Dalits and Muslims women are the worst off. The cultural orthodoxy of Muslim community is yet to disappear for the better treatment of women. For women, exclusion and disempowerment begins at home. Violence against women remains critical challenge which the new mantra of empowerment has not been able to prevent. Extensive field surveys have verified this assumption to be true (Dahal and Kumar 2009; Chakravarti 2008: 10-17; World Bank/DFID 2006).

11. Perhaps because of the variation in methodology, the HDI 0.616 given for Newars in the Human Development Report (HDR) 2009 is different than in Table 2.8 cited above. Likewise, the HDI for Hill Brahman and Hill Chhetri given in the HDR is 0.612 and 0.514 respectively which is lower than that of Newar (UNDP/N 2009: 44). But Table 2-8 suggests otherwise with 0.765 HDI for Hill Brahmans which is higher than Newar and HDI 0.549 for Chhetri, better than the HDR (Lohani and Vaidya 2009).

12. Interestingly Sarlahi district comprising more than 700,000 people that has always enjoyed a privileged position in the central cabinet either under the king's direct rule or democratic system is one of the most backward districts in the country. The incumbent cabinet is composed of 4 ministers from Sarlahi with powerful portfolios but the district remains in a pitiable situation. Former Prime Minister Madhav K. Nepal is from Rautahat district, which is also the most backward district crowded with Muslim population. Earlier, there were several times prime ministers from the Far-West and Mid-West development regions both during the panchayat rule and under democracy, the fate of these regions however remains miserable in socio-economic sectors as the power elites migrated to Kathmandu abandoning their places of origin.

13. For an overview on Muslims in Nepal see (Hachhethu 2009).

III

Assessing Government Policy

Policymakers are increasingly concerned with the problems caused by the exclusion creating structural anomalies in social relationships. Inequalities in various forms have become the most common concern. Income inequalities and regional disparities within the state fundamentally caused by disproportionate government spending have endured social exclusion by design. Government has thus taken some important decisions to change the overall socioeconomic situation through adoption of strategies for removing the barriers against inclusion. These are the commitments posited in the Comprehensive Peace Agreement (CPA) for 'political, economic and social transformation' followed by the constitutional processes with adherence to progressive restructuring of the state to resolve the existing class, caste, regional and gender related problems through competitive multiparty democratic system (Preamble of the CPA 2006 and the Interim Constitution 2007). Social justice[1] through social inclusion is a crucial agenda in Nepal's efforts towards human development. Translating commitments into reality providing social security, social justice with inclusion of deprived and marginalized people in the development process remain a challenge.

Exclusion has been perpetuated in Nepal on the basis of the multiple identities categorized as caste/ethnicity, culture, religion, location, age and gender. Individual/personal experience of exclusion in society has become relational but differs significantly based on caste and class, gender and race with power and powerlessness. This constitutes the identity politics. Narratives of identity are reflected in the contending issue of federalism determined by ethnicity in the state restructuring process. Unitary state with excessively centralized system of governance presided over by the constitutional monarchy had exemplified bad governance. Systemic change with reform in governance had been public demand reflected in the Jana Andolan-II. This made the change in the institutional structure of the state based on the policy of exclusion an imperative. The structural issues perceived as the prominent reasons of prevalent inequality, poverty, unemployment and discrimination are briefly discussed below.

On Religious Inequality

Dominant religious ethos remains Hinduism long pursued as the state promoted and protected religion by constitutionally declaring the country as a Hindu state on a majoritarian basis in a multicultural and multireligious society. Popular alienation hit the rock bottom with the first ever drafted democratic constitution promulgated in November 1990 stipulating Nepal as a Hindu state. It became controversial as it contravened the religious freedom in the country. This perception was strongly embedded in the minds of non-Hindus who expected to live in a secular state under democracy. This exclusionary provision was conceived by the non-Hindus, though in minority, as a process of derecognizing and deconstructing their social identity, therefore, debased. The government's position on religion after the success of the April 2006 popular movement has changed for the better.

With the abolition of monarchy, Nepal has become a federal democratic republic and constitutionally a secular, inclusive state as well (Article 4, Interim Constitution 2007: 2). Article 23 of the Interim Constitution, providing 'religious rights' to each individual, has however, restricted religious conversion by discouraging any act of infringement on others' religious belief. Secularism has ultimately become the state religion commensurate with the idea of social inclusion. This shift in the identification of the state confined to an exclusive religion towards a secular state draws cultural legitimization of power of the state.

Though Nepal has witnessed occasional religious tensions, particularly between the Hindus and Muslims, these are in rarity. Undercurrents of religious tensions erupt due to external cause and influence. For example, Hindu/Muslim communal violence in neighbouring Uttar Pradesh following the demolition of the Babri Mosque in Ayodhya in 1992 had exacerbated tension and sense of insecurity among the Nepali Muslims. The 1 September 2004 riots in Kathmandu by the Hindu fundamentalist group, the *Pashupati Sena*, an arm of the *Indian Shiv Sena* that occurred against the background of the killing of 12 Nepalis in Iraq by the anti-American resistance group on 31 August, destroying Muslim mosques, and properties belonging to the Muslim citizens had caused trauma and insecurity amongst the minority community (Kumar 2008a: 286-89). Again, protests by Hindu fundamentalists in India against the declaration of Nepal as a secular state in 2006 and support by the *Nepali Shiv Sena* reflected in the events such as that occurred in late 2006 in Nepalgunj, a Muslim majority city, were averted in the midst of heightened tensions. The regional and global connection of the Muslims as a religious group is both strength and weakness of this community.

Christianity also has its influence in Nepali community. Christians in Nepal are a tiny minority who lived in peace until some Hindu fanatics bombed their Church in Lalitpur city in Kathmandu Valley in 2008. Secularism is a practice that has to deconstruct the religious mindset. Majoritarian syndrome constructs the religious mindset in Nepal, which is a common South Asian attribute. Thus it is claimed that religious conversion has occurred in the name of secularist identity. Certain political parties like the Rastriya Prajatantra party, Nepal (RPP, Nepal), committed to their anti-secularist ethos, have adversely remarked that tens of thousands of people are converted into Christianity in the post-2006 period. Massive influx of foreign fund in Nepal is suspected to have played a pivotal role in religious conversion. Perhaps the bombing of the Church exemplify the fanatical reprisal of the Hindus. This is a clear symptom of religious conflict as the Hindu fanatics think their religious sanctity has been infringed with. These cases show legal guarantee of religious freedom is not enough.

Poor people from religious minorities (Buddhist, Muslim, Christian), however, have yet to experience the benefits of Nepal government's declaration of a secular state on 18 May 2006, including equitable access to public funding for religious facilities. This study suggests that poor Muslim communities are especially vulnerable, experiencing multiple and overlapping sources of social and economic exclusion. Religious minorities would like their religious identity respected. Muslims in particular have become a disaffected group as their independent identity has not been recognized by the state. Despite their distinct history, tradition, culture and religious identity, the state restructuring committee of the CA has not recognized their separate existence by the act of lumping them together within the framework of the larger Madheshi community of Nepal Tarai.

This has become one of the most serious points of contention in the deliberations of the Constitutional Committee. As a matter of fact, the Muslim community dwelling in all the three ecological zones of Nepal has its own identity, consciously preserved and distinct culture in practice. They celebrate their own religious festivals such as *Bakare Id* and *ramajan*; the government has declared the day as national holiday. Their demand, thus is, they should be treated separately recognizing their rightful place in the society. Moreover, it naturally suggests that religious tensions exist beneath the surface in parts of Nepali society and there is thus a need for more research and sensitive monitoring of this situation as well as policy efforts to promote tolerance, mutual complicity and greater social inclusion.

Identity politics has both ethnonationalist and religious fervour sensitizing the social and political space. As Samuel Huntington provocatively views, religious identity has become a worldwide phenomenon compartmentalizing the world divided by the fault lines of civilizations making conflicts on religious grounds inevitable (Huntington 1993; 1996). This pessimistic but diagnostic politics of identity has led scholars like Amartya Sen to examine the unfortunate connection between violence and tendency to identify it either with ethnicity or religion. According to him, "violence is promoted by the sense of inevitability about some allegedly unique – often belligerence – identity that we are supposed to have" (Sen 2006). Identity in many cases has categorically become divisive and hostile. Such a situation is gradually seeping through the debates on federalism crucially tied to the question of a single-identity or multiple-identity federal and provincial units in the state restructuring process in Nepal.

Rising ethnic assertion has forced the dominant groups into defensive leading them to consciously revive their *Khas* identity comprising mainly of Brahmin, Chhetri, Thakuri and Dashnami group who constitutes over 33 per cent of national population.[2] The point to ponder is if there will be a federal unit based on the ethnic population of 0.04 per cent of national population, would it be sensible to deny such identity and recognition to the people representing one third of the total population (Lohani 2011). Such a case makes it clear that the concerned authorities of the state require being vigilant and alert to any eventuality involving identity politics. The minority assertion is in vogue. Demand for inclusion of the minorities providing appropriate political space has become central to policy debates on hitherto neglected and suppressed issues. Adopting secularism is not enough. The secularist agenda is a contested one which is under fire both at home and abroad. But being republic is obviously being secularist.

On Caste, Ethnic Discrimination

The Muluki Ain 1854 was considered the first instance of social segregation introduced in Nepal in modern times, the crucial ingredient of which has been the system of touchability and untouchability. Conceptualizing the state in such a state of relationships between the citizens with rules framed in accordance with the caste and kinship had continued as human bondage in Nepali social system. This uncivil social code was abolished in 1963 by the new Muluki Ain. Numerous legal measures against untouchability were taken but it persists in social relations along with discrimination on the basis of caste and ethnicity.

This is the persistent problem and challenges it posed in the social relations are apparently unending despite prohibitive regulations. The government had established 'Neglected, Suffered and Depressed Class Upliftment Development Board' in 1997 in relations to discriminated and oppressed communities. Following this, the National Dalits Commission was established by the government in 2002. Dalits are the most deprived groups in a situation where casteism prevails. Recognizing their genuine grievances the Ministry of Local Development has initiated several Dalit focused poverty alleviation projects (Sharma Pokharel 2004). The government has introduced Caste-based Discrimination and Untouchability Act 2011 to discourage the practice of social malice, yet far from being implemented.

Caste inequalities can be traced in social relations, which are degradingly and regularly reinforced in the case of poor Dalit communities in rural areas. Livelihood insecurities emerged as top priorities among Dalits; landlessness as central to their vulnerability; and injustice and indignity of the untouchability practices to which they are still subjected have been a cause of serious concern. A sample of their wretched existence and backwardness is reflected in the following Table providing statistics on Gazetted 3rd class officers, from mid-April 1983 to mid-April 2002, the Dalits' representation was not more than two in a given year. Their poor educational background is notably one of the crucial reasons for their failure to qualify both for application and selection in the Public Service Commission examination.

Table 3.1: Number of Dalits in the Gazetted 3rd class officers in the Government service

Caste	1983/84		'86/87		'88/89		'90/91		'92/93		'94/95		'96/97		'98/99		2001/02		2006/07	
	No.	%	No.	%	No.	%	No.	%	No.	%	No.	%	No.	%	No.	%	No.	%	No.	%
Dalits	0	00	1	0.4	3	0.5	3	0.7	2	0.4	2	0.2	1	0.1	0	00	0	00	74	0.9

Source: UNDP, Nepal Human Development Report 2004, Table 13: 178; Tiwari 2009.

The indigenous minority groups known as Janajati or the ethnics are a community of highly diverse people. This community differs in terms of poverty levels, level of political organization, language and sense of identity. The Janajatis can be classified into three categories: advantaged, disadvantaged, and highly disadvantaged. Newar and Thakali fall in the first category whereas Chepang and even Limbu fall into the third category. They are mostly outside the Hindu caste system, except Newars who are also adherents of Hinduism; they are for greater political representation and recognition of their language and culture. However, ethnopolitics has yet to become a pan-Janajati nationalism bordering on violence despite the ethnics feel they have been treated unjustly by the state in its historical formation ranging from repression of language to their cultural ethos.

The National Federation for Indigenous Nationalities (NEFIN) has identified 81 nationalities as against the previous record of 59 nationalities in the country. It has recorded 11 vanishing, 50 marginalized, 17 excluded and 2 opportunity holders groups along with 1 another unidentified nationality groups. However, this revised report on nationalities is yet to be the final one.[3] NEFIN is an umbrella organization working towards greater equality of Janajati groups with that of other caste people. Likewise, there is Nepal Indigenous Women's Federation (NIWF) and several affiliated agencies are constantly engaged in exercises seeking social justice and equality in the society.

The recognition of multiculturalism and multilingual identity by the state with constitutionally abolishing the caste system has been a positive step towards the formation of state into a social compact in view of the policy debates raging on the role of indigenous people in the state restructuring processes (Malla et al 2005). The directive principles and policies of the state have vowed to end 'all discriminatory law' from the state to promote equity and justice. It should also end the customary practices traditionally followed in actual human relationship. Facets of liberalism expounded in the Interim Constitution have however become problematic in practice. Societal relationships and customary practices are difficult to change overnight. Differences are betraying political consensus even on the previously agreed agendas. Therefore, the future remains indefinite so far the proposals of creating federal units either on the linguistic or ethnic basis are concerned as the challenges are mounting in the Constituent Assembly debates.

On Gender Inequality

Discrimination against women features prominently, among others, in three social spheres. Political participation, employment market and ownership and decision making are all skewed against women. Though numerous laws have been passed in favour of ending inequalities and discriminations, the majority of people in power are actually detrimental to change the traditional value system. As a study records, there were "118 legal provisions and 67 schedules, spread in 54 different laws, including the [1990] Constitution, that are discriminatory against women" (FWLD 2000). Another study on discriminatory provisions on Nepal's legal system conducted through the perspective of the Convention on Elimination of All Forms of Discrimination against Women (CEDAW-1979) has found 15 acts, 18 laws discriminatory and over 100 flaws (Sigdel 2009). Domestic violence against women remains pervasive (KC 2010).

Recent data on domestic violence suggest verbal abuse endured by women is 66 per cent followed by 33 per cent related to emotional ones. 77 per cent of the perpetrators of such non-physical violence against women are the family members. Dowry deaths in the Tarai region are moreover also caused by the family machination. The data compiled by a study conducted by the Women's Rehabilitation Centre (WOREC) comprising 1,594 women throughout the country reveal 76.5 per cent of women suffering from various sorts of violence were married prominently victimized by their husbands and family members. Social violence accounts for 21 per cent and rape amounts to 9 per cent (WOREC data cited in Kathmandu Post, 5 December 2010a). Notwithstanding the passing of the 'Domestic Violence (Crime and Punishment) Act 2066' (2009) against Women as an additional legislative measure for establishing a just society women have continued to suffer.

The situation of women is desperate, particularly, in the Far West and Mid-Western Nepal where polygamy has been the foremost reason for domestic violence followed by the suspicion of infidelity by the absentee husband along with their alcoholism and gambling habits. Domestic violence is a common practice despite forbidden by the law. In some districts like Jajarkot, torture and violence had led more than 12 women to commit suicide and more than 200 complaints registered at the police posts without any legal remedy due to political interferences (Singh 2011). Similarly, the police posts in the Dandeldhura district are regularly visited with the complaints of domestic violence by the victims – both young and middle aged married women. As per the data there were 37 complaints received in the month of July that increased to 27 complaints within the first two weeks of August 2011, but initiative to stop domestic violence is faltering (Pant 2011).

However, with the adoption of statutory measures on women's rights the legal constraints are being eliminated to ensure gender equality. In 2006, the Gender Equality Act 2063 BS had discarded several provisions of 17 other Acts and Nepal Code was amended. Followed by this, the Twelfth Amendment of Nepal Code 2007 was introduced, which also made significant changes from gender perspective. Steps towards this has been taken by the Interim Constitution of Nepal 2007 in Article 13 (rights to equality) and Article 20 (rights of women) guaranteed by the Fundamental Rights for changes in existing provisions. Article 20 (2) is in lieu with the ILO-183 involving maternity rights of women endorsed by the Labour Act in Nepal.

Amendment was also made in the provision related to women's property and land rights making the rights of women of unmarried or married status equal in sharing parental property, thus, recognizing their rights to control over resources. Equal inheritance right is indeed a battle won by the women's movement simultaneously launched as an offshoot of democratic movement in Nepal since the early 1940s. Rights to inherit parental property are certainly a measure to change the social and economic status of women and their children to avoid being denied the patrilineal link after their marriage. The constitutional changes have made certain other positive contributions in relation to women's rights. The Gender Equality Act 2063 (2006), for example, has even broadened the definition of rape to include marital rape providing a married woman's rights of consent.

Similarly, the Citizenship Act of 2006 also qualified women's right by allowing children to obtain citizenship certificate through their mother's name. But certain misunderstanding on the issue remains. Controversy over the citizenship as fundamental right of women on the basis of hereditary inheritance or accreditation, and the children of the Nepali women as single parent is pending at the Constitutional Committee. Resolution to the question of lineage or naturalization citizenship to a child born to a Nepali woman remains. Obtaining citizenship by the children born of Nepali mother and foreign father is also problematic. Transfer of citizenship of a Nepali woman to her foreign husband is also complicated by the need of the person's presence in the country for at least 15 years unlike in the case of a Nepali male citizen marrying a foreign female. In the later case the female requires a two years' stay with renouncing previous citizenship. This precondition has also been changed recently. It is said that any foreign woman married to a Nepali male citizen can obtain accredited citizenship at once if she desires so by renouncing her former identity. On the question of citizenship, the girl child or woman by birth has been continued to be discriminated. This is widely viewed as patrilineal bigotry. For example, two women members of the CA view that the top guns of their political parties have discarded both the principles of equality and nationalism on the question of citizenship to the people of Nepal (Pandey 2012; Rai 2012).

The women's caucus composed of the members of the CA is genuinely concerned over equitable treatment to their demand in relation to citizenship rights. Understandably, their reservation is especially focused on the draft of the Fundamental Rights and Directive Principle Committee of the CA, which they term discriminatory. Particularly on the provision of citizenship by lineage, as stated above, the draft assumes the necessity of both of the parents being Nepalis. However, in the case of foreign nationals, particularly, a woman married to a Nepali citizen, that woman will be instantaneously eligible for Nepali citizenship and so will be her siblings from Nepali husband to claim citizenship by lineage. This rule, does not, however, apply in the case of a Nepali woman married to a foreigner. The women's caucus is drawing attention to such discriminatory practice. Awareness campaigns on the rights as such to inform the poor and excluded women living in remote villages and activate them are unfolding. Children born out of a conjugal relationship between a Nepali female and a foreign male are facing difficulties in obtaining citizenship.

However, all the ministries have appointed gender focal points. The constitutional provisions and the decision to secure candidates proportionately from different social and regional groups in the election to the Constituent Assembly 2008 also increased participation of women and men from different social and regional groups in the political field. The Constituent Assembly is presently composed of 197 (32.77%) women representatives from diverse sections of society. This is one of the major indicators of women's empowerment in participatory politics. But in other competitive areas like in civil service and judiciary the proportion of women is very low reasonably because of their low education attainment as well as the social disapproval. Women's representation in Special and Class I levels in Gazetted civil service increased from 2.4 per cent in 2000 to 4.5 per cent in 2007.

At the time of writing there are two women serving at Secretary Level (Special class) in the government. Conversely, their representation at the officer level (Gazetted Class II and III) rather decreased from 6.2 to 5.3 per cent in the same period (Nijamati Kitabkhana 2064 (2007). This scenario is gradually changing with the introduction of reservation system after the second amendment of the Civil Service Act in 2006. According to the statistical record of the Nijamati Kitabkhana (civil employees' record office), there were a total of 11,303 women serving in the government at different levels 2009/10. A comparable data of women serving in the government in the fiscal year 2000/01 was 8,768 that increased to 10,456 in 2006/07. This has not happened in judiciary however; judges are very few: two out of 20; four out of 110 and one out of 135 judges are women in Supreme Court, Court of Appeal and District Court respectively (Administration Section, Supreme Court 2009).

This does not however mean to suggest that the participation of women is disappointing. The reality is that women are no more caged within the households; their participation in society is rather increasing despite numerically low. Take for instance, the civil service. There are 8,731 women out of 72,838 employees; of 56,077 police personnel 3,169 are women; there are 1,115 women in the 95,000 strong army; 60,000 teachers and 3,000 medical practitioners; 1,000 lawyers and 800 journalists. Over 4,000 women are serving in the banking sector in the country (Shrestha 2010: 20-22).

The Ministry of Women, Children and Social Welfare (MWCSW) is alert to the gender related problems. However, it has not been able to deal with the challenge of ensuring gender equity in resource allocation in decision making of the government. This is reflected in the proportion of the budget indirectly supporting gender equity declining from 1.8 per cent in 2008/09 to 1.5 per cent in 2009/10 despite increase in programme budget of MWCSW in the proportion of directly supportive budget from 17.9 per cent to 34.5 per cent in the same period (cited in NPC 2010: 55). The MWCSW is allocated with Rs.8.66 billion (3.38%) budget in the fiscal year 2009/10 besides mega-spending on the women related programmes under different headings that indirectly benefit the gender issue. Despite this, the gender mainstreaming programme is yet to be implemented sensitively (NPC 2010: 55-56). This creates the gap between commitment and implementation.

Gender sensitivity by the government in Nepal was first expressed in the Sixth Five Year Plan (1981-85) under the Panchayat system recognizing the need to improve their social situation. In other words, women's welfare was made a development issue. Not until democracy was restored in 1990 and the Eighth Plan drafted women's rights were recognized and treated as equal to their male counterparts in principle. The Tenth Plan has incorporated women's empowerment through affirmative action as a part of the PRSP with a perspective of providing equal access to decision making power in the long run. This process against discrimination and deprivation should however be acknowledged in the initial stage. The National Women Commission is also working as a watch dog asserting gender right and equality.

The long enduring gender movement in the cultural context involving freedom and independence for women with assertion for sharing political rights with equal opportunity through income generation activities beginning, especially, in early 1970s, has graduated to both income and right based activities against discriminatory social practices in the post-democratic polity. Recognition of political rights of women was initially made through reservation of 5 per cent of seats for representation with constitutional dispensation in 1990. The Local Self-Governance Act 1999 had mandated the representation of deprived, disadvantaged and marginalized people constituting women, Janajatis and Dalits in local bodies by further liberalizing the political space.

Presently, the constitutional rights that women in Nepal have acquired through positive discrimination are 33 per cent representation in every aspect of public life, although they constitute over 50 per cent of the country's population. This right is asserted through different medium as freshly exemplified by the demand for 33 per cent seats for women in the 35-member council of ministers. The representation of women in the present cabinet is just 14.28 per cent, which is not even meeting 50 per cent of the policy commitment. Women's representation, however, remains always below the stipulated number in the cabinet or the council of ministers. Even the 44-member cabinet formed in 2009 had 5 women ministers, which was a lowly 11.36 per cent.

The collective effort of the interparty women's caucus in the CA perhaps would have positive effect on the prospect of power sharing on decision making with adequate representation and participation of women in the national life. Comparably, four of the fourteen Constitutional Committees of the CA are headed by women also with commendable number of representation in parliamentary committees. They have also raised voice for their proportional representation in all state organs as their entitlement. Women are thus working as lobbyist in the CA as well as in the legislative-parliament to safeguard their broader interests despite their position till date appears only as dissenting voices.

On Regional Inequality

The pervasive feeling of long subjugation among the people living in the Tarai exploded in January 2007 in the shape of Madheshi Andolan that led the Government formed after Jana Andolan-II to recognize the Madheshi plight and agree to their demands. This was another dimension of ethnic upsurge in Nepal besides the Janajati movements taking place in the hills. Consequently, the Interim government has signed a 22-point agreement with the leaders of the Madheshi movement – the Madheshi Janaadhikar Forum (MJF) – agreeing to provide national recognition to their dress, language and culture (point 7) and facilitate proportional representation in all political appointments, Military and Foreign Service and education service and Commissions instituted by the government of Nepal (point 8). More crucial agenda of the agreement has been the provision of federalism with autonomous provinces in due consideration of the sovereignty, national unity and territorial integrity of Nepal (point 6).

The Madheshi movement has strived for proportional representation, provincial autonomy and federalism for self-rule making momentum towards inclusiveness of the traditionally excluded community (Deshantar Weekly, 2 September 2007). The Madheshi uprising was indeed a national awakening for many of the political leaders belonging to the hill high caste community but represented mostly from the Tarai regions forcing them to put the neglected region at the centre of the national political agenda of inclusive democracy.

The disadvantaged Madheshis have shown their moon-lightening force during the Constituent Assembly (CA) elections.

The Tarai based political parties have emerged with strong regional appeal and electoral support. Consequently, the CA comprises of 84 representatives elected to the 6 Madheshi political parties. To their satisfaction, the post-CA Nepal has the first elected Madheshi President as the head of the federal republic. And another Madheshi is elected as the Vice-President of the country as well. Despite this, the Madhesh based political parties are concerned over the inclusion of the issues and agendas raised in the new Constitution during the signing of the 22-point agreement. The crux of the problem, the Madheshi leadership and the people in general feel, is in the implementation of the commitments.

There is also a persistent problem caused by the state exclusionary policy of denial of citizenship to Madheshi people and Muslims as well denying them the voting rights and participation in the national decision making process with the sense of belongingness. Though their disenfranchisement, to a larger extent, has been eliminated through the distribution of citizenship to some 2.6 million people on the eve of the Constituent Assembly elections in 2008, the Madheshi dissatisfaction remains as they are yet looked at suspiciously by the hill people. Citizenship does not only provide national identity, it also guarantees political rights to a person as the citizen of the state. Such an arrangement has drawn the Madheshi people directly in the mainstream national politics through their enthusiastic participation in the CA elections despite continued political dissension.

Despite this, the Madheshi movement has succeeded in opening up the vista of possibilities for the inhabitants of the Nepal Tarai that was hitherto closed to them. This is the most significant change that the Madheshi movement has brought about in the hill-centric national politics. No longer can Madhesh or the inclusive aspirations of the people of the Tarai be ignored in the political equation of Nepali state. Assertion of the Madheshi identity nevertheless has made power sharing and broadening of participation through providing them the political space an imperative.

On the other hand, the most disheartening case of regional disparities and discrimination is the Karnali Zone and the Jumla district in particular. Social exclusion, if understood as denial of 'a right to have rights' is the fate of Karnali Zone, the most underdeveloped region of Nepal. Some mountainous districts of Mid-West and Far-Western Nepal are virtually abandoned by the government; these are the economically deprived and dirt poor regions always facing food scarcity and thus starvation.[4] Most of these districts fall into different anticipated federal units, though disputed, in the proposed concept paper submitted to the CA. The economic feasibility of the federal units is questionable on account of the perennial food scarcity and persistent poverty as well as low density of population. Of the proposed 14 federal units, there are Jadan, Khaptad and Karnali federal states in the Mid-West and Far-Western hills and mountains with mostly questionable economic viability and with highly negligible and limited revenue generating capacity for fiscal management of the provinces in making (Pyakuryal et al. 2009).

On Language Discrimination

Language is a critical variable that plays a crucial role in identity politics. Multilingualism has become the national policy drive with the change in the political environment. Electronic media, including FM radio services and television, have aired news and programmes in different ethnic languages. The *Gorkhapatra*, a vernacular national daily, has continued to devote two pages in print on various languages and related subjects. The government has adopted a policy of primary level teaching in local language or mother tongue. However, the problem is that preparation of textbooks in several languages is facing difficulties.

Being a multilingual state some 126 languages/dialects are spoken in Nepal of which 92 are officially recognized.[5] But only 18 languages are live, safe and secure and the rest are endangered and moribund along with some 40 languages of minorities have been virtually extinct (cited in Subba 2008: 17-18; Yadav 2009: 95-121; Toba 1992). The government has reached understanding with various lingual groups to adopt a trilingual policy for conducting official works, education and international communication in (i) Mother tongue, (ii) Nepali language, and (iii) English, for example, while signing agreement with MJF (Deshantar Weekly, 2 September 2007; Yadav 2009).

Maintaining vernacular *devnagari* Nepali as the national language and other languages as language of nationalities was the elite interest in the past as reflected in the 1990 constitution. Previously, the language policy of the government was thoroughly discriminatory with the promotion of single language in official communication and uses, in education and general conversation. The spread of Nepali language throughout the country, though a process of bonding together of nationalities living within the territory of the Kingdom, had a negative impact on the flourishing of other languages. Nepali becomes a *lingua franca*. Spoken and understood throughout the country, the language is rich in vocabulary as other national language. It has formal and informal words in addressing the people at conversation. For example, words used for "you" as 'ta', 'timi', 'tapai' and 'hajur' express social position of the person addressed as well as degrees of intimacy.

The word hajur, though derived from the Urdu language 'hujoor', is normally used by high caste people, royalty or their affiliates in mutual exchange indicating their high civil and social status. It has become the elite language of conversation. This word is also an indication of the language use by the ruling class groups. These people never use that word in addressing their subordinates or commoners in the society. It is thus rich in hierarchical and impersonal construction. Hajur, as honorific word, now has become as common as other words in the daily use of people. Linguistic diversities, however, have brought up complexities to ethnically heterogeneous population. Though the Interim Constitution 2007 has recognized all the mother tongues spoken in Nepal as national language and their uses in local administration are being legalized, the *devnagari* Nepali language and script has been declared as the official language (Article 5). As Nepali language is spoken and understood by the majority of population, its acceptance as a language of communication has become a reality.

However, the elites' interests remain their preference for vernacular language – Nepali – as a means for communication, legal administration and public service examination. It is on the record that a majority of people who fail in public service examination are those candidates whose mother tongue is not Nepali language. The people with Sanskrit language background with Nepali as their mother tongue score better and scale high in the public service examinations. One of the fundamental reasons for the high percentage of Brahmin caste group of people in civil service, mostly in the decision making level, is their command in the official language. Proficiency in spoken and written Nepali language is the basis for opening opportunities in civil service and other professions including media and journalism.

On the other hand, the need of interlingual balance is acutely felt. Recognizing Nepal as a multilingual state the 1990 Constitution had stipulated for providing primary education in mother tongue; the Interim Constitution 2007 has accepted it as the fundamental rights of the children. Yet this mandate of constitution remains ineffective in the absence of textbooks in mother tongues, absence of trained teachers and even in the absence of policy directives. Bilingual teaching for non-Nepali speaking children, though favoured, has become more confusing both for the teacher and students. The government has seriously considered the necessity of linguistic survey in Nepal to concretize its language policy in the future. The NPC has launched a four year programme on the linguistic survey of Nepal in collaboration with Tribhuvan University. There are linguistic groups with disappearing languages. The government's objective has been promoting language and literature; in other words, cultural preservation of the people. This, indeed, is a reversal of the role of the government in language policy as the motivation of national politics has changed from exclusivity to inclusivity.

On Decentralization

The country is raged with the debates on local autonomy, self rule and self-determination to preserve and promote participatory rights and electoral representation of the people in decision making apparatuses even at the grassroots level. The Local Self-Government Act-1999 was adopted after long deliberations. The major objective of the Act was 'equity, inclusion and empowerment' of women and disadvantaged groups. The practice of discouraging their involvement in the decision making either in the local bodies or in the community organization had continued. The high caste/low caste segregation also continued as the Dalits in the local bodies had to face humiliation from other members of the community. Likewise, the donor funded gender equity programme in local bodies' activities had become cosmetic.

Similarly, in the absence of any policy link between poverty reduction and decentralization, the local bodies are superseded by the line agency of the government in implementing such programmes. Thus the local bodies, particularly at the VDC levels and other community organizations, being capable of addressing poverty reduction issues at the grassroots, are denied the opportunity to function as it involves the elite interests in utilizing the fund. This happened before the country was rendered local government-less since a decade after the tenure of the elected local bodies expired in July 2002. This constitutes a lapse of two terms of the formation of the representative local authority of popular choice. The absence of local bodies has caused anomalies in governance constraining the process of inclusion, representation, and participation for implementing development programmes in accordance with the local needs.

The priorities of the people in rural areas are largely context-specific. The local decision making is critical to ensure that people's development priorities are effectively met. The situation today is that most of the local bodies among nearly 4,000 village development committees are even without secretaries appointed by the government due to the growing insecurity caused by unsocial elements and serious threat posed by the Maoist cadres. In 2009 there were 58 per cent of VDCs that had secretaries but were not available to expedite necessary works. Development activities at the local level have become more exclusivist catering to the influence, preference and discretion of the political elites in control of the line agencies like ministry of local development, central level political representatives and local development officers appointed by the government (Kumar 2008b: 30; ADDCN 2001).

One of the primary objectives behind decentralization policy is to enhancing the capacity of the local communities to manage social sector services such as schools and health posts through formation of management communities after devolution of power by the central authority. Despite certain difficulties in meeting the target of 15,200, transferring of 9,810 schools to local communities was successfully made in March 2009 (MOF 2010:179). Altogether 11,410 schools out of a total of 33,160 schools are transferred to local communities within the decade of the programme initiated with the financial assistance of the World Bank.

However, the plan has not been well received in the communities. As per an assessment of the Ministry of Education, the programme has utterly failed to address the sensitivities of the principal stakeholders – the teachers – and encourage them to implement it responsibly. According to the Director-General of the Department of Education, Lava Dev Awasthi, "conflicts between teachers and government increased with the formers' refraining from taking any responsibility as a consequence of which community school has weakened.... The unlimited power disposed to the management community has politicized the situation with misappropriation of financial resources leading to vandalism and "anarchy" implicating on teaching-learning situation with very few schools being exceptional to common woes" (Poudel 2011a). The local people think that the government has shifted its burden of responsibility by transferring schools to the community level. Inefficacies of the communities to manage the schools have led to degeneration in the quality of education, decline in enrollment number and guardians' concern on the conduct of school affairs. Thus, it is observed some "70 per cent of community schools are in crisis" (Sayapatri 2011). The adverse impact is reflected in the declining percentage of SLC (matriculation) graduates from the public schools.

A comparable data available for community health services transferred till 2005 were 1,412 ranging from sub-health posts to primary health care centre. Though initiatives for transferring the control of these institutions to local communities are taken with good intension, they are mostly seen by the local communities as the consequence of the policy of government to refrain from any responsibility of people's genuine needs and the strategy to dump the problem of managing local affairs. The government has announced "health cooperative as an imperative of new Nepal" with the promise of introducing an "integrated public health policy" in view of the problems faced by the people living in the remote and disadvantaged districts (GON 2011). It has, however, to face challenges even in managing the ultra-modern BP Koirala Cancer Hospital, Bharatpur (Chitwan district) over the staffing disputes for several months. Excessive political interferences in social sectors have destroyed the norms and values related to professionalism in service delivery to the people in general.

The absence of local bodies has further defeated the primary objective of improving the system of governance through participatory local level development programmes and the key agenda of empowering the people for self-government in totality. This exemplifies the case of the dismal failure in institutionalizing democracy in the grassroots level. Neglect of the local bodies has negated their contributions in fighting against poverty. Power sharing at the grassroots level remains crucial to change in the governance process. Hopefully, the situation, however, is likely to change. In case federalism materializes, with the federal authorities working to benefit the federal state, they would have to focus more on managing their immediate constituencies through fiscal decentralization as a prerequisite for establishing direct link between local self-governance and poverty reduction programmes.

On Employment Problems

The future of Nepali politics, its political stability, economic development and prosperity depends largely on the youth employment invariably of the political and structural design of Nepal and the organizing ideology governing the Nepali state. Unemployment is creating grievous situation and impeding the poverty reduction objective of the government. The population joining job market is increasing by 400,000 in number per annum but the government has failed to create jobs; hardly 10 per cent of them are absorbed in internal market. On the average, some 300,000 youths go to foreign employment market per annum. This is authenticated by the data of Foreign Employment Department of the government for the fiscal year 2009/10. There are 7.3 million people aged between 14 and 30 years in Nepal. Some 60 per cent of unemployed youths are from 15-29 years of age group.

According to the Nepal Labour Survey 2008 data, nearly 1 million youths of 15-29 age groups are economically inactive. On the whole, some 2.5 million population of working age group are totally unemployed. Youth unemployment is also a serious sign of exclusion. Thus, the youth bulge, if not managed properly, could be a cause for destabilization. Unemployment is singularly becoming the cause of poverty and insecurity. Unemployment could cause severe income poverty adding to grievances making it a catalyst for conflict, as witnessed in the successful mobilization of unemployed rural youths in a week-long general strike by the CPN (Maoist) between 1 and 7 May 2010. Unemployment, poverty and exclusion are crucial factors causing civil unrest that Nepal has experienced in the recent past. The unemployed youths actually constitute the post-conflict powder keg.

Table 3.2: Number of Economically Active and Inactive Youths

(in '000)

	Presently Active			Presently Inactive		
	Male	Female	Total	Male	Female	Total
	1421	1924	3345	445	597	1042
Rural	1202	1729	2923	264	386	650
Urban	219	204	423	181	212	393

Source: Nepal Labour Survey 2008.

People's expectation is tied to the government to resolve their unemployment problems as the government itself is the largest employer[6] in the country where private sectors could hardly provide job guarantee. On the top of it, the trade union movements have made the private sectors more cautious in providing employment opportunities. Unemployment of the youths – both educated and uneducated – is the cause for instability and volatility undermining the political processes and disrupting national resilience. Sen (2000: 19-22) fears "persistence of unemployment can cause deprivation in many distinct ways", for instance, with immediate consequence of the loss of productivity, loss of motivation for future works, weakening of social values by psychologically affecting human relations and disrupting social order. Youth's alienation from the society they belong to has severe consequence – both social and political. The future of Nepal depends more on the productive use of this ever growing manpower for development and stability than making 'revolution' championing democracy in abstraction.

The government has outsourced employment opportunities for Nepali youths by providing foreign employment opportunities through manpower contract companies. From mid-1990s to date, the number of youths engaged in foreign employment is unofficially estimated to have reached 3 million, besides those seasonal migrants and settled in India. Some 80-85 per cent of migrants head across the border; the traditional workplace where they are lowly paid. The rest 15-20 per cent migrants, who are relatively well-off than the dirt-poor people, go beyond the subcontinent by taking loan from moneylenders and mortgaging land and other properties. Some 95 per cent among them are employed either in Gulf States or in Malaysia. Kuwait is another oil-rich country where Nepali youths are destined to go. Some 41,000 Nepali women are working in Kuwait as housemaids. Qatar and South Korea have become other attractive destinations for the unemployed Nepali youths. Some 60,000 youths, for example, have applied to sit in the Korean language test for labour contract within four days in the first week of May 2011.

The number of youths leaving the country is swelling year after year. For example, comparably 24 per cent more young men and women had left the country on foreign labour contract in the first seven months of the fiscal year 2010/11 than a year earlier. In the first seven months of the fiscal year 2009/10 a total of 149,729 persons had left the country on foreign labour contract, which subsequently increased to a number of 185,652 in the same period, the Foreign Employment Department says (Kantipur, 23 February 2011). The destinations of the majority of Nepali youths are five Islamic countries where menial labour is in abundance. Rich Muslim countries Qatar, Malaysia, Saudi Arabia, United Arab Emirates and Kuwait are followed by another officially promoted country South Korea for the Nepali labour forces. For example, the comprehensive official data on

Table 3.3: Youths in Foreign Labour Contracts

Fiscal Year	Number of youths	Destination	Number of youths
2006/07	204,433	Malaysia	361,464 (within past 5 years)plus 72,460 (2012)
2007/08	204,951	Qatar	351,544(within past 5 years)plus 91,243 (2012)
2008/09	219,965	Saudi Arabia	246,448 plus 63,867(2012)
2009/10	294,094	United Arab Emirates	178,535 plus 47,833 (2012)
2010/11	354,716	Bahrain	020,303
2011/12	313,093*	Kuwait	020.145. South Korea 3,763.

Source: Department of Foreign Employment, GON, July 2011.
* Data for 10 months only.

Table 3.4: Youth Leaving the Country for Foreign Labour in 2011

Month	Number	Month	Number
January	72,000	July	68,000
February	56,000	August	64,000
March	65,000	September	61,000
April	76,000	October	52,000
May	63,000	November	79,000
June	67,000	December	65,000

Source: TIA Immigration Department, Government of Nepal, 2012. The figures are rounded.

youths leaving the country reaching 1,591,252 in nearly six years of the post-Jana Andolan-II period is tabled in next page.

The above statistics show 788,000 Nepali youth had left the country in 2011. Besides those seasonal migrants to India, Nepalis leaving the country for foreign employment are 2,165 on average per day. Their remittances amounting to USD3.5 billion in 2010/11 comprising 23 per cent of national GDP sustain consumerism at home. Despite remittance has become the backbone of national economy, foreign labour employment is yet to become a serious concern and issue of overriding national priority. Though remittance has generated income for the rural households, the youth exodus to foreign employment has also emptied the rural areas of the much needy work force for their development. The social implications of foreign labour migrants in their family are worse; increase in infidelity, divorce, communicable diseases, untimely deaths or even heinous crimes. Another repercussion of remittance in relation to poverty is that neither has it helped inequality decrease at the village level, nor resolved the ever growing problems of unemployment at home.

At home, the need of creating some 1.5 million jobs (MoF 2007: 77) involving youths in productive income generating activities and contributing to national development has forced the government to prioritize labour intensive works such as infrastructure development putting emphasis on road building and irrigation system. Currently, employment to population ratio is reportedly 81.7 per cent of which the ratio of male is 85.5 per cent and female 78.5 per cent (NPC 2010: 21). The first post-CA government budget had proposed to constitute local literacy volunteer in each ward of each VDCs recruiting a total of 35,000 youths with the cost allocation of Rs.1 billion in fiscal year 2008/09 (GON 2008). The budget statement also stipulated a youth self-employment fund with Rs.500 million by the Maoist-led government providing easy financial services to the youths with 'requisite skills and entrepreneurial zeal' to launch their self-reliant business/work. Provision of non-collateral loan of Rs. 200,000 on concessional rate was considered with the cooperation of commercial banks. The government has also deducted a day's salary from all the employees, including of the university service, with a circulation letter from the Finance Ministry to create the 'Youth Self-Employment Fund'.[7]

In view of this, a National Action Plan for youth employment for the period 2010 to 2017 has been reportedly drafted. The government has also announced to create 200,000 jobs per annum for youth employment. It has allocated over Rs.220 million for the 'Karnali Employment Programme' (GON 2009: 37). Sensitive focus on youth employment was the priority laid on Three Year Plan. Further, the concept paper for another Three Year Plan (2010-2012) prepared by the NPC has committed for creating internal employment opportunities through agricultural reform, infrastructure building and market management inclusive of making foreign employment more secure and respectable. The concept paper however has not addressed the cultural and structural aspects of employment policy of the government impeding the job prospects for Dalits and other disadvantageous groups.[8]

Though the Youth Self-Employment Fund intends to promote the unemployed youths of the poor and disadvantageous groups, especially from the remote areas inclusive of women, indigenous people and even the victims of violent conflict, it has been able to bring some 4,000 people only under the scheme. Thus, the result is not propitious. On the other hand, employment opportunity has been found allegedly skewed to a particular caste group in the more competitive public sector, as data below indicate.

Employment prospect has also been fundamentally skewed against Dalits and Janajatis, particularly under democracy. Imprints of continuity in exclusionary policy are evident in composition of the Gazetted rank officials in the civil service. According to Harka Gurung, the number of Hill Brahmins serving in national bureaucracy doubled within the past 16/17 years period, although it increased by slightly over 10 per cent. Despite the rise in the number of Chhetris in national bureaucracy, their representation declined by 2 per cent. Comparably, the percentage of Newars is slighted by almost half, whereas the representation of Dalits remains pathetic.

Gurung maintained that the social structure of power elites has not changed meaningfully since mid 19th century. The hill high caste Brahman/Chhetri constitutes 83.1 per cent in national bureaucracy compared with just 3.4 per cent ethnic groups in 1997-98. In 1983/84, there were 69.3 per cent of high caste officers and 3.0 per cent ethnics. This figure in 2000/2001 rose to 87.0 per cent for high caste and fell to 0.5 per cent for the ethnics (Gurung 2003:17). This is the reflection of reality of continuing discrimination in the state policy. Though such a situation is reflexive of group culture and tradition in choice of occupation, it can, nevertheless, be considered as a pattern long discouraging employment in government by making knowledge of *devnagari* Nepali language compulsory in the public service commission examinations. Language constraint for non-Nepali native speakers prima facie is the continuity of the situation of relative deprivation in relational terms by denial of capacity.

This bitter reality has led the government decision on making the civil service inclusive by adopting the reservation policy for the disadvantageous groups. The civil service (second amendment bill) led the cabinet to decide on the reservation of 45 per cent seats for the underprivileged sections of society in August 2006. Arrangement has been made to reserve 33 per cent for women, 27 per cent for indigenous/janajati people, 22 per cent for Madheshi, 9 per cent for Dalits, 5 per cent for disables and 4 per cent for the people belonging to the backward communities assuming that 45 per cent seats taken out of the total seats advertised for the open competition as 100 per cent. The Police, Armed Police and Nepal Army followed the suit. Tribhuvan University has also followed this practice by advertising seats for teaching positions on quota basis in early 2010. Flexibility in eligibility age for women to compete in civil service examination has also been presumably raised to 40 years. But given the retirement age limit to 58 years, it is not apparently promising.

Though popular, affirmative action, however, is not a panacea to social bondage. For many it is not a good idea with respect to equality and social justice to remedy the needs of historically excluded. It is the other way to promote the policy of inclusion by exclusion. Affirmative action grants preferential treatment to some against the others which is not in conformity with the provision of 'rights to equality' as stipulated in the Article 13 of the Interim Constitution 2007. As the falling poverty rate in the country has not improved the lot of poorer Dalits living in the hills and the Tarai, and the other underprivileged groups, so has the affirmative action or reservation in relations to them. Discrimination and social injustice are conspicuous even in addressing their problems. This can be a subject for another study.

Notes

1. The notion of social justice could be jeopardized in case the CPN (Maoist) succeed in bringing the national judiciary under the control of the parliament along with appointing the judges and chief justice of the Supreme Court and quashing independent judiciary in "New Nepal". This issue was one of the 18 crucial disputed agendas at the CA.

2. The 2011 National Census data put the percentage of the said dominant group at 31.2 per cent of the total population. It has notably reduced this groups's size by 1.8 per cent than in the 2001 census report.

3. The High Level Task Force Committee formed in March 2009 to identify the number of nationalities in Nepal, while submitting its report to Prime Minister Madhav K. Nepal on 13 May 2010 ("81 Janajatiko Suchi Pesh", Kantipur Daily, 14 May 2010).

4. Currently Humla, Jumla, Rukum, Dolpa, Kalikot, Mugu, Jajarkot and Dailekh in the Mid-West and Achham, Bajura and Bajhang in the Far-Western Nepal are under the threat of starvation in the absence of food supplies caused by difficulties in transportation (Baniya 2010).

5. The 2011 National Census data have recorded only 123 mother tongue/dialect groups.

6. The applicants' data on the seats advertised by the Public Service Commission for the post of non-Gazetted 1st class officials of the government in various service categories are indicator of the growing unemployment problems. There were 10,875 applicants for 46 seats in the General administration; 11,685 for 133 seats in the Revenue Department; 4,167 for 23 seats in Foreign Service; 2,801 for 28 seats in Account; and 520 applicants for 9 seats in the Audit Services (Dristi Weekly 11 May 2010:2).

7. However, the youth self-employment fund and programme related to it has vanished along with the fall of the Maoist-led government on 4 May 2009. On the other hand, the Finance Minister Baburam Bhattarai was put under scrutiny by the Public Account Committee of the legislative-parliament with

the suspicion of embezzling over Rs.1.11 billion undermining the fiscal discipline. Even his social programmes as mentioned in the text are accused of being pro-cadres. For the programme announcement see (GON 2008) and for misuse of the state exchequer see (Pandey 2009). This programme has been revived with the appointment of Baburam Bhattarai to the post of the prime minister of the Maoist-led coalition government on 28 August 2011 and enriched the Maoist cadres by distributing money amounting to Rs. 600 million. Institutional corruption continues unabated.

8. Dalits, being untouchables, for example, are rarely employed as peon (the lowest rung in the public service) in the government offices where they are meant to do different odd jobs along with serving tea/coffee/snacks to their high caste officers.

IV

Prioritizing Social Security

The Jana Andolan-II symbolized the assertion of rights by the people who had nourished a pervasive feeling of denial by the state even after the success of the Jana Andolan-I and under the provisions of subsequent democratic constitution promulgated in November 1990. It was a mass uprising for rights denied historically with policy of exclusion and marginalization. It was indeed a political struggle entailing transformation of state by confronting the structural inequalities underlying the negation of human rights. The Jana Andolan-II was therefore a political movement for assertion of inclusive and participatory rights for development through power sharing. State restructuring remains a priori commitment to the signing of the 12-point understanding on 22 November 2005 that led to Jana Andolan-II in April 2006.

General welfare of the people is integral to the processes of state restructuring and social inclusion. Service provision meeting the minimum expectations of the people has become inescapable obligation of the governments formed after popular uprising. A minimal level of social security provisions already exist in the organized sector under the Acts and Regulations adopted by the government. The elected government of the

Nepali Congress party had adopted the Social Welfare Act in Nepal in 1992 for the first time aiming to:

> ... provide humanistic livelihood to the weak and helpless individual, class and community and make them enable; in order to provide status and respect to the welfare oriented institutions and individuals and in order to develop a co-ordination between social welfare oriented institutions and organizations.

Besides this, some social security related measures are also taken in the development sector. Further advance was made by the government or the concerned agency providing compensation security cover to the affected person or the family in case of certain unfortunate eventuality after 2006. And philantrophic works and corporate social responsibility taken by private sectors have contributed commendably to social security needs. Needless to say, expectations are high as social security is an expensive endeavour. As per the available data expenditure on social security has risen significantly. In fiscal year 2011/12, the last budget reviewed in this study, the allocation for social security amounts to approximately NRs 9.61 billion, besides pension distribution. However, a national policy on social security is still void. [1]

The governments formed after the success of the Jana Andolan-II have incorporated some important facets of social welfare provision as national priorities in the six national budgets in preparation for the enabling environment to the people. They are briefly highlighted below to depict the commitments on human development.

Mapping Sectoral Allocation in National Budget

The first post-Jana Andolan-II national budget (2006/07), inculcating the welfare provision, had announced a pro-poor and inclusive economic programme with increasing investment on social sector to institutionalize democratic system as an objective and priority of the government. In view of the development thrust on creating an environment for the emergence of an inclusive society the budgetary allocation on social sector was made Rs. 52 billion (36%) out of Rs. 144 billion total budget. Of the total social sector allocation nearly Rs. 23 billion was devoted to education along with Rs. 9.3 billion on health and Rs. 6.19 billion on drinking water.

Substantial investment on these basic services was meant to further the objective of human development. Priority was also laid on the upliftment and empowerment of the oppressed and marginalized people with programmes on raising their social awareness and providing skill-oriented trainings. Women's upliftment and empowerment with securing their property rights along with institutionalizing gender responsive budget was allocated with Rs.100 million; allocations were made for providing education facilities to Dalits and girl child; increment in the allowances for the elderly citizens, widows and women victimized by the insurgency along with physically handicapped and disabled citizens.

Similarly, infrastructure development, particularly, road building as the foundation of rural economy has been emphasized along with employment generating works by training 9,066 persons as primary teachers and some 44,743 persons for various with skillful trainings. The budget also did not miss to mention details on the Karnali Zone Development Programme from infrastructure building to continuity in lunch package to some 24,000 lower secondary level students and free education up to class 10 for the girl students. Nearly Rs.200 million was allocated for launching Animal Husbandry programme collectively in 22 districts densely populated by the Dalits and freed Kamaiyas (bonded labourers) to help income generating activities of 18,700 poor peasants. The budget had allocated Rs. 3.96 billion in agriculture sector. All in all, the total development expenditures amount to Rs.67.28 billion (46.72%) of the budget (GON 2006).

The budget that followed in the next fiscal year 2007/08 was not substantially different. There were hosts of development

Table 4.1: Essential Services for Human Development
(% of Total Expenses)

Sector	2006/07	%	2007/08	%	2008/09	%	2009/10	%
Education/ Sports*	23.00	15.99	28.39	16.61	38.98	16.51	46.52+9	16.27
Health/ Sanitation	9.30	6.41	12.18	7.21	15.58	6.60	18.68	6.53
Drinking water	6.19	4.39	5.33	3.15	7.96	3.37	9.04	3.16
Local Development	9.40	6.53	13.08	7.74	20.42	8.66	25.24	8. 82

Source: Budget Speeches from FY 2006/07 to 2009/10, Government of Nepal.
Note: Sports segregated from education to form a separate Ministry of Youths and Sports from FY 2008/09.

programmes laid with budgetary commitment of Rs. 75.25 billion with Rs.28.39 billion for education and sports, Rs. 12.18 billion for health, Rs.5.33 billion for drinking water projects. Poverty alleviation, human development and increased investment on women's empowerment remain the focal points with rebuilding, rehabilitation and relief for strengthening endurable peace, stability and democratic system in the country. An allocation of Rs.5.82 billion was made for rural infrastructure building indicating an increase of 47.3 per cent from the previous year. The Ministry of Local Development was allocated with Rs.13. 08 billion for development works.

Agriculture and rural infrastructure are identified as foundational measures for poverty alleviation and economic upliftment with the commissioning of 3,500 projects targeting to lift the living standard of 80,000 households. For this programme, the PAF had been allocated Rs. 1.77 billion. This followed the social welfare programmes for elderly citizens, disables, widows, orphans and the needy ranging from free treatment of heart patients for both children under 15 and elderly over 75 years of age and 10 per cent additional assistant in the pension of the retired civil servants above 75 years of age etc. An amount of Rs.950 million was allocated to welfare provision of the elderly citizens in the budget (GON 2007).

The state policy (Article 35 [9]) is to undertake specific measures to provide social security to single women, orphan, children, helpless, old, disable, and disappearing national minorities and reduced their vulnerability as their livelihood concern becomes paramount. The disables, senior citizens and widows in particular face challenges to their welfare and livelihood in the absence of family to look after them and even with the family unable to support them properly. These are the reflection of policy programmes of the government in relations to oppressed, suppressed, downtrodden and marginalized people, including the Badi women. Deprivation amongst them is the acute problem.

Several gender equality programmes for women's empowerment were launched along with the implementation of the concept of Gender Responsive Budget with allocation of Rs.19.09 billion for programmes directly benefiting the target group. In addition to the poverty alleviation, gender equity and social inclusion programmes introduced in 1,624 VDCs, a decision was made to expand programmes to 54 VDCs along with continuity in the socio-economic and legal empowerment and institutional development of women project in 15 districts of Nepal. Special programme were designed to launch in 40 more districts in order to make the oppressed, ultra-poor, landless, Dalits, indigenous Janajati and Madheshi women economically self-sufficient.

Understandably, the first post-CA government led by the CPN (Maoist) had increased social security expenditure by 440 per cent to Rs. 4.41 billion in fiscal year 2008/09 with considerable provisions of monthly support to elderly citizens, single women and physically handicapped people from Rs. 175 to Rs. 500. A pertinent decision was the reduction of the age threshold from 75 years to 60 years for eligibility to receive social security allowance. Similar level of monthly allowance of Rs. 500 (later increased to Rs. 1,000) has also been provided to the people of fast disappearing nationalities irrespective of their age. A Rs. 1,000 allowance for fully disabled and Rs. 300

for partially handicapped persons was also considered in the budget 2008/09. This decision along with the health care by providing free medicine facility to the level of district hospital and health posts; provision for free of cost operation service to children below age of 15 and senior citizens above of age of 75 along with all endangered ethnic people was universally appreciated despite implementation of such decisions remain uncertain. Karnali Zone received the attention of policymakers as its dependency increased rather than decreased with increment of allowances to Dalits, single women and people over 60 years of age.

Women's empowerment has become the prominent focus of the budget 2008/09 making impressive commitment under the Gender Responsive Budget with appropriation of Rs. 32.91 billion (13.9%) of the total budget directly benefitting women from different programmes (GON 2008:41). A gender sensitive budget with commendable financial commitment has, therefore, been a step towards inclusion and human development as women's contribution to even household economy has never been truly assessed.

Table 4.2: Gender Responsive Budget (in Rs. Billion)

Agenda	2006/07	2007/08	2008/09	2009/10	2010/11	2011/12
Women's Empowerment	100mn*	19.09	32.91	49.45	60.61	73.33

Source: Budget Speeches from FY 2006/07 to 2011/12, Government of Nepal.
Note: * Gender Responsive Budget was viewed to initiate women's empowerment programmes. Just Rs 100 million was allocated directly for the purpose in the beginning (Budget Speech 2006/07: 7).

The budget for fiscal year 2009/10 announced by the CPN (UML)-led coalition government has become more ambitious than the Maoists' one. It laid priority on social security with Rs.7.78 billion investment. This is Rs.3.37 billion increase over the previous year. Incentives are offered for changing modes of social relations. For instance, the budget declared inter-caste marriage with Dalits by non-Dalits would be awarded with

Rs. 100,000 grant; Rs. 50,000 grant would be given to widow marriage couple; Rs. 3,000 allowance to women volunteers; state facility identity card for the poor; allowance raised from Rs. 500 to Rs.1,000 to vanishing *Raute* community and free medical services to elderly and children are all populist measures that the budget has undertaken. An amount of Rs. 2.72 billion is stipulated for expansion of poverty alleviation programme in all the 75 districts. Self-employment schemes are announced with allocation of some Rs.355 million for skill-oriented trainings free of cost. Provision for soft-loan from self-employment fund is made to make 5,000 rickshaw pullers masters of their own rickshaws.

The government has announced mega-investment on education amounting to Rs. 46.52 billion, which is an increase of approximately over Rs. 7 billion from the previous fiscal year. Similarly, Rs. 18.67 billion is allocated for health services and Rs. 9 billion to drinking water projects. It has also proposed an amount of Rs. 49.45 billion for launching programmes to directly benefit the women as against Rs. 32.91 billion in the year 2008/09. This amounts to 17.30 per cent of the total budget of fiscal 2009/10. Besides this, Rs. 30 million is allocated for the welfare of the women of Badi community; Rs. 200 each for the dirt poor, Dalit and children of Karnali Zone below 5 years of age to benefit 400,000 children with expenses of Rs. 720 million. A scholarship scheme amounting to Rs. 60 million is stipulated for Assistant Nurse Midwife training of Dalits and poor Muslim girls from Bara, Parsa, Rautahat, Siraha, Sarlahi, Saptari, Mahottari and Dhanusha districts provided they have obtained grade 8 pass school certificate (GON 2009). If properly implemented[2] this budgetary trend on women's empowerment programme is certain to make its imprint in the future. Besides this, the Local development Ministry has claimed that it is spending to the tune of Rs. 40 billion per annum on 43 projects related to poverty reduction (Kantipur, 27 January 2010).

An interesting aspect of the FY 2009/10 budget is that it has decided to introduce a broad-based social safety net encompassing health, education, social security services by focusing on senior citizens, disadvantaged and underprivileged groups in the community. For this obvious reason the budget has made the provision to collect one per cent tax from regular income earners. Limited cash grants to the old and needy is thought to be inadequate social security provision in reducing their vulnerabilities. As a matter of fact, social security has indeed been one of the long festering demands raised by trade unions. After consultative meetings among the private sector employers, trade unions and government an official task force headed by revenue secretary of the government was set to study the problem and provide recommendations. Initially, the beneficiary of such policy will be roughly 800 thousand employees working in the organized sector. There are about 400 thousand persons working in the organized private sector (Pyakuryal 2009). However, the coverage is only around 10 per cent of the people employed in the formal sectors; the majority of people working in informal sectors are still denied any protective coverage.

The budget 2010/11 has tremendously increased allocations in the social sector, though it was first announced through an ordinance and later regularized by the legislative-parliament through tripartite compromise. Allocation for social sector reached a total of Rs.150.03 billion, which is 44.40 per cent of the total budget of Rs.337.9 billion. Allocations increased commendably on Education: Rs. 57.64 billion; Health: Rs. 24.51 billion; Drinking Water: Rs. 9.34 billion; along with allocation directly benefitting women has gone up to Rs. 60.61 billion. The "Children Security Grant," targeting the children below 5 years of age from the extremely poor, Dalit and Karnali Zone beginning since the last fiscal year, has continued.

The budget for the Fiscal Year 2011/12 presented at the legislative-parliament of the CA on 15 July 2011 by the CPN (UML)-led coalition with the Maoist and MJF, Nepal, government is termed the most populist till date, despite its priorities have not shifted from the previous pattern. Emphasis on social sector, agriculture, and infrastructure building has continued. Allocation on education reached Rs. 63.91 billion; followed by transport Rs. 37.16 billion; agriculture Rs. 29.73 billion; health Rs. 27.12 billion; energy Rs. 23.99 billion; and social security Rs. 11.34 billion. Compared with the previous year, drinking water, however, received low priority with just Rs. 9.0 billion. Allocation directly benefitting women has appreciated by Rs. 73.33 billion from Rs. 60.61 billion of the past fiscal year. Of the total budget amounting to Rs. 384.90 billion, Rs.202.56 billion is allocated for the development programmes and the rest Rs. 182.34 billion for general administration (GON 2011).

The reality, however, is different. There is a wide gap between the budgetary allocation and disbursement actually reaching the targeted people. Gender equality and women's empowerment have remained a mirage; best exemplified by the continuing discrimination in providing citizenship to children of single Nepali mother. The budgetary allocation for resolving the livelihood challenges of the dirt-poor women in the villages, preventing them from falling to worst situation, providing them justice and fare deal in the society or even taking care of the school drop-out girls, has yet to become productive investment. The women empowerment agenda begun with the allocation of Rs.100 million as Gender Responsive Budget in FY2006/07 reaching over Rs. 60 billion in 2010/11 has hardly changed the face of women in Nepal. Despite the stipulation of stipend to women the day they become widow irrespective of their age by the FY2011/12 budget, many measures remain cosmetic.

Similarly, on the education sector, as per a documentary featuring the life of the school going children of the Karnali Zone shows, the promise of free education is not encouraging. Notwithstanding the rhetoric of "Education for All" teaching-learning situation there is devastating. The documentary made with special focus on the lives of the students of Dolpa district is a disclosure of the mismanagement of funds by the responsible government personnel. The documentary is the evidence of falsification of the governmental commitment. Similarly, the situation of both health and education sectors in Jumla district is deplorable (Kunwar 2011).

Many schools throughout the country are in appalling stage; they are schools in name only; where, in some cases, a single teacher runs three classes at a time in the open grass-field or in a roofless classroom or within a concrete skeleton called school (Appendix VI). As recently revealed by the Ministry of Education Report, the school level education sector, for example, has been highly infected with corruption and malpractices committed by the District Education Offices of the government as well as school Head Masters. It reports Rs. 738 million has been misappropriated out of Rs. 1.63 billion disbursed for textbook printing and distribution all over the country. Some 1.7 million students had not received the text books at all; the report says (Poudel 2011b).

The education scene therefore remains horrible. Excessive politicization of national education system is reflected on the level of literacy rate of the Nepali population that remains 39 per cent. Despite decades of government's involvement in literacy campaigns some 5 million people between 15 and 60 age groups are illiterate in the country (Kantipur, 8 September 2011). Though in the past three decades since 1980 an estimated expense of approximately Rs.10 trillion on school education have added schools and pupils in numbers, it has, however, not improved the teaching and learning situation in the country. Both the community as well as institutionalized school systems are rotten with no practical utility of the knowledge acquired.

Some 90 per cent of budget is spent on administrative use in the name of capacity building and technical training of government officials rather than teachers and infrastructure building. Consequently, there are thousands of schools without buildings to house the pupils; 20 thousand schools are without toilets and other amenities for the girl students; 50 per cent of schools did not receive the standard textbooks; thousands of subject teachers' post remains vacant; under-qualified teachers are engaged in upper-grade class teaching in thousands of schools; along with nearly 22 thousand schools running classes under 100 days a year, in spite of the standard 220 regular days (Wagle 2011).

Likewise, there are reports on the misuse of the social security allowances by the concerned authorities. For example, the case of Dolkha district obviously presents the degree of manipulation and misappropriation and irregularities of social security allowances by the District Development Committee. The government has released Rs.83 million for the district in FY 2009/10. But the allowances have been distributed in the names of deceased persons as well as fake names which the living elderly persons and widows were entitled to get at the rate of Rs.500 per month (Manandhar 2010). Reports on manufacturing and manipulating records of the people deserving allowances by the VDC secretaries have been published, so has the record of the sharing of the spoils by the powerful local politicians of the district and villages drawing the attention of concerned ministries for expediting investigation on the issue.

Underspending by ministries and line agencies on development expenditures persists reasonably because of the delay in budget approval, thus, obvious delay in disbursement and project implementation. This makes the target unattended and unfulfilled. For example, of a total of the Rs. 123.7 billion sanctioned for expenditure in the first seven months period of the fiscal year 2010/11, the government spent only Rs.108 billion representing a shortfall of Rs. 15.7 billion (EIU 2011). Development expenditure problematic, particularly at the district and village levels, is the absence of the elected local bodies. The Local Development Ministry has continued to allocate budget for development of VDCs every fiscal year after 2002, even when the term of elected local bodies had already expired.

In the current Fiscal Year 2011/12, an amount of Rs. 8.68 billion is appropriately allocated for village development. This amount is billed accordingly for each and every VDCs ranging from Rs.1.5 million to Rs. 3.5 million as per the estimated needs. However, the most frustrating situation presently is that the personnel in the ministry that allocate the budget for the VDCs have no idea how the amount allocated would be spent. Notwithstanding the reports of massive misappropriation of the development funds by the VDC secretaries appointed by the government and the local cadres and workers of major political parties with undue influence, the government has failed to take any initiative to curb the corrupt practices. This anomaly has a direct effect on beneficiaries – the people. This way, the allocated budget, even if disbursed, never reach the target population.

Net Assessment

It is very difficult to assess the achievements of policy, not least because of uncertainty of knowing what would have happened in its absence. The time lag between introduction of any policy measure, investment decisions, and, for example, the actual implementation of the project is often so long that there can be no certainty of cause and effect relations. Although development policy is ostensibly concerned with economic issues, the underlying justification is usually political. Disparities in economic opportunities between one part of the country and another are potentially divisive, especially when influenced by ethnic or cultural distinction.

Net assessment based on the review of the impact of the policy in details, however, concludes that the commitments made so far have not ascertained desired results. Nepal has long been planning for the prosperity of its people, but in vain. Ten Five Year Plan past the National Planning Commission has issued two three year plan documents without achieving any substantial results of the goals set. Meanwhile, the importance of social sector for human development is irrefutably recognized as the increased share of budgetary allocation implies. However, the reality is that development activities in Nepal are donor dependent. Delay in disbursement of fund and implementation of the project have raised the cost incurred with negative impact of the programme. Another shameful reality, as widely reported in electronic media and news dailies, is quite the contrary to all the exuberance and pious announcements made by the finance ministers.

Politicians with powerful position are stealing money from the people they promise to serve. The budgetary practices influenced by the powerful cabinet members disparage the concept of distributive justice. Allocation of development funds for the districts (constituencies) of the influential ministers/politicians has led to the marginalization of the already marginalized. Budgetary allocation for the five development regions in the fiscal year 2010/11, for example, was a case demonstrating exclusion and injustice than inclusion and distributive justice, a pattern continuing since the erstwhile Panchayat days.

Although the Far-Western Development Region is the most underdeveloped, it received the least priority in budgetary fund with merely 8.23 per cent in comparison to 19.72 per cent to Mid-Western, 19.26 per cent to Western, 31.72 per cent to Central, and 21.07 per cent to Eastern Development Regions. The budget that was brought through ordinance was sliced by the powerful politicians/ministers taking major chunks for their own constituencies (MoF 2010a). This exemplifies the deliberate case of exclusion than thrust for inclusion by the privileged politicians against the underprivileged population. Distributive justice is absent in the policymaking frame even though it is affirmed in principle.

Reports on the gross misappropriation of development budgets by the local leaders of the major political parties have surfaced time and often. The education minister representing the Tarai Madhesh Loktantrik Party (TMLP) in the coalition government, Ram Chandra Kuswaha, for instance, was fired on bribery charges in late February 2010. Another minister from the Madheshi Morcha, Mahendra Yadav is also accused of stalling several irrigation projects in the Tarai for want of money – the prepaid commission/bribe to the minister to get the budget disbursed (Nagarik, 28 November 2011). But the more corrupt leaders belonging to the hill caste/ethnic stock, the TMLP claim, are ignored. Such a case is exemplified by the government's indecision to bring the culprits involved in the "Sudan APC Scandal" to book.

The alleged mastermind of the scheme and some prominent political leaders directly involved in the case, however, remain scot free. [3] Tendency like this means discrimination applies even in the corruption cases. As a matter of fact, endemic institutional corruption is eating the vitals of the state's development aspirations. It was evident recently in the disputes over the Value Added Tax (VAT) and the backdoor attempt to adopt 'supplementary budget' at the fag-end of the fiscal year between the Finance Minister Bharat Mohan Adhikari and the Finance Secretary Rameshowar Prasad Khanal, forcing the latter to resign from the post disputing the minister's "illicit decision" (Kantipur, 31 March 2011; Nepal, 2011: 18-21).

On the other hand, when the more needy people are dying from easily curable diseases like dysentery; even not getting para-cetamol as free medicine; hospitals/health posts are empty of medical practitioners despite tremendous rise in health budget; politicians are paid lavishly for medical bills. [4] Though improvement in basic health services in the areas of child and maternal mortality rate is appreciable, much remains to be done in National Health Service. Notwithstanding health care being declared free as fundamental right and irrespective of increase in public health expenditures, for example, health services have become expensive beyond the reach of general public. Both health and education sectors have become thriving business.

Similarly, although, when students had to spend their entire education calendar year without books, the government had announced free education up to class 12 to the students of Karnali Zone out of the Rs. 38.98 billion allocated under the education heading in 2008/09. Karnali Zone, in fact, epitomizes the state of the failed state of Nepal. The government has also established 24,773 community based child development centre and 2,000 more centres had been planned to add in FY2009/10. Though the 'Food for Education Programme' launched in the 10 districts of the Mid-West and Far-Western Nepal between 2008 and 2010 has brought positive impact by discouraging dropouts with serving day-meal, its continuity, however, is doubtful as the programme depends largely either on donor's preference or policy of international organizations like the United Nations (MoF 2010b). The national predicament is that Nepal has long adopted 'food for work' programme as development practice for labour intensive works. It has also been airlifting food for the needy since early 1960s that has yet to stop. But situation has not changed; it has rather worsened along with the increase in Nepal's donor dependency. Table 4.3 below exemplifies the aid situation in Nepal.

Table 4.3: Foreign Aid Commitments and Disbursement

(in percentage)

Descriptions	2001/02	2002/03	2003/04	2004/05	2005/06	2006/07	2007/08
Total Aid/Total Budget	43.29	36.77	79.67	62.01	105.34	69.83	59.57
Social sector	32.57	33.50	46.16	45.43	50.64	58.71	62.09
Share in development expenditure (per cent)	58.07	71.06	81.89	86.53	74.45	65.08	54.75

Source: MoF, Economic Survey from 2001 to 2007 annual issues.

The problem with donor dependency is that the donors' commitments are not always forthcoming. Records in 2007/08 show less than 60 percent of the committed aid was disbursed. And the 'reality of aid' is that nearly 80 per cent of amount returns to the same donor agency through advisory services as Action Aid Nepal reported in 2003. The officials directly engaged in aid negotiation have usually lamented about difficulties in getting assistance in national priority sectors as donors have their own wish lists and preferences. Deepening dependency makes government unable to reject the aid package. Foreign Direct Investment (FDI) can work as an alternative to aid in the long run. But the Nepali situation at present is repulsive to FDI. The share of foreign aid in social sector, however, has been impressive. The donors' support in this sector has steadily increased and almost doubled as it also caters to humanitarian interests.

Table 4.4: Projects involving Foreign Assistance in FY 2009/10 in Social Sector

(in Rs'000)

Ministries	Government	Foreign Grant	Foreign Loan	Total
MWCSW	92, 900	60,251	146,623	299,774
Education	3,011,275	11,162,397	3,391,426	17,565,098
Health & Population	3,197,654	8,132,694	390,000	11,720,348
Local Development	6,386,972	9,995,100	1,796,748	18,178,820

Source: MoF 2009.

Tremendous investment on social sectors, for example, in education (under Education for All Programme), health and drinking water and sanitation, is made and projects are launched successfully. But many un-projected stories remain.[5] Policies and programmes undertaken by the government have failed to address the structural problems that lead to social exclusion. The dominant national ethos remains the ruling elites comprising the high caste hill Hindu group that structured the social relationships. The coalition of this dominant group's interests remains preserving their privileged position by protecting their customary rights, which is founded on unjust social system. As Shucksmith says, any "attempts to address inequality and social exclusion must seek both to alter the structures which constrain individuals' actions and also to build the capacity to act of those actors with the least power and opportunity. Arguably these are both core concerns of development... ." (Shucksmith 2000: 2).

Challenges to development, however, are not limited either to difficulties of terrain or technological lag or even resources scarcities but the social complexities influencing human relations based on ethnic and caste diversity and religiously influenced social system of touchability and untouchability, purity and impurity and approval and denial. Again, social complexities are caused moreover by the problems of over-politicized state. This phenomenon is prevalent in Nepal where leaders' preoccupation remains their own and regime survival rather than political participation and economic development. However, the importance of the latter two is made relevant in case of deriving semblance of legitimacy by the leaders to rule, hence, weakening of the commitment and disposal of development. A testimony to this can be found in excessive centralization of economic activities and political authority, enduring political instability, crippling strikes and *bandh* along with implicit and explicit threat of violence making harrowing transition thereby defeating development aspirations of the people. Government without governance is the case of enduring disorder in Nepal.

Such an anomaly was reflected in the revised estimate of the total expenditure incurred in the FY2008/09. The share of central level expenditure was 75.57 per cent of the total government expenditure as against 15.91 per cent of the district level expenditures in that fiscal year. As the share of the central level spending was around five times higher than that of the district level spending the differences in priorities are starkly revealed (Pyakuryal 2010). As noted, this has also pointed towards a deteriorating investment environment impacting on poverty, unemployment and growth rate along with weak budgetary implementation and project management (GON 2009a: 4-5).

The challenges posed by such a situation are reflected in the difficulties in below-target capital expenditure in the first seven months of the FY2009/10, which amounts to only 14.8 per cent of the budget estimate. A surplus of Rs.8.4 billion, roughly similar to that of the year earlier when the surplus was Rs. 8.8 billion, has been announced by the government in the first seven months of current fiscal year. As a result, the unspent government balance stood at Rs. 20 billion, up by 30.7 per cent compared with the figure of a year earlier. The budget surplus is the manifestation of difficulties in spending the allocated amounts in the targeted development programmes (EIU 2010: 14). This trend is also noted in the current fiscal year (EIU 2011: 17). Thus the allocation, disbursement and implementation are not consistent with the commitment made. State fragility has, hence, compounded the development challenges.

Notes

1. The beneficiaries of social security are mostly in the organized sectors of the government, public and private enterprises. The Civil Service Act 1992 and Regulation 1997 detail the social security provisions for the employees. Like in the Military and Police Services, the government has also built a Civil Service Hospital for the civil employees under the Chinese aid. Besides the benefits in person, inclusive of disability benefit, the employees are getting education benefits for their two children.

    In the development sector, free medical facilities along with medicine and maternity and child allowances are provisioned in government policy under the primary health care sector. Educational benefits are provided to the girl child, literacy classes for women, free meal for school going children along with scholarships to the disadvantaged and marginalized children. Some specific economic programmes, inclusive of monthly allowances to marginalized communities have also been undertaken by the government.

    Initiatives on social security allowances to elderly, widow, disable and other needy people are taken by the government for a long time. These programmes are however drawing severe criticism at the implementation level due to the rampant corrupt practices involving the concerned agencies. There are flaws in the programme at delivery and monitoring stage. However, the government's commitment to socioeconomic welfare of the people cannot be questioned as it is overspending money than the goal set by the Copenhagen Social Summit in 1995 earmarking at least 20 per cent of budgetary allocation for social expenditure. Of late, the government has also taken compensation security measure providing Rs.1 million to the kith and kin of the person in case of the unnatural death caused by accident or public riots. Despite this, the government spends very low amount of money for social protection/security provision both in terms of per capita per person and as a per cent of GDP.

2. This programme has now understandably hit a snag. There is some misunderstanding over the admission issue between the stakeholders and the CTEVT. The Muslim girl students who had passed the examination taken by the CTEVT for the 29 months course of the assistant mid-wife have been informed about the inability of their admission to PQ (qualified) technical schools located in Siraha and Saptari districts from where 132 girl students have been selected for the training basically meant to poor and disadvantaged female students from Dalits and Muslim communities. Though the fiscal year is coming to a close soon, they were yet to be admitted for the training course and receive scholarship. See Appendice V for the joint statement published by the stakeholders against this decision of the CTEVT, Government of Nepal.

3. The scandal in question relates to the equipment purchase, including Armed Personnel Carrier (APC), to the personnel of the Nepal Police posted in Sudan as a contingent of the UN Peacekeeping Force. Of the equipment purchase amounting to Rs.450 million, it was alleged that Rs. 310 million was embezzled by the responsible authorities ranging from the then Home Minister, Home Secretary, IGP of Police and other high level police and civil officials. Despite the State Management Committee of the legislative-parliament has given a green signal the Commission for Investigating Abuse of Authority (CIAA) has initially developed cold feet against arresting the corrupt officials. Once the case is filed, the Special Court has summoned 34 police officers, including three former Inspector General of Police and two agents supplying the goods raising Rs.500 million as bail amount from the accused. One of the agents, a British citizen, is absconding.

4. Though some 1,100 applications from the sick and needy people for health aid were pending since over a year at the Ministry of Health, Uma Kant Chaudhary disbursed Rs.23.86 million under health aid to party leaders, ex-ministers and lawmakers as health

minister since last 10 months. The release of Rs. 70 million for health assistance was spent within 6 months; another Rs.20 million was sanctioned later for the same purpose. Smelling a rat, the Commission for Investigation of Abuse of Authority (CIAA) had directed the Office of the Prime Minister and Council of Ministers to stop releasing more money (Kathmandu Post, 1 June 2010).

Earlier the CPN (Maoist) Prime Minister Prachanda had distributed Rs.1billion to the party's supporters and cronies during his 9 month's tenure. However, Prime Minister Madhav Kumar Nepal had superseded his predecessor by embezzling the largest amount from the state purse initially distributing over Rs. 75 million to different party stalwarts for medical and other expenses from the national coffer (Dristi Weekly, 22 March 2011:5), and squandering Rs.78 million in foreign junkets accompanied by his coteries on different occasion.

Approximately Rs.290 million from the state coffer was distributed as financial assistance to persons ranging from the former Prime Minister Sher Bahadur Deuba (NC), former Deputy Prime Minister and Home Minister Bam Dev Gautam (UML), former Deputy Prime Minister and Home Minister Narayan Kaji Shrestha (Maoist) to the leader of Bhutanese refugees Tek Nath Rijal and other luminaries between October 2008 and June 2011, a recent report says (Bania and Miya 2011). Another report discloses the outgoing Prime Minister Jhal Nath Khanal has distributed more than Rs.10 million as financial assistance mostly to his cronies within a month (Mahat 2011: 15). Unfortunately, there is no law to prevent such misappropriation by the authority. Along with such institutional corruption, the loot has continued in different shape. These looters and wicked politicians, unfortunately, have become the destiny makers of the people under the democratic republic.

5.   Though 'education for all' campaign has helped improve the percentage of primary school enrolment along with other literacy activities, a study had also revealed many are also excluded from the programme. Some 83 per cent children of 600,000 squatter families numbering some 2 million were found illiterate (Acharya 2002: 82). Similarly, a finance minister had noted in his budget speech that over Rs.12 billion spent on school education was a sheer waste in view of the massive failure of public school students in the SLC examinations (MoF 2003: 4). There are reports on

the 'school enrolment campaigns' launched under the 'education for all' to 'achieve universal primary education' programme of MDGs targeted towards deprived children completed without the knowledge of the stakeholders. The enrolment campaigns led by the District Education Officer (DEO) were confined to the district headquarters, for example, in the Rukum district of mid-western Nepal (Thapa 2010: 10).

As a matter of fact, everything is forgotten after enrolment season lapses and aggregate data collected by the officials for the record; school inspectors rarely visit the remote rural areas and the dropout rate is hardly accounted for. One study has found 'higher the grade, higher is the dropout rate'. Magars, an indigenous Janajati people, have the highest dropout rate after class five (Dahal and Acharya 2008: 12-13).

Expansion of health posts and hospitals throughout the country with provision of free medicine to poor and needy is another success story. But doctors in government hospitals and trained health practitioners in health posts are rarely present. One notable problem is that even basic health service has not reached the target population (MoF 2007: 165). Otherwise, a number of people would not have died from easily curable dysentery or diarrhea diseases in Jajarkot and other districts in Mid-Western Nepal. Maternity deaths in the Far-West are common due to inaccessibility of health services. Scarcity of potable water even in the city of Kathmandu – the capital of Nepal – is obvious to all. Water in Kathmandu is proven arsenic contaminated; supplies are irregular. So urban and rural drinking water projects have their justification to continue indefinitely, not to talk about the festering of mega-Melamchi project begun a quarter of century past, the tunneling work for which is inaugurated this year.

A report based on the deliberations on the Melamchi Project at the Public Account Committee of the Parliament recently notes only 8 per cent of the tunneling work completed in two-and-a-half-year period out of the 26.21 kilometer long tunnel. The contract was rewarded for 4 years period but only 2500 meter tunneling is completed so far (Baniya 2011:4). On sanitation, the media advertises over 14 million Nepalis are without toilets. Actually, 51 per cent of Nepali households are without toilets (NPC 2010: 147).

V

Social Inclusion, Human Development and Nation Building

Social inclusion is a political project. It is a liberal mode of policy that a state undertakes. It is also a policy of recognizing rights; opposed to the denial of rights. Thus, social inclusion is manifestation of the pluralistic and liberal concept on human relationships. The idea of social inclusion is contemporaneous to national discourses as it has become the most crucial agenda of state restructuring process in the 'post-conflict' situation. Simply defined the post-conflict situation is a period absence of violent conflict but not the attainment of peace. In other words, it denotes a period central to peacebuilding. It is a period in transition between a violent past and uncertain future that should be managed for socio-political stability by discouraging dissension and disputes.

The post-conflict situation, in fact, is blurred with pulls and pressures of different dimension wherein socioeconomic and political interests of various groups coalesce. These have to be addressed to discourage recurrence of dissent and encourage institution building by delivering public goods, including public security. Economic recovery is integral to constructing peace, not the guns for policing the state. Security and development have become tied concepts. Peace cannot prevail in the absence of the either. Thus the priority should be rebuilding public order destroyed by the violent conflict.

Constitutional and Social Relationship

To lend credibility to this central task the Interim Constitution was adopted with collective measures in 2007. The constitutional provisions of adult franchise, proportional representation with affirmative action, reservation for women, Dalits, Madheshi, Janajati and disadvantaged and marginalized groups, relaxing citizenship act, abolition of discriminatory laws are all liberal streaks instilled in the policymaking process contributing to create human resources enabling them to freely participate in the nation building process. The discourses on social inclusion are, therefore, articulated on the state-society relationships level. Social inclusion has made the role of the state as a facilitator of the societal empowerment abnegating the antiquated social hierarchies and replacing them by equity and justice.

Rights involve struggle for access to resources, demands for recognition, and social justice. Articulation of rights to participation is the demand for opening the avenues of power sharing. And, decision making on the issues related to their interests with power sharing is expressed through consummate passion for equality and justice. Inclusion can help empower countless impoverished and illiterate people and uplift them from their dehumanizing existence. It provides the sense of belonging together to the hitherto neglected people and gives them the unison of purpose through participation and representation. Inclusion, in other words, relates to the process of acceptability of the hitherto marginalized persons in the society they belong to with opening of social space for their participation. Social inclusion has thus become a core concept for human development and nation building. It has also become the foci of development agenda; the objective of pro-poor governance sustaining the policy of poverty reduction in

Nepal. In sum, as the MDGs, for example, has reinforced, it is the rights based approach to development (Shetty 2005: 73-75).

It should however be recognized that most of the strategies conceived of social inclusion are at the inventory level. Policies on social inclusion are yet to influence the degree of inclusion of previously excluded groups. Though demands channelled from below have been met by policies formulated from above, societal norms have not changed as power structure remains inflexible. Persistent disparities and discriminations have encroached upon egalitarian policies and programmes such as poverty alleviation (NESAC 1998; UNDP 2001; 2004; World Bank/DFID 2006), women's literacy (Acharya 2002; Parajuli 1995), Dalits upliftment (Pokharel 2004), and Madheshi participation and representation (Shah 2006; Dahal 2005), thus equity and social justice. Experience has shown that constitutional dispensations and legal measures are not enough to change the discriminatory practices.

The erstwhile 1990 Constitution, for example, had extensively treated individual rights curtailing ethnic, caste, and gender based discrimination. However, structural conditioning of the constitution defining Nepal as a Hindu, monarchical state continued the religious-cultural practice of denial and exclusion defeating the liberal mode of the democratic constitution. Governments were formed with flawed premise of exclusion deriving legitimacy from traditional sources and destroying identity and unity of the people by institutionalizing exclusion. Electoral politics under the 1990 constitution had further marginalized the aspiration of representation of the people other than the hill-high-caste-Hindu groups, particularly, the Brahmin-Chhetri combine. Thus, Nepal's identity as a Hindu state was presumed unscrupulous to other religious ethos. State construed on the particular religion was considered uneven development under democracy. This requires being undone to construct a democratic identity of a multicultural state. Such a perception has charged the ethnic consciousness amongst the people long denied their rights to participation and representation in the national mainstream.

Structural reforms through state restructuring processes stipulated in the CPA and the Interim Constitution are reflections of such popular consciousness, although they are yet to be initiated by the drafting and adoption of a new constitution by the CA. State transformation agenda thus has bogged down by political bickering resulting into uncertainty. Initiatives for empowerment through politics of participation are also constrained duly because of the absence of elected local bodies. Participation and representation at the local level is dissipating the prospect of the formation of the citizens' state. State in transition thus tends to make policies fragmentary.

People, Poverty and Development

The concept of development has assumed a human face when it strives for human security, presumably with provisions on social security rather than emphasising on economic growth if it do not serve the human needs. It has also become a development perspective reflecting on the importance of human capital mobilizing the manpower capabilities for human development. Fundamentally related to poverty impeding human development is the "livelihood insecurity intensified by chronic unemployment, malnutrition, poor housing, sanitation with educational lag, [and] deprivation of sorts like denial of citizenship constraining the social relationship". Being excluded from social relations deprives the people essentially from the social opportunities resulting into intense suffering, mental agony and humiliation (Sen 2000: 20). Deepening poverty is seen and interpreted as a case of expanding human vulnerabilities that might result into increasing social conflict and insecurity.

Poverty, thus, has overwhelmingly influenced the international perspectives on development and security. This has found authentic expression in the assertion of the former World Bank Chief, "When we think about security, we need to think beyond battalion and borders. We need to think about human security, about waging a different war, the fight against poverty" (Wolfensohn 2000). Paul Collier (2007) endorses this view when he said, "Poverty is the ultimate systemic threat facing humanity. The widening gap between rich and poor.... [If] poor are left hopeless, poverty will undermine societies through confrontation, violence and civil disorder." The "poverty trap" as Collier maintains, would undermine development, but the more dangerous one is the "violence trap" that may constraint development, the World Bank says. The *World Development 2011* published by the World Bank has concluded that violence is not just one cause of poverty; it is becoming the primary cause.

Poverty reduction, therefore, is central to state transformation through human development, a theme that the *Nepal Human Development Report 2009* has projected. States like Nepal emerging out of over a decade of armed conflict need escaping from poverty even to maintain some resemblance of peace. Notwithstanding the receding of violence of both state and non-state nature, the Nepali society has become more vulnerable to shocks caused by the frequency of political protests, stoppages, labour unrest and shutdowns resulting into increasing social anomaly, tension and economic breakdown. Spread of light weapons, homicide and other types of violent crime has accompanied the unsavoury trend. Risk of such events increases as the state fails to regulate and control the occurance opening up the vulnerability of common people. State fragility has, therefore, become crucial challenge to both stability and economic development.

This state of affairs has forced large-scale exodus of Nepali youths to foreign countries mostly as menial workers. Unemployment begets poverty and poverty begets violence as the rural youths had demonstrated by becoming the Maoist guerrillas in the past. These two empirical facets have contrary features. Both of these features however are the crucial causes of bad governance. The government's irresponsibility and unaccountability therefore had ignored the prospect of livelihood of the citizenry, which is sensitively related to the essential perspective of human security ingrained in social justice and public security.

Changing this situation requires first, an inclusive perspective on social mobilization for nation building. Secondly, there should not be any precondition attached while articulating systemic reform. Unitary state symbolized by the monarchical control had been exclusive, exploitative and discriminatory in the past. The governments formed in the post-CA period had said to have tried to be effective in their commitment, but none is. So they have failed. Espousing federalism integral to state building or state restructuring process is thus a popular choice, as unitary state being excessively centralized impinging development. Participation, power-sharing and self-determination are features embedded in federalism potentially making it less discriminatory than unitary system (UNDP/N 2009).

The recent report on MDGs assessment (NPC 2010) is positive on the poverty reduction efforts in Nepal. Earlier, it was also found that poverty has decreased. This success has made planners optimistic on reducing poverty further to 21 per cent level within the three years between 2010 and 2012. The NLSS-III further heightened this optimism. However, inequality is severe among the economic groups in view of the poverty incidence that ranges from 2 to 54 per cent with major incidence in agriculture wage earners (53.8%) and self-employed agriculturists (32.9%). Moreover, caste, ethnicity and gender have been found as significant factors influencing poverty (World Bank/DFID 2006). Variation in poverty by caste and ethnicity range from 14 per cent in Newars to as high as 45 per cent among the Dalits (Tiwari 2006:5). Inequality remains high as the social opportunities denied. Human development thus is skewed when exclusion persists.

Conversely, social inclusion is broadly understood as a concept developed as a policy entry-point for expansion of participation to improve the condition of human wellbeing. The MDGs agendas are indeed compatible to human development, prominent among which are the goals 1, 2 and 3 defined as eradication of poverty, acquisition of knowledge for leading a decent life standard through occupation. Health and environmental sustainability related goals are integral to the quality of human development. Simply put, human development is 'capability expansion'. In other words; it is the acquisition of freedom of choice by an individual to pursue civil occupation without social exclusion. This freedom entails political, economic, social opportunities as principal means for development (Sen 2000a). Haq's 'freedom from want and freedom from fear' has led to a critical paradigm shift in the thinking on development. Central to all economic activity is the human being. In his reasoning, 'equity lies at the heart of human development'. He said,

> Human development has four essential pillars: equity, sustainability, productivity and employment. The human development paradigm is concerned both with building up human capabilities (through investment in people) and with using those human capabilities fully (through an enabling framework for growth and employment). The purpose of development is to enlarge all human choices, not just income (Haq 1996:21).

It thus led to the development of Human Development Index (HDI) to measure the differences, discriminations, disparities, denials and gaps between various caste, class, gender, geographical region and ethnic groups by disaggregating their income reflecting on the human condition (Haq 1996: 54-55). Following Haq's perspective on human development, the NESAC (1998) study provides the disaggregated HDI by ethnicity and caste groups. Trends in disaggregated HDI across regional and social collectivities show the level of human development in rural areas is only two third of the urban areas. It thus concludes 'poverty in human capability in Nepal is very high as well in comparison to other countries of South Asia. People in Nepal are much more capability poor than income poor'. Indicating the lowest level of human development the report has noted 0.378 HDI for Nepal with 45 per cent of global HDI as its absolute value (NESAC 1998: iii-iv). The 0.509 HDI value recorded for Nepal by HDR 2009 for the year 2006 is definitely a sign of steady progress made by the country on poverty question (UNDP 2009: 34).

However, on the question of unemployment and inequality the country's performance has been dismal. The dirt poor people overwhelmed by chronic poverty are the consequence of unemployment. People remain capability poor, therefore, economic opportunities are denied in the absence of job creation. Such a stagnant situation further intensifies rural poverty. This is starkly demonstrated in HPI value gaps between rural (38.2%) and urban (20.7%) areas (UNDP/N 2009: 41). This is not merely a statistical gap, this is a gap created by the continuation of the policy of deprivation. Poverty reduction strategy has been strongly influenced by the need of rural orientation for rural development (The irony however is that ever since the period it was thought as an imperative there is the absence of local government in Nepal as its tenure ended in 2002). Concerns with the people's wellbeing with expansion of their capability enabling them to improve their personal income and live a comfortable life with fundamental freedom

Table 5.1: Human Poverty Index across Areas and Regions between 2001 and 2006

Areas/Regions	2001	2006
Urban	25.2	20.7
Rural	42.0	38.2
Mountain	49.8	43.3
Hill	38.8	32.7
Tarai	39.6	36.9
Eastern	37.1	33.7
Central	39.7	35.3
Western	36.7	33.2
Mid-Western	46.3	38.7
Far-Western	45.9	39.0
Nepal	39.6	35.4

Source: UNDP/N 2009: 41.

are the crucial ingredients of human development (Gurung 2007: 3; Sharma 2006: 1). Investing on education and training has been prioritized to transfer the unskilled human resources to human capital for aiding equitable and inclusive development objective of the state. This gives a new impetus to carve social relations with a hitherto ignored community by the state recognizing differences and diversities.

Diversity entails necessity for nation building. Nation building is a process of forging a sense of common nationhood in order to overcome ethnic, sectarian and communal differences and counter alternate sources of identity and loyalties of the 'imagined communities' (Anderson 1987). Citizenship is the thread weaving diverse nationalities together to sensitize the process of nation building (Bendix 1964). Citizenship, indeed, is the glue that binds the multitude of nationalities together. The concept of citizenship is not only confined to rights and duties but also entails the notion of power which confirms equality under the law, access to social rights and rights to franchise of an individual as an essential component of democratic political order (Marshall 1950 cited in Byrne 2005: 39; Delanty 2000: 14-22). Democracy that has invented citizenship as a rule to social order and legitimating state-society relationships has been challenged with the demands of self-determination as the rights of citizenry (Delanty 2000: 3). It involves freedom of choice for the people.

In this context, ethnicity has strongly politicized the notion of federalism based on ethnic boundaries. Sub-nationalism, thus, has lately emerged as a formidable challenge to nation building; the main reason behind which has been the pursuit of exclusionary policies by the state that has also manifested into political violence and insurgency in Nepal making the state weak and fragile. State fragility in itself is not only a situation, it is also treated as a concept defining the absence of political will or capacity to provide basic functions needed for poverty reduction, development and safeguard fundamental human rights with security assurance to the people.

Social inclusion therefore is context-specific in the case of Nepal where the need is to lead the state from fragility to resilience for nation building through human development activities. The crucial element for nation building is the expansion of citizenship and of rights to political participation. Poverty reduction, minimizing unemployment and bridging inequality are integral to the efforts towards nation building. Education that imparts awareness among the people, thus, would be central to such an endeavour of nation building. Education is obviously thought to be a great equalizer.

Citizenship and Belongingness

Discriminatory practices have led policy decisions even to the extent of denial of the citizenship, thus, fragmenting social solidarity through derecognizing their rights to belonging together, rights to equity and rights to opportunities. Citizenship is the identity of an individual who becomes an integral link to the national socio-political community in which the person recreates roles to evolve a culture of solidarity by linking private and public spheres (e.g, Delanty 2000). Only citizen of a state enjoys the fundamental rights aside from the human rights. Delanty concludes, "Human rights are basic ethical rights that all individuals enjoy by virtue of their common humanity, whereas citizenship rights are specific to a particular political community" (2000:69). Citizenship provides the voting rights legitimating the person's participation in the national electoral process. As voting right is enjoyed only by citizens it symbolizes their identity with the state. The delinking of such a process through denial does not only create a 'tribe' of popular apathy but also relates it to the question of poverty with the exclusivist social setting making the poor helpless and powerless and increasing their alienation towards the state. Denial of citizenship is the denial of national identity to the person making him poor and vulnerable as social opportunities are dissuaded.

Citizenship, by contrast, sensitizes the person assuming responsibility with the sense of belonging to a community and the state. Citizenship forms an integral link for solidarity with the state through social integration contributing to nation building that relates to freedom and liberty imparted to its citizenry by power sharing and distributive justice, and by integrating the sub-national aspirations in the political process. Nation building is a process that imparts the sense of national identity and loyalty to the state. Neglect of sub-national identities and aspirations by the state has eroded the thin veneer of Nepali national identity creating a condition for resurgence of ethnopolitics with increasing impetus for self-determination. State's disinclination towards preserving minority rights has manifested in conflicts related to language, religion, cultural and educational issues coupled with the increasing demands for devolution of power.

The prevalence of structural violence commonly defined as the deliberate pursuit of social exclusion by the state is at the root of ethnicization of the domestic politics that the state building enterprises through homogenization of culture has failed to arrest. Nepali state that is prefaced by the notion of 'national unification' through the forces of single language, for example, has become a contested concept in a multilingual society with tensions brewing *reasonably* because of the suppression of the genuine identity of the people characterized by diversity. The policy of national assimilation has failed to evolve a collective identity. Assertion of identity leading to the clashes has created traumatic situation with obvious consequences of ethnic dilemma. Struggle for preserving identity thus has become reclaiming history and culture.

Nepali historiography is now under scrutiny. Debates range from misconstruction of national icons to 'heroes and builders' and historical narratives surrounding them. Heroes of yesteryears are presented as the villains in the context of the state restructuring process. Even the process of the state formation of Nepal is under critical inquiry. Was it a national 'unification' or a sheer military conquest? And how Nepal was governed: through exclusion or inclusion? Assessment of Nepali historiography provides certain stereotype images of heinous court politics and state repression against peoples' urge for democracy. The alleged cruelty of Prithvi Narayan Shah (the first Shah King of Nepal), the exploits of Jang Bahadur Kunwar Rana and the cunningness of King Mahendra is paraded along with Lakhan Thapa Magar's rebellion, Bhim Datta Panta's defiance and the struggle of BP Koirala, Ganesh Man Singh and Pushpa Lal Shrestha against the dynastic tyranny in Nepal.

Deconstruction is a significant sign of post-conflict Nepal in which the 'Bir Gatha' (Onta 1996a) and construction of nationalism through school texts and cultural practices (Onta 1996b; Onta 1994) of the past in the state building enterprise central to monarchy are forbidden only to be replaced by the 'Mahan Jana Yuddha' of the UCPN (Maoist). School text books of Panchayat era (1960-90) are forsaken. They are replaced by the texts for indoctrination by the 'Maobadi Shichhya' in districts controlled by the Maoists during their insurgency (1996-2006).[1] As identities are primarily constructed and reconstructed locally, school as an important agency of socialization contributes to identity formation during the childhood. School children trained with the texts written by the Maoists' leadership glorifying the armed insurgency and socialized accordingly could be dangerously exposed to the merits of violence. Such imprints need to be erased and the children are required to be taught and given lessons from the standard texts with different meaning and connotation to the alphabets and words they have previously learned from the Maoists' texts.

School children are also to be given lessons on the changing context and political transformation of Nepal from a kingdom to a republic. Till recently, the self-definition of Nepal as a nation state was the "only one Hindu Kingdom in the world". The construction of the state then was rooted in the Hindu religious hegemony and situated in the specific cultural space with the recognition of the coreligionists of the world. Such an assertion was made by the ruling elites and championed and promoted by the state beneficiaries throughout the history as a module of state building set on the unitary principle and unidimensional cultural context. Challenged by ethnopolitics that coupled with the Maoist insurgency in the 1990s later culminated into the Jana Andolan-II in April 2006 have finally decontextualized the entire structural edifice of the monarchical regime. This led to the collapse of the dominant cultural ethos dislodging the unitary state by transforming it to the imaginary of federalism.

The imprint of such transformation in perspective is exemplified by the change of national anthem glorifying the monarchy to promotion of multicultural unity. Nepali people are now consciously undertaking the present as a part and task of nation building project as a multiethnic state based on the ideology of secularism and multiculturalism. Cultural liberty and ethnic identity exalt the nation building process. Nation building has become a design to protect and preserve the rights of individual citizens through a diminution of the prerogatives of the state. In other words, nation building in Nepal should be based on the rights-based democratic ideals.

The Crux of Nation Building

Nation building in post-conflict situation is an uphill task, however. Despite the setting of a clear objective of peace and stability, people mostly need a functioning government and its reassurance for their safety and security. Minimally, they need certain opportunities for their life sustaining woks. For this any government in Nepal should prepare itself in setting national priority central to the people's need and work accordingly rather than making high sounding rhetorical commitments on populist programmes like "jivikako laagi krishi, digo vikaska laagi krishi" (agriculture for livelihood, agriculture for enduring development) and "gaon, gaon ma sahakari, ghar, ghar ma rojgari" (cooperatives in every village and employment in every home) to increase agricultural productivity (GON 2009) without any meaningful investment on farm land, labour and irrigation system. Similarly, the exclamation like "janatako rahar, ujyalo sahar" (when the country is usually undergoing 16-18 hours of load-shedding a day) made in the 'policies and programmes' of the government announced at the legislative-parliament of the CA on 3 July 2011 is another instance of absurdity. These homilies are elitist communist jargons uttered for self satisfaction and deceive the gullible mass.

Nation building initiatives for Nepal are actually very ambitious. It ranges from far reaching cultural, economic, political and eventually military development projects in one of the most thoroughly motivated efforts in the post-conflict and post-monarchical period. The project include a design for federal democratic republic and building of an effective civil service and responsible national security and defence forces with required reform in these public institutions. Change in the nation building strategy from the concept of unitary to a federal state structure with constitutionally stipulated self-rule means uprooting the centralized power structure in favour of distributive justice.

This has led to a perceptive change in the nation building processes as suggested by Walker Conner (1972) from historical ambition of "destroying nations" to derive "primary allegiance to the state generally considered *sine qua non* of successful integration" to recognizing diversities and accommodating multicultural aspirations with power sharing for state resilience. The right-based approach to nation building as ascertained by the ethnic assertion and identity politics has compelled governments to uphold inclusive policies, even reluctantly in certain cases like the recruitment of Madheshi in the national armed forces.

Nation building is inherently a long-term and arduous task. Nation building in Nepal ultimately aspires to transform the social structure by fundamentally reshaping values, principles, interests and power relations in the anticipated political system.

Unlike state building, nation building is not simply maintaining jurisdiction over the territory, administer the realm, collect tax and revenue to function and derive legitimacy, but ensuring national coherence through participation of diverse population as stakeholders in developing the state with mutual compliance. For a country coming out of conflict, the foremost priority should be one of stabilization and security. Political leadership with a firm vision for the future followed by systems and institutional mechanism is a necessary feature during the transition. A cohesive society provides bases for restoration of order, peace and stability founded on the rule of law. In essence, this is a precondition for successful nation building.

Social inclusion thus is the core of nation building that opens up the public sphere for participation and representation of the people in public institutions. Along with this, the provision of the 'rights to work/employment and social security' (Article 18) and 'rights to social justice' (Article 21) incorporated as fundamental rights in the Interim Constitution 2007 are premised on the value espoused by inclusion. It then perforce the state to embrace an inclusive policy to bridge the gaps created in the social relationships by the past exclusionary policies through reversing the trend. Unless the pervasively unequal social relationship is changed in practice and replaced by equitable and just social order the objective of human development would be impeded and nation building lost. The thrust of nation building should thus be poverty reduction, job creation providing social justice and equality nurturing the democratic values with emphasis on human development to sustain peace and welfare in the society. Nation building, in fact, implies democratization of the social sphere founded on the notion of federalism to perpetuate peace as explicated in the Kantian philosophy of the 17th century. Article 138 (1A) of the Interim Constitution that declares Nepal as a 'federal democratic republic' is instructive on this process.

It should, however, be remembered that the nation building is a never ending process. It is a long, complex, arduous, challenging and continuing political process. Equity and equality are the governing criteria of nation building process in the absence of which the task of national integration would become more contentious than consensual. Article 3 of the Interim Constitution 2007 has recognized all people of Nepali nationalities as the collective embodiment of the nation called Nepal. This is the testimony to the principle of equity and equality endorsing social justice rectifying injustice. Their participation and representation to build the society, the economy and the polity to meet their basic needs so that they would not be driven by the fear of animosity and grievances related to poverty, unemployment and inequality and create a palatable and just society should be indigenously negotiated and evolved.

People build the nation. Adjusting to their unique circumstances through the conscious cultivation of a national identity, the sense of belonging, based on shared values, tradition, history and collective aspirations they build the nation on the foundation of social cohesion. Similarly, state-society relations are established with formal institutions of governance abiding by the rule of law by making the state functionally responsible to the governed. Participation of citizens in the governance process through power sharing to the grassroots level, by choosing a system, electing leaders and playing an active role in decision making becomes the democratic norms.

The economic well being of common mass leading to the qualitative improvement in their lives has become the cherished aspiration of the people in the nation building process. Part of nation-building, therefore, includes establishing an enduring atmosphere for economic development for the whole nation. The process of nation building can only be internally generated and led and achieved. A sensible leadership thus is pivotal to institutionalizing nation building process successfully in the face of political transition. Others, inclusive of the donors, can support in their efforts providing sufficient funding and technical skill along with sincere advises to the government they work with. In their involvement in nation building processes the donors should be vigilant of the possibility of the elite capture of disproportionate benefits accrued through the efforts that could become an alibi for conflict.

The donors' initiatives should be sustaining transitional authority by helping to prevent any likely conflict by discouraging improper expectations. The motive behind the donors' engagement is creating an environment for sharing opportunities for common benefit. Their support should be oriented towards building up the national response capability.

Thus the triangle – social inclusion, human development and nation building – should be a significant motive behind the institutional processes reflecting on the commitment made while signing the CPA on 21 November 2006, for 'socio-political and economic transformation and conflict management' as the enduring objective of human development through poverty reduction. It is expected that the government in Nepal can enhance its capacity for democratic governance, improve its economic situation and ably address the persistent problems of social exclusion and poverty by integrating these three variables. This requires the consensual rule for reducing uncertainty and good governance fostering accountability. The institutional framework remains drafting and adoption of a constitution corresponding to the need of setting rules, rights and duties guaranteeing pluralistic and inclusive democracy under federal political system with primacy of the people.

This way, the long persisting patron-client nature of state-society relations and the societal tensions brewing underneath could be minimized by reordering and redefining it through creating an enabling environment to the people through inclusion, opportunity, competition and governance based on social justice. Thus nation building should be provisioned on the premises of human security. As a concept, human security is primarily linked with practices of human rights. That right is provisioned on the concept of citizenship which, in turn, is a crucial facet of nation building. Citizenship implies the identity of and belonging to a nation, which was previously denied mostly to the people of Tarai origin, thus, making the process of nation building incomplete and raising insecurity and human suffering. Citizenship flows both ways: the narrative of state maintains control over the person and his/her movements as its citizen, and the person as a citizen beomes a rightful claimant to the opportunities provided by the state.

In this context, it should be understood that people in Nepal are living within the confines of a territory of a weak and vulnerable state which remains grossly unaccountable to its citizenry. This makes people more insecure as bad governance cause sociopolitical chaos generating conflict, environmental and economic breakdown, population displacement, poverty and social exclusion. All these reflect directly on the condition of human security. Failure to ensure human security risks disillusionment; it threatens state from within as the inefficacy of the government increases. Human security embraces a notion of security that approaches an expanded range of social, political and economic developmental issues in relations to state capacity building provisioned on wellbeing of the people. Human security in Nepal is moreover concerned with the development aspiration of the people leading to poverty reduction in the country.

The Maoist insurgency lasting over a decade has clearly marked an increase in human insecurity particularly in the poverty pockets of Mid-Western and Far-Western Nepal. Poverty has also provided recruiting grounds for the guerrilla leadership. Insurgency violence caused the already deprived areas foregone by development works further making the challenges of livelihood critical. With the beginning of the Maoist insurgency the Nepali society has undergone a traumatic change, nothwithstanding social suffering as the Maoists had transferred their role into a paragon of cruelty. This led the state and the Maoist as the non-state forces to reproduce violence by strengthening their countervailing strategies making the poor and defenceless people suffer the most.

However, the political violence has also raised understanding of their wretched situation among the people and, thus, opened up the avenues for assertion of hitherto suppressed social issues. It gave the voice to the voiceless people and worked as a catalyst in bringing social awareness by changing social thinking. Inequality, discrimination, patrimonialism and social exclusion have been persistent causes of underdevelopment that tempted violent insurgency. Political violence however rendered the state dysfunctional. It weakened the institutional capacity of the state to function, undermined and ctrippled the national economy, encouraged capital flight and kept away foreign direct investment. Conversely, the upsurge of violence caused societal breakdown with the spread of arms and light weapons heightening public insecurity. The situation, therefore, remained the same: both democracy and development have merely become the culture of aspiration. Thus, poverty and insecurity persist.

Human Development and Human Security

The reverse should have been the case as poverty is deeply entwined with the concept of human insecurity. Humanitarian sufferings, for instances, are the causes of widespread poverty, scant welfare provisions and abuse of authority by the functionaries of the state. There is therefore the high risk of misuse of the welfare provisions or structures in existence (say, the Poverty Alleviation Fund, Selfemployment Fund, Primeministerial Fund and Natural Calamity Fund) for the legitimation and maintenance and support of the leadership of a certain political party in government through neopatrimonial distributive system that has nothing to do with the need of human security: food security, health security, personal security, economic security, and, political security (UNDP 1994: 24-35). Simply defined, to repeat, as the "freedom from want and freedom from fear" as the fundamentals of human security, the plight of mostly poor and least developed countries like Nepal is underlined in the concept. As an architect of the concept, Mahbub ul Haq defines:

> Human security is not a concern with weapons. It is a concern with human dignity. In the last analysis, it is a child who did not die, a disease that did not spread, and ethnic tension that did not explode, a dissident who was not silenced, a human spirit that was not crushed. ... Human security is a concept... emerging from the daily concerns of people – from the dread of a woman that she may be raped in a lonely street at night, from the anguish of parents over the spread of drugs among their children from the chocked existence of prosperious communities in increasingly polluted cities from the fear of terrorism suddenly striking any life anywhere without reason.... [H]uman security is reflected in the shrivelled faces of innocent children, in the anguished existence of the homeless, in the constant fear of the jobless, in the silent despair of those without hope (Haq 1996: 116-17).

Human security is thus central to the poverty-development nexus. The thrust of human development, as argued, should be oriented towards the provisions related to human security (Kumar 2008a). In the context of human development the Nepali situation is becoming worse even in comparison to its South Asian neighbours (UNDP 2010). The economic malaise with shrinking development expenditures in practice, irrespective of the high budgetary allocations, makes the situation more pathetic. Increasing unemployment and soaring inflationary trend have critically compromised the life chances of the poor people as their sustainability and survival become questionable. This situation directly relates to poverty and hunger. People still struggle to make ends meet; they have not enough to eat and living on a meal a day. Such a plight of the people magnifies the poverty concern, which is multidimensional and relates critically to unemployment and underdevelopment. Suicides of individuals and families caused by joblessness and hunger are sadly reported (e.g., Kumar 2011).

The question of malnutrition and food insecurity then follows when food subsidies are not available and market control and job creation lapse in a situation where social security is beyond the reach of the poor and disadvantaged. The interplay of "want and fear" has become integral to structural complexities of human security in Nepal where public authority remains corrupt and unaccountable, the regional imbalance signifies public expenditure and investment and poorer people are neglected and left out to fend for themselves as they are uneducated, therefore, unproductive. Widespread corruption of public fund, indeed, has become an unsurmountable detriment to human security. So whither the poverty alleviation funds!

Interface between development and security is not new. The paradigms of both development and security have been sensitively changed further by making them human centric rather than emphasizing on growth and territorial integrity. This conceptual shift has understandably reinforced the relationships between state and society along with the underlying measures for the formation of the former in pursuit of the preservation of the latter. The threats inculcated in the context of human security are social and economic threats, particularly, in relations to poverty, health and environmental degradations. Broadly speaking, the basis for discouraging such threats to arise is the maintainance of a liberal political order with churning of public goods. Denial may constrict normalcy and disaffection may result into generating contention and conflict in a situation when public protests, riots and violent assertion of rights have become a common texture in the course of social unrest. Further terrorism remains a potential factor in damning both development and security with explicit use of survival instincts of poverty striken people in case of the continuing government's neglect.

Provisions of basic needs are tied fundamentally to the context of human security in Nepal where chronic poverty coexists with suprarich people. This is the consequence of inequity not equity as a policy pursuit. Thus obtaining human security lies within the framework of governance wherein political leadership matters the most. Henceforth the politics and the priority of political leadership and government in Nepal should be pursued for human security rather than waging incessant struggle for power leading to institutional atrophy and state fragility (Kumar 2008a: 309). State fragility makes the situation more insecure. Challenges multiply as state becomes incapable to resolve the public concern. A step towards managing the public contention should, therefore, be reversing the exclusionary practice of governance with the measured policy of social inclusion in relation to governance with accountability.

Democracy versus Ethnocracy

The state restructuring process is fundamentally encased in ethnicist explication of national polity. Ethnocracy, in reality, has pushed democracy to the extreme politicking. The establishment of the High-Level State Restructuring Commission and its two separate recommendations, for example, are the consequences of deep-seated ethnic anomalies prevalent in the socio-political setting never so obviously expressed. Another example is the breakup of established political parties on ethnic line despite their political philosophy remains the same laden with the doses of Marxism-Leninism. Thus ethnic diversity creates identity politics that in turn makes incipient democracy difficult to hold. However, ethnicism thrives under democracy rather than dictatorship. Nepal in itself is evident to this analogy.

The furor in Nepal about ethnopolitics is understandably the cause of repression and marginalization of indigenous people under autocracy or the monarchist's regime in the past. This has to be reversed. Ethnics thus are demanding both political space and share in the national mainstream. The Comprehensive Peace Agreement 2006, indeed, is an agreement on power sharing. This is the context in which the process of social inclusion has begun reverently. Enthused with the entering of the revolutionary elites in the national polity the dimension of social relations changed reflecting a meaningful representation of people from diverse social setting in the Constituent Assembly.

Never before there had been 197 women in the national parliament functioning simultaneously with the CA, of whom 29 were elected through direct contest (FPTP) and the rest through proportional representation. Similarly, of the 50 Dalits representing at the CA, 7 had won direct elections. The representation of indigenous people (Janajati) and Madheshi as well are comparable to the women's representation making the CA most inclusive. The chamber of national decision making thus has widened to make the presumed democratic republic more cohesive as representative polity. Such an encouraging trend however is compromised by the reality of the ruling group being homogenous in all major political parties with the dominant Bahun-Chhetri combine. The secularist ethos thus is in ferment with the assertion of making Nepal a Hindu state that had much to do with the priestly Brahminic caste people patronized by the Chhetri/Thakuri rulers. Ethnicism brought conservatism to fore. Religiosity has become avid commitment for some groups to sermonize their role in national politics. Therefore the risk-averse political leaders have put the secularist agenda on trial. The phenomenon of ethnicity, on the other hand, not only has become a ticklish challenge but also a fervent problem awaiting satisfactory resolution.

Nepal has successfully managed certain crucial aspects of challenge obtaining in the post-conflict situation. Nepal sends peacekeepers abroad in dangerous places to discourage recurrence of violence in post-conflict countries. Peacekeeping forces are sent abroad to help manage state building by externally induced initiatives in most of the post-conflict states. But Nepal is an exception. It is keeping peace without the presence of the blue helmets on its soil. Though it had invited UNMIN with exclusive mandate for helping conduct CA elections and monitoring arms deposits, the mission left Nepal in 2011 with dipping popularity incurring heavy expenses. But it failed fundamentally in rationalizing democracy without being able to help draft a constitution as mandated by the Jana Andolan-II and as a consequence of CA elections. The electoral politics thus failed in sustaining democracy leading the political leadership to lose accountability and legitimacy in the eyes of the electorate. The process of nation building thus has stagnated with vacillating of the national consensus among the political parties. Governance, as a result, has become a charade.

Notes

1. The Maoists introduced "Janabadi Shichhya" in the rural areas during the course of their insurgency that continues till today. The following two books published by the CPN (Maoist) in 2005 are examples of the text developed for indoctrination of the pupils at schools in Achham, Jajarkot, Jumla, Kalikot, Rolpa, Rukum, Salyan, Surkhet districts etc. These texts were taught to students at schools beyond the reach of district headquarters. Complete texts for grade I to III and Social Sciences text for grade IV to X were drafted and developed under the leadership of the Western Command of the CPN (Maoist) and endorsed by the highest leadership with Chairman Prachanda's authentication (Lohani et al., 2005; Mukunda et al., 2005). Examples of entries of meaning for alphabet in these books are 'revolutionary' as A stands for Army, G= Gun, H=Hammer, R=Rifle, S=Sickle, T=Tunnel and so on.

VI

On Social Policy and Nation Building

Policymaking in Nepal is adverse to the indigenous knowledge developed on the basis of the reality of the situation. Decision making practices are fundamentally based on *ad hocism* and leadership idiosyncrasies. As most of the development agendas are donor driven and funds for development works in some cases are exclusively met by the donors, the national government lapses in the ownership of the project. Therefore, national development projects mostly survive on donors' choice and commitment. In Nepal, donors are everywhere. From the prime minister's office (PMO) down to some obscure NGOs, donors command influence and authority making their presence and penetration in decision making processes acute. For example, bills are theoretically legislated by the parliament; decisions are made by the government and placed in the parliament for endorsement whenever required. But in practice, the momentum for drafting bills by bureaucracy and decision making by the political leadership is steered only with the doses of foreign aid and guidance of the donors. This is the shining reality of the post-monarchical Nepal. The post-conflict recovery process depends virtually on the donors' democratic zeal. It is ironic that donors, in reality, have become service providers. NGOs are the trusted partners of the donors in mobilizing resources and involving poor people than the government with limited capacity and corrupt mentality.

Next, the degree of aid dependency defines the level of control over policies and programmes by the national leadership. The donors' trap is entrenching more than ever before in the Nepali context. The visionless and incompetent political leadership have compromised their freedom in governance compelling them to accommodate even untenable issues in domestic politics by appeasing the opposition for their mere survival in power. Besides donors in policymaking in development dramas, external penetration in the national decision making process even in making and unmaking of the government is increasingly felt. Nepal's neighbourhood policy is increasingly being tasked to take cognizance of their respective security interests as nothing but uncertainty creeps in its national politics. Following this, there are policies influenced by social and political movements. Policy decisions related to indigenous (Adibasi/Janajati) and Madheshi people are moreover the consequence of social and political movements forcing the dominant groups to concede to popular urge for inclusion.[1] For example, the government's commitments to certain genuine issues of federalism and proportional representation along with signing of several other agreements are the consequence of activists' pressure tactics.[2] Perhaps the Madheshi movement has been the largest social mobilization for assertion of identity and inclusion in the history of the country. This movement has led the government to change the policy of denial (Kumar 2007). Thus, rather than being proactive the government is becoming reactive to the popular sentiment and public pressure.

Social inclusion as a policy perspective has become an imperative for the national leadership duly because of critical international upsurge in identity politics translated into ethnic rivalries for space and status and transformed as national agenda by the Maoist insurgency at home. The fundamental objective of the Maoist insurgency, in fact, has been to improve their position through violence by increasing chances of accessibility to state power under the pretext of inclusion in the name of equity and social justice. Despite resistance, their ultimate motive remains state seizure, then, translating their ideals of making Nepal a communist state. Participation in the Maoist insurgency has become a gate-crashing incident for many Janajati groups and Dalits who had long been excluded from the political mainstream, and thus had nurtured grievances against the state. The Maoist insurgency, therefore, had subalternity in its appeal.

Despite being classified as 'hybrid democracy' in essence (EIU 2010; 2011), trouble begins in democracy when servants of the people start behaving as masters. As observed, the relationship between government and society has long been that between master and servant. The images of the government in Nepal, be that under autocracy or democracy, remain irresponsible to the people. Governments formed even under democracy have largely been unaccountable to the people. What the people now want; how they view their government should be; and how they expect their government should act in response to their needs? Features as these are the larger concerns in the principles of governance. The term used in defining the relationship between the government and society is "'partnership' (Micklethwait 2011:3-6) with the state creating a right environment for work and being efficient, transparent and accountable" to the people. Micklethwait asks 'What is government for?' Minimally, the state should be responsible for better schooling, health care and infrastructure to meet the basic needs. Maximally, state matters because it has inevitable impact on people's lives.

> The quality of state you live in will do more to determine your well-being than natural resources, culture and religion. In the surveys that measure people's happiness, decent government is as important as education, income and health (all of which are themselves dependent on government) (citing Geoff Mulgan, Micklethwait 2011: 6).

A decent government or good governance in popular lexicon is always the missing link in the statecraft. This is what Carothers has noted in the case of the country like Nepal.

> Political elites from all the major parties or groupings are widely perceived as corrupt, self-interested, and ineffective. The alternation of power seems only to trade the country's problems back and forth from one hapless side, to other. Political elites from all the major parties are widely perceived as corrupt, self-interested, dishonest, and not serious about working for their country. The public is seriously disaffected from politics, and while it may still cling to a belief in the ideal of democracy, it is extremely unhappy about the political life of the country. Overall, politics is widely seen as a stale, corrupt elite-dominated domain that delivers little goods to the country and commands equally little respect. And the state remains persistently weak. Economic policy is often poorly conceived and executed, and economic performance is frequently bad or even calamitous. Social and political reforms are similarly tenuous, and successive governments are unable to make headway on most of the major problems facing the country, from crime and corruption to health, education and public welfare generally (Carothers 2002: 10-11).

The utmost challenge Nepal faces is lifting millions of impoverished people out of poverty. This policy should be the premium responsibility of an elected leadership. Carrying out commitment with infrastructure development and job creation to the youths aspiring for their freedom to live on their own earning should be the minimum resolve for governing the state. These need investment on the young people, proper management of available resources along with expertise and channelize them to productive use. The problem is that the Maoists have politicized poverty utilizing it for their insurgency mobilization that helped their pursuit to state power by fusing poverty with violence. Thus poverty continues to remain a problem and a significant means to attract foreign aid and use it for the vested interests of the leadership by turning the state as a significant source of personal wealth. *Fiefdom* is what the undergoing situation at present can be described. Besides the pure cynicism in describing the way in which the Nepali state has functioned irrespective of whatever brand of political system created in the history the invariable choice of the political leadership has remained creating poverty purposively. The political culture nurturing the state leadership remains extractive. This is the bitter reality.

Reversing the State of Denial

The idea of social policy has originated in the developed economies of the West. Its relevance in our national context is more pertinent as the majority of people living in the country need state intervention in social sector providing them service and protection. Debate has continued on what should be the appropriate mode of social policy influencing the process of poverty alleviation in Nepal. In relations to this, a provision for social security is made, which is crucial to state obligation as a service provider to its citizenry. But the gap between need and policy is stark in the context of an underdeveloped economy and unstable political situation in the country. Social policy is meant to bridge and resolve this gap in the due course. Social policy promotes the potentiality for social stability. Thus rural poverty should be contextualized while setting policy priorities with identification and consideration of actual needs of people living in the villages. This requires discarding the state-led top-down policymaking process by patronized experts appointed at the National Planning Commission[3] – a model unsuitable for democratic decentralization and federalization as well.

Although promoting social welfare has been the pivotal policy of governments formed, however, the economic situation prevalent in the country makes every effort inadequate to address challenges related to poverty and vulnerability of the citizenry. The state thus is tasked to undertake social policies benefitting the needy particularly after reclaiming the multiparty democracy in 1990 by upholding measures for social sector development. Provisions for promoting social welfare intensified after the success of Jana Andolan-II in 2006. The post-conflict narrative has begun with the focus on social responsibility of the state, which is reflected in the budgetary allocation on social sectors, inclusive of social safety nets and social security. Although the shifting sands of policy priorities of governments of the period have influenced the practice unduly even in the works of the Ministry of Peace and Reconstruction, the commitments to children and senior citizens welfare have been appraised positively as a sign of socioeconomic security. Despite this the thrust for social promotion or protection in overall context has been considered limited as the social protection index (SPI) developed by the Asian Development Bank suggests. The SPI score of Nepal is 0.048 which is below the South Asian average both in terms of median 0.081 and mean 0.117 values (ADB 2011). This is, indeed, pathetic.

However, the momentum gained thus far needs to be preserved. The fragments of dissension should be amenably resolved with engaging dialogue. This is necessary to avoid or discourage the incendiary effects of grievance, dissension and conflict. Democracy is a practice for dialogue and consensus with confidence building between groups with varied interests. Politics is competitive and citizens are contentious. Engaging in dialogue means recognizing others' points of view and their experiences with honesty and coherence. Interaction should sequence with engaging dialogue, influencing the negotiating side, responding to the opposing grievances and restoring peace and stability. Therefore, the imperative of social cohesion should never be undermined for political expediency.

A cohesive society, as Wetherell (2007: 3) asserts, is one where (i) there is a common vision and sense of belonging for all communities; (ii) diversities of people's different backgrounds and circumstances are appreciated and positively valued; (iii) those from different background have similar life opportunity; and, (iv) strong and positive relationships are being developed between people from different backgrounds and circumstances in the work-place, within schools and within neighbourhoods. To simplify, this is to recognize cultural differences and circumstantial variant. Political awakening of the people aspiring for a political order is founded on the recognition of rights of all cultures and communities. In a multicultural society neither of any culture is superior or inferior. Cultural pluralism encourages respect for identity and freedom of all cultural groups. Differences in cultural practices not necessarily lead to tensions and clashes between the groups in communities. Nepal celebrates cultural practices of all nationalities with equal enthusiasm bonding a relationship among the people contributing to strengthen social cohesion. The identification of freedom of all cultural groups can enhance and entrench democracy rather than weaken its values.

The *mantra* to achieve this is social inclusion. State, actually, is a big apple pie and people aspire to have a share of it. Access to the state power makes inclusion or exclusion in simple sense as exclusion becomes the symbol of denial. In sum the struggle between the assertion of ethnicity for their cultural freedom and citizens' rights and its denial has textured the template of political development in Nepal with inclusion-exclusion matrix.

The vision of a multicultural state is comprehended by the Interim Constitution 2007 obviously making inclusion as an imperative of state transformation, politically named as state restructuring process. State formation therefore would much base on liberal democratic framework despite the ensuing quarrel on the organizing ideology of state. The Jana Andolan-II of April 2006 has been a step towards nation building in essence by reversing the course of state denial.

Social Policies, Donors, Political Leadership and Governance

One of the most commendable social policies ever initiated by the government of Nepal has been the decision on "Janata Awash Karyakram" (People Housing Programme), a Habitat project for the destitute under the leadership of the Prime Minister Madhav Kumar Nepal. The low cost housing project has been targeted towards the Dalits, disadvantaged and marginalized people living in the Tarai and Hill districts of the country. The project was allocated a sum of Rs.300 million to accommodate some 3,000 families with a provision of low cost dwelling (GON 2009a). Efforts made by Finance Minister Surendra Pandey towards its successful completion remain exemplary. However, the corrupt practices of the Physical Planning and Construction Minister Bijaya Kumar Gachhedhar of the Madheshi Jana Adhikar Forum (Loktantrik), a coalition partner of the then CPN (UML) government, who mobilized his henchmen mostly in the Tarai-Madhes districts, for example, Siraha, led to embezzlement of funds for the housing project with many structures of the housing units left incomplete (Bohara 2011:20-22). It was also reported that housing units built for the disappearing minorities Chepang groups of Makawanpur district are leaking and breaking down due to the use of low quality construction materials. This development endeavour worth a name with humanitarian service is now under a cloud because of continuing political instability at the centre.

Likewise, another significant social policy espoused by the government is for the elderly care. This measure of crucial import was begun early in 1995 during the minority government of the CPN (UML) led by its august leader Man Mohan Adhikari. With the introduction of the 'universal pension scheme', the first of its kind in the South Asian region, following the recommendation of the International Conference on Population and Development held in Cairo (Egypt) in 1994, the government stipulated elderly pension scheme initially for people of 75 + years of age and 60+ year old widows with a token amount. Though the government has endorsed the identification of the elderly in conformity with the World Health Organization's (WHO) definition as "people who are 60 years and above", it does not concur in practice. Despite this the government has continued allocations for the elderly allowances in the annual budget disbursing through the local

Table 6.1: Janata Awash Karyakram: Data

Fiscal Year 2066/67 (2009/10)
Districts

Saptari: 1,000 units of design selection, all (972) Housing units completed.
Siraha: 1,000 units of design selection, construction of 848 units begins but remains incomplete.
Kapilbastu: 426 Housing units selected; 260 constructed; stopped construction of 43 units.

Fiscal Year 2067/68 (2010/11)
Districts

Saptari: construction started on 347 units.
Siraha: construction started on 444 units.
Kapilbastu: 474 housing units selected.
300 housing units for Chepang ethnic people in Chitwan, 200 units in Makawanpur, and 100 units in Dhading and 70 units for Raute in Dandeldhura in the Far Western Nepal along with 12 housing units for Kusunda (the disappearing ethnic group) in Dang, Gorkha, Pyuthan and Rolpa districts constructed.

Fiscal Year 2068/69 (2011/12) planned
Districts

10 housing units for the people of Surel ethnicity in Dolkha.
5 housing units for Raute in Dandeldhura.
136 housing units for Badi people in Banke, Bardiya, Dang, Dailekh, Jajarkot, Kailali and Surkhet districts.
100 housing units for Gandharva (musicians Dalits) in Arghakhachi, Bardiya, Dang, Gulmi, Kaski, Surkhet and Tanahu districts.
8 housing units for Kusunda in Dang, Pyuthan and Surkhet districts.
15 housing units for Bankariya people in Makawanpur district.
525 housing units for Chepang in Chitwan, Dhading, Gorkha and Makawanpurdistricts.

Source: Bohara, 2011; Budget Speech, July 2009:32; and the Statement Delivered by the Finance Minister, July 2010:5.

bodies. Currently banks have replaced local bodies in disbursment of elderly pension making it difficult for old persons to collect their pensions as over 80 per cent of the people in that age bracket are illiterate. Banking services are also not available in thinly populated rural areas.

Following the Senior Citizens Act 2006 numerous other Acts like the Elderly Population Act 2006 and Elderly Population Rules 2008 are introduced making special arrangements for the elderly in the transport and service sectors. Likewise, enactments concerning social security system, Senior Citizens Policy and Working Policy 2002, National Action Plan for Senior Citizens 2005, Senior Citizens Health Facility Programmes Implementation Guidelines and Senior Citizens Regulations 2009 were adopted to benefit the old people (Bhattarai and Bhattarai, nd). The monthly allowance for senior citizens is Rs 500 as per the rule (GoN 2009: 14), though nominal and inadequate, it subsidies certain basic expenses of the elderly people. However, the fixture of age limit in the case of women for their entitlement to get social security allowance has been removed with the provision that women will receive the allowance from the day and date of widowhood (GoN 2011). Similarly, the eligibility for elderly pension for men has been brought down from 75 to 70 years; it, however, makes no sense as the life expectancy of male in Nepal is still below that age. The average expectation of life at birth was 59.7 according to the 2001 Census. By 2011, the estimated life expectancy at birth of the female has reached 67.44 years and 64.94 years for male populations in Nepal (CBS 2012).

Nepal's elderly population has increased from 6.5 per cent to 9.1 per cent respectively between 2001 and 2011 census period.[4] During the same period population increased from 23 million to 26.6 million of which 2.4 million constitutes the elderly people. Factors contributing to the growth of elderly population are decrease in fertility and mortality rate as well. As the traditional family structure is breaking down with changing social mores and increase in nuclear families, the elderly are more or less in a state of despair as they have become human bondage in several cases. If the old age allowances are distributed properly by the responsible agencies this may serve as a relief to the persons receiving pensions. It would also be certain incentive to the members of families taking care of the old or even disables in the house (Bhattarai and Bhattarai, nd).

Similarly, although domestic violence and child abuse have surfaced as issues of public concern and rights groups are pursuing the cases both at national and international forums, elderly abuse by family members remains a private matter despite being a social crime. This universal phenomenon, of lately, has drawn the attention of democratic governments like in Nepal. Preventive measures against this type of family violence in physical, verbal, emotional and financial context or even accusation of witchcraft particularly against women are conspicuous by their absence as there is no law. Their neglect in the society as spent force in general leads to discrimination and marginalization with the loss of their self identity. The social policy thus requires addressing this growing problem of 'domestic violence' against elderly and terming such treatment as inhumane criminal folly and design appropriate law and intervention procedure protecting the human rights of the elderly. Simply distributing allowance is not enough. With rapidity in breakup of the family tradition the vulnerability of ageing people has sharpened and their invisible sufferings are rarely noticed in a rush to individual welfare and happiness. Government thus can make a difference.

Thirdly, the CPN (UML) party and the government led by it deserves appreciation for encouraging widow marriage with some financial incentives. Though widow marriage is not strictly discouraged for a long time, it is however treated as a taboo and not appreciated, particularly, in the high caste families leaving the young widows languishing for life. The step against the conservative tradition prevalent in the Hindu society has been boldly taken as a policy issue by the Finance Minister Surendra Pandey of the CPN (UML) party, though resisted, repudiated and criticized alarmingly. Although being largely a social tradition, marriage system is a personal and a private affair related to the human rights and freedom of an individual. But a widow or a woman becomes something like a commodity or property in the household of a patriarchal society. The effort towards breaking out of such a tradition was remaking the society anew, which, however could not be materialized at the policy level. Similarly, the introduction of the government programme encouraging inter-caste marriage, particularly, between the Dalits and non-Dalits created a chasm in the social taboo. Such policy initiatives are meant to make society more tolerant, accommodative, egalitarian and fundamentally inclusive by constructing a new social tradition for the future of the Nepali state. However limits in practice are yet unavoidable.

Another crucial agenda that also relates to social policy of the government is pensioning the *Rastra Sevak* – its former employees. As the number of retired and retiring government employees in the civil, military, police and education (teacher) sectors is increasing annually, the government is obliged to provide pension. In the FY 2011/12, the pension amounted to Rs.18. 5 billion for an estimated 185,000 recipients. As per a report, presently 83 per cent in the civil service, 58 per cent in the military, 42 per cent in the Police and Armed Police Force and 17 per cent in the Teaching service are receiving pension in comparison to the incumbent employees in these sectors (Bhattarai 2012: 44). Pension is paid in lieu of the service of an employee who retires after a fixed tenure or the service age limit of the person. It is usually thought as the employer's gratitude to the employee for sustenance in the old age. With more service holders retiring due mainly to the age factor, the government is burdened with the challenge of taking care of its former employees and the ageing population. Pensioning of its ageing employees requires a serious reconsideration of policy as the size of this population is about to increase naturally demanding heavy expenses covering their needs. The governmental measures towards the pensioners would eventually be preventing social suffering of the country's ageing population. In response to this, the health care and welfare provision needs to be reconceptualized to address the burgeoning challenge.

Similarly, the growing challenge posed by the child care of divorced couples, abandoned or street children and child labour like children working in the public transport sector and teashops in urban centres and labouring in the brick kilns require a rigorous policy oriented towards their elimination by making the lives of such children socially normal and congenial for their progress in the future. Like the bonded labour, child labour is also a curse in Nepal. Contributions of NGOs in these areas are commendable yet inadequate. The government needs to learn from the work experiences of the NGOs while developing policies approaching the problem. Policymaking requires being effective based on the evidence or fact rather than hypothesis or assumption. The government should initiate a process of mapping out the difficulties and challenges for framing the responses. This could sustain policy to be driven by the evidence rather than ideology or prejudice. If the government is committed to deliver its decision should be based on the concrete evidence, not on dogma for human progress. This may help the prospect of human development that relates poverty to exclusion. Evidence of denial can only be upturned with the adoption of capability enhancing approach by the government providing opportunity to each aspiring citizen of the country to participate in development.

The Question to Address

Have we ever discussed the consequences of change; the transition from monarchy to republic and the impact of political transformation on the general public? Has the government been responsive to the people? Are the social policies pursued by the governments adequate to meet the social needs? Have the governments been able to alleviate poverty through implementing policies or remittances have helped reduced poverty artificially? Have the governments ever thought about the serious consequences of social anomalies caused by the exodus for remittance earning? All these seemingly relevant concerns are jettisoned in the context of the state being overpoliticized. Relations between the state and society remain so close but so distant that the political process commencing in the country revolves around power struggle and political equation among the major political parties leaving the societal concerns and demands apart. Political parties are usually indifferent to the public concern. Parties in government have designed paper plan, which is never being implemented. The National Planning Commission prepares bogus reports to suit the government objectives. The credibility of government remains in doubt.

The finding of a recent study published by Arjan De Haan on social policies in South Asia in general laments that "deeprooted inequalities continue to pervade government, public institutions, and the public debate" (De Haan 2010:191). These inequalities manifest particularly in the cases of gender empowerment, inadequacy of education, health and certain other crucial provisions of social opportunities tied to local development. Inequality and exclusion are also consequences of cultural practices and locational disadvantages: The glaring example is the hilly and mountaineous districts of Mid-and-Far Western Nepal being excessively in denial by the state. Thus the case of Nepal, as discussed, is not exceptional to what De Haan has observed.

However, the story is nowhere near complete: Every government formed in the name of serving people has worked otherwise. Economy is crumbling and prospect of economic development is low so long as political impasse continues. National budgets allocated for capital expenditure or commonly known as 'development budget' are meant for embezzling the amounts at the end of every fiscal year by releasing sometimes more than 70 per cent of unallocated budget within the last month of the fiscal year at the expenses of the deliberate lag for the past eleven months. Such amount is released in the name of 'people's participation' in the local development efforts designing the fake projects to fulfill the fraudulent motives of the parties in government. For example, a report on the distribution of Rs.1 billion in different local constituencies of the leaders of major political parties with their connivance has recently appeared in the press (Gyawali 2012a). Misappropriation of budget in this manner has continued as a legacy of the erstwhile panchayat regime before 1990. This development practice has emptied the coffers of the state making the country lurching in waste and underdevelopment.

This trend, however, has become more dangerous in the absence of the elected local bodies, particularly, after Jana Andolan-II. After the expiry of the term of the local bodies in 2002, government servants (secretaries appointed at VDCs, DDCs) had initially managed the official development works. The mantle was later taken over by the *Sarva Daliya Sanyantra* (All Party Mechanism) in the post-CA period. The *sanyantra* retained the ultimate power to decide and decisions were always made in favour of the politicians controlling the purse meant for local development. Corruption flourished rampantly. Over the decade of the absence of the local elected bodies even the social security stipends were grossly misappropriated. There are cases of Dhanusha and Saptari districts in the Tarai region where the secretaries appointed by the government have recently been found stealing multimillion rupees allocated as widows and senior citizens stipends under political protection. In Saptari district alone, for example, Rs. 300 million has been found embezzled (Gyawali 2012b). Consequently, the people suffer.

Social suffering is not limited to the reminiscences of the torture and violence that the people had directly experienced in the past. Villages in Western and Mid-Western Nepal are toiling in the tales of the past violence. The sufferings and traumatic memories of the villagers are recounted through reports, writings and documentaries. The images of sufferings are vividly portrayed and presented. People dislocated from the villages after confiscating their household, property and land and villagers forced to abandon their domicile after arson had similar fate to share by becoming the object of terror of both state and non-state. The able-bodied persons have also abandoned the farmland becoming unproductive both because of the lack of modernizing inputs and land fragmentation further complicating the productive cycle. Lack of development works in the districts and villages is making unemployment perennial for unskilled and semi-skilled labour that crucially affects their livelihood by deepening rural poverty. Despite the budget for local development has increased tremendously the situation in the villages has hardly changed against the reality of decaying practice of corruption.

Table 6.2: Budget Allocation for Local Development

Fiscal Year	Budget	Expenses on	Previous Year
2007/08	13.08 billion	Donation for DDC	3.61 billion
2008/09	25.31 billion	Donation for VDC	9.31 billion
2009/10	35.69 billion	Donation for Metro	1.19 billion
2010/11	41.84 billion	Social Security Stipend	8.60 billion
2011/12	44.50 billion	Participatory Programmes	500 million
		Constituency Dev. Programmes	600 million

Source: Budget Speeches, Different Years Indicated; Ministry of Local Development, Government of Nepal, August 2012.

Damages and destructions caused by unimaginable violence of the Maoists' "people's war" have lasting imprint in the social conscience. The decade of the Maoist insurgency was the case of extreme form of social suffering coupled with hunger and starvation of the people, particularly in Western Nepal. The Maoists in Nepal thus have been presented as a source of social sufferings although they had launched the violent struggles apparently to abolish the persistent discrimination and exploitation from the society. But along with these inhuman practices, miseries and destitution caused by poverty persist, which the World Health Organization has determined in 1995 as the "World's most ruthless killer" (WHO 1995). Thus, we can argue to hell with good intentions. The Maoists' declared intention was to transform the country with state restructuring and pursue the egalitarian policy by providing social justice. It however remains a mirage despite the Maoists had led the two coalition governments in the post-CA period. The Maoists have failed to articulate any policy related to social cause generating optimism among the people rather than becoming a cause for political dissension, public consternation, social disapproval and pessimism. Alienation, hence, is widespread. The incumbent government headed by the Maoist Vice-Chairperson and Prime Minister Baburam Bhattarai is presided over the volcano of social disruption. The magnitude of the outburst could be unimaginable.

Social policy, therefore, needs to be framed in consideration of the future based on the structural transformation of the state. A federal state means empowering the political units functioning with local autonomy endeavouring for economic development and national integration. It requires changing the nature of the state from being a rent seeking and extractive to becoming an institution providing incentives and opportunity through equity, social justice and inclusion. Merely the provision of rights to employment and social security as stipulated in the Article 18 of the Interim Constitution 2007 is not enough (IC 2009:6).

A sentiment of exclusion with overriding concerns for unemployment, poverty and consequent marginalization of the young having been unable to find a job, however, has led to hopelessness of the situation deepening certain malaise that may contribute to invoke violence in the absence of economic policies addressing sustainable growth. Social policy needs to address and accommodate the sense and sensibility of the people living in the down south. Despite holding tremendous economic significance as Nepal's rice bowl and gateway to the hills and mountains, the region has been left neglected for long; consequently for breeding discontent. Nation building fosters national integration. This needs opening access to the aspiring people to the system that the state promotes by maintaining democratic order. Prima facie public accountability is an imperative of good government. This however is conspicuous in absence making the government a farce. Though an economy sustaining the aspiration of people indubitably has become one of the crucial facets of nation building, it remains an aspiration not a reality.

Notes

1. The author is indebted to Kailash N. Pyakuryal for drawing his attention to this reality. It is also well known that Government policies in Nepal are normally influenced by donors' preference and pressure. Besides this, political pressure has become insurmountable and political parties in government accommodate such pressure even for expediency. This is freshly exemplified by point-3 of the 5-point consensus reached between the political parties agreeing to extend the three months tenure of the Constituent Assembly that expired on 28 May 2011. Point-3 has included the claim of the Madheshi Morcha agreeing to effective implementation of the previously undersigned agreements on recruitment of Madheshi citizens in the army to make it inclusive with national character.

2. Take, for instance, the "Eight-Point Agreement signed between the Government and Samyukta Loktantrik Madheshi Morcha" on 28 February 2008 with adherence to the demand of group entry of Madheshi citizens into the National Army and increasing their quota from 20 to 30 per cent in the constituent assembly seats. Similarly, the "Agreement between the Government and Janajatis" signed on 7 August 2007 has also led to further opening up of social and political space. The 5th amendment to the Interim Constitution has mandated the entry of Madheshis, Janajatis, Dalits, Women and people from marginalized and disadvantageous groups into the Army to make the institution inclusive bearing the national character. The "Four Point Agreement" signed between the UCPN (Maoist) and the United Democratic Madheshi Front (UDMF) or Samyukta Loktantrik Madheshi Morcha, popularly known as Madhesi Morcha, on 28 August 2011 that help the formation of the Maoist-led government under the leadership of Baburam Bhattarai has also reiterated the bloc entry of 10,000 Madhesi youths in the national army with distinct identity.

3. Actually, the National Planning Commission (NPC) that functions as an adjunct to the Prime Minister's Office has become a charade under the republic. The culture of *bhag-banda* (sharing of spoils) among the major political parties has been reflected in the appointments of 12-members instead of the stipulated 5, initially along with the gender representation but discontinued later. With the size of its honourable members the NPC become so congested that it had no office space to provide. The NPC

Vice-Chair appointed by the CPN (Maoist) Chairman Prachanda as the prime minister during 2008-09 tenure of the first coalition government formed after the Constituent Assembly elections, had resigned over dissatisfaction on the selection of the other members for the Commission.

4. The 2011 National Census records it at only 8.1 per cent, not 9.1 per cent as previously assumed.

VII
Transforming Governance

Despite policy and promising budgetary allocation, official measures regarding social inclusion lack serious commitments; it's simply treated as political rhetoric. The government programmes do not address the structural problems that led to social exclusion in the first instance. Patrimonialism and rampant corruption feature the socio-political and economic system in which development priorities are to be set and situated. Continuation in the composition of the historical elite compact despite the earthshaking political development impedes any meaningful change. Political power remains within the confines of the same elite structure regardless of the entry of the aspiring group through violent momentum. The behavioural pursuits of neoelites have been observed to have become more centrist, selfregarding and ruinous than the traditional elites.

Authority is maintained through personal patronage rather than through ideology and law. Leaders occupy public office less to serve the people than to acquire public wealth and status. So, Nepali political/power elites are not divided by any crucial political agenda or social cleavage irrespective of the Maoists' musing. The political and power elites in Nepal are indeed united, unified and dominant over the socioeconomic and political landscape. Their differences are over distribution and sharing of power: electoral, contractual and preferential. They take poverty as given and exclusion as systemic imperative to maintain dominance through social hierarchy and hegemonic control.

> For members of hegemonic groups, their language must be the only official language; their religion must be followed by all citizens; and their institutions must be enshrined in government and society. Hegemonic elites often believe that their narrow group is the legitimate ruler of the polity. To ensure their rule, they must promote the group's culture, language, demographic predominance, economic welfare, and political hegemony at the expense of other groups (Byman 2000: 29).

Thriving on the policy of exclusion such was the situation ideally prevailing in Nepal for a long time. The system that was institutionalized by the cultural, political and power elites in Nepal has been projected as the "*afno manchhe* syndrome" (Bista 1991). Thus the social system remains thoroughly exclusionary. Nepali society revolves around a concentric circle where "Nepali individuals feel themselves and treat others almost like non-person" who belong "outside of this circle". As an astute observer of Nepali social relationships, Bista further says,

> Nepali mind is very clearly structured into several types of divisions. This structure automatically leads into a very well organized hierarchy too. The distinction between the ingroup of "us" and the rest of the outsiders [is clear] as "they" manifest in every walk of social, cultural and economic life. Everything inside the circle of "us" is predictable and manipulable, and outside the circle is unpredictable. So there is a constant need to maintain the line of that circle. There is no security without the existence of this circle. The persistence of ethnic or regional identity in addition to the social and ritual hierarchy is a manifestation of the need to have one's own circle defined clearly and maintained permanently (Bista 1989: 178).

Social inclusion is against such a practice. It does not seek to compartmentalize the Nepali society. Rather the motive behind the concept of social inclusion is bonding society together for mutual trust, survival and progress. The dominant discourse in Nepal has therefore continued against the dominant group in search of socio-economic and political space by the marginalized groups.

Although social inclusion has become an entry point to anti-poverty agenda; little has changed in the elite perception of poverty, which is crucial to influence policy decisions. Challenges to the future, therefore, are posed by the persistent political divisions as sub-national groups have largely been undermined. Assertion of identity by the sub-national groups has become a cause of consternation for the traditionally dominant groups encouraging polarization of interest beset with the probability of social conflict. On the top of it the unsettled political agendas of federalism, the organizing ideology of state and the feature of governance all point towards a difficult time ahead. The situation is presently compounded further by the deepening economic malaise in the country as the belated impact of global economic crisis with increasing imports and harrowing trade imbalances.

The triad of reduction of export revenue earning, rising imports and simultaneously increasing unemployment is likely to foster support for more radical groups such as the Maoists. Uncertainty continues to haunt the political sphere with the situation of "two armies, one state" remaining constant till November 2012 defeating the objective of peace and stability. However, the threat of renewal of conflict exists when the state suffers from fragility and unsettling social challenges (Kumar 2011). The only remedy to such risks is the imperative of building institutional capacity by the political leadership through forging a trustworthy state-society relation. Indeed, the need is to make every possible effort to move out of conflict rather than indulging in contending bargains to drag on the differences. Indifference to economic malaise is opening up potential social vulnerabilities in the midst of restive populations.

The Rapid Credit Facility amounting to USD 42.05 million provided by IMF on 28 May 2010 was perhaps a testimony to an impending economic crunch. Nepal's total debt in 1990 was Rs. 37 billion. The outstanding foreign loan was Rs.234 billion in FY 2005/06 (MoF 2007: 21). By mid- 2011, Nepal's indebtedness has reached USD 7.0 billion along with foreign grants amounting to USD10 billion, although still safe from the debt trap. Nepal inescapably faces stabilization challenges in both political and economic dimensions. Regenerating economy and rebuilding social order require institutional capacity, which is, however, weak with low social capital[1] in a situation where distrust predominates. Economy is pivotal in sustaining human development programmes in the absence of which everything will be standstill and the concept of republic could be prematurely dead. Hence the leadership on which the future of the state depends. The gap between commitment and implementation can be bridged only in case the leadership pursues policy stringently towards the targeted groups. The leadership is the one who is going to make this happen.

Much will therefore be determined in the near future by the political process. Cautious assessment should be made with understanding the reality of the rise of the factionalized political elites who could upset the development trajectory for serving self-interests and lead the state to a worst situation. The national reality is the 'post-conflict' situation where the existing institutions have failed to function and protect the nationals by maintaining legitimate monopoly over the use of force; where new institutions are to be created and made functional, where 'legal culture' is yet to be practiced to make transition sustaining democratic order; and where different norms and values require reconciling and setting for evolving a peaceful future. An effective nation building plan entails an understanding of the interests and priority of the poor and excluded. Thus there is urgency in taking steps for legitimating the nation building process by adopting a framework of responsive governance founded on rule of law. Creation of a depersonalized bureaucracy and an independent judicial system is fundamental to institutionalizing effective governance.

All the three: governance founded on rule of law; creation of depersonalized bureaucracy; and, independent judicial system are under a cloud as political transition stagnated and instability delayed the constitution making framing the state governance system. Again the priority of political parties differs on the organizing ideology of the state. The UCPN (Maoist) as the largest political party participating in the constitution drafting process adheres to the communist ideology preferably making the constitutional system integral to the rule of the communist party, not the rule of law as understood under the democratic system. In the democratic system public officials act in accordance with the power and authority prescribed by the legal norms. By contrast, the Maoists seek to establish government with unlimited power. Their fascination for absolutism is based on their ideological adherence to Maoism.

The Maoists have reiterated that they do not recognize the prevailing law governing the state. State power is manipulated and exercised as per their interests penetrating the civil service. Their preference for making judiciary subordinate to both the legislature and the executive is the classic case of their interests in evolving the Maoist party as the superstructure of the state. With the rule of law and protection of rights abandoned and the judiciary becoming subservient to the communist party, the desire and objective of creating a federal democratic republic on the line of multiparty parliamentary democracy would definitely be jeopardized. The Maoists are, indeed, not in favour of federal democracy either. Instead their stakes are on the federal People's Republic. They are still dancing with the concept of 'democratic centralism' with a strong presidential system contravening the ideals of multiparty democratic parliamentary system. Such anomalous situation facing the state in transition reflects on the different facets of nation building objectives.

Similarly, there are a number of significant issues related to the question "what is happening to poverty and inequality?" The importance of this question cannot be undermined as the repercussion of this could be three dimensional: social, economic and political. First, the social cost of inequality includes crime, corruption and problems of accessibility of the poor to basic services such as education and health care, particularly in need of children and women. Second, the economic cost of inequality creates discriminatory behaviour in the labour market place discouraging participation thus reducing labour supply along with exploitation of the weaker sex. Third, the political cost of inequality creates chronic political instability affecting social relationships. Inequality and poverty are considered as the most potential sources of conflict in relation to systemic stability. Therefore, it is an imperative for both the government and donors as development partners to pay particular attention to challenges posed by rising inequality while designing the future of Nepal.

The idea of an inclusive society is based on peace, freedom and equality. The task ahead is clearly nation building requiring a long term strategy and multiyear funding for capacity building through institutional processes absorbing the structural challenges posed by social inclusion and human development in the fragile state. Building institutional capacity thus is premised on the state capability to face transitional challenges. In the view of the World Bank, "Capability refers to the ability of societies to respond to such [transitional] stresses. Successful responses depend in part on resources and technical capacity (e.g. availability of finance, legal and organizational systems, skilled personnel, equipment) but also, critically, on leadership in the collective interest, shared values and social cohesion. Capability and resilience grow over time, on the basis of repeated success in tackling stresses" (World Bank 2011: ii).

It should be recognized that Nepal is a critically fragile state. It requires to be saved from falling apart. Preventing state failure with transitional administration making the state responding to the vulnerabilities with the objective of developing state capacity to address the agenda of human development, as inequality and poverty remain the dominant concern, should receive the priority in decision making. A functional state is only the vehicle of success. And the primary objective should be the recovery from the legacy of the armed conflict on the society. Restoring legitimacy should follow the institutional building efforts, which, in turn, sustains the state capacity to respond to societal stresses. State capacity should simply be conceptualized and understood as a process of managing governance through transparency, accountability and responsiveness while interacting with citizens and society in the policymaking process under the premise of the rule of law. For this to happen, politicians need to change old habits and transform them from behaving like rulers to servers of public interests by making the state a facilitator and a provider. Experience has shown that pursuit of ideology by political parties and their leadership makes no difference when governing the state. Every government formed and departed has left the mark of corruption irremediably in the bodypolitik. State power has continued to be abused and misused with the imprint in the society that such a tendency remains the systemic order and the struggle either to oppose or change it would be myopic. Any attempt to make the future better than the past has been resisted and discouraged by none other than the politicians, except in their rhetoric.

Political culture and tradition remain unchanged despite changes in the political landscape brought about by the political movements like the Jana Andolan-II in 2006. New political elites emerging as a consequence of the Maoist insurgency and the Madheshi movement, recognized and established by the Constituent Assembly elections in 2008, imparted no sense of change in their behavioural pursuits than the existing elites. Circulation of elites through widening the vestige of power and participation in the aftermath of Jana

Andolan-II was largely thought as representing the rising social aspirations. But, politicians at every stage manoeuvred rules and regulations to enrich themselves by embezzling the state coffer and foreign aid. The Maoists have become the 'capitalist-roaders' reaping the profits from spoils of democracy even to the extent of misappropriating government largesse meant for keeping their guerrillas robust in the Cantonments. The top leadership echelon of the Maoist is accused of amassing wealth by misusing state power by none other than the colleagues in the party hierarchy, cadres and combatants. Maoist leadership, including the party chief Prachanda, was investigated on the charges of corruption and embezzlement by a committee formed by the party ostensibly.

Once in power, the Madheshi political elites swarming on the ministerial portfolios at Singha Darbar – the Government Secretariat – also did not look back as some of them asked for pre-paid commission without blinking their eyes. Criminal enterprises flourished and the nation and the people as a whole suffered. No respite to political change is felt by the people despite momentous change has occurred with the abolition of monarchy. The electorate had put their fate on the Constituent Assembly mandated for peacebuilding and constitution making. What transpired to their dismay is the uncertainty of their future with the betrayal of their trust by the politicians. But none of the political parties has taken the responsibility and ownership for the bitter end and the prolongation of the political transition. The people, at large, are now left with delusion with the cruel end of the Constituent Assembly without promulgating the constitution on 27 May 2012.

It is therefore advisable that national polity in transition should be managed with serious consideration of following agendas to steer the state out of current impasse.

Governance through Authority Building

Systematically, governance is the overarching priority of nation building in which political parties are the real stakeholders.

Political processes based on the articulation of the rule of law governing the state-society relations through reconciliation by addressing inequities and inequalities and promoting accountability would help strengthen national resilience. Being a state in the post-conflict situation Nepal requires the recovery from the armed conflict permeated by the socioeconomic as well as political fragility. What a fragile state in transition needs most is prudence in governance while the political leadership engages itself to evolve a viable political order for making a functional state. Governance provides institutional authority to public officials legitimating the exercise of public authority to deliver goods and services to the people in exchange for their public performance.

Building authority, thus, is a prima facie requirement of leadership during political transition. The challenge to Nepali leadership in the post-Jana Andolan-II situation is both regime building and nation building; the structural transformation of the state is an imperative that can be achieved only through gaining performance legitimacy; a government formed with fragile coalition is doubly vulnerable to internal push and pull that jeopardizes even the sense of direction in decision making which the core leadership must overcome to pursue the central agenda by matching goals with capabilities. Leadership commitment, therefore, can make up with their inexperience in governance, if they set their agendas correct and clear them from their apparent self-interests.

Towards this goal, political parties must stop the practice of sharing spoils of democracy. Patrimonialism and partisan interests should be discouraged and right man in the right place encouraged in civil, judicial and security services. Excessive political interferences in the civil service and patronage politics have corrupted the institution. Government, despite being elected under democratic system, is the most mistrusted institution as it remains indifferent to the livelihood security of poor and excluded, insensitive to gender equity and reaching out to the people through providing service accessibility. Any government in Nepal therefore needs to change its attitude towards governance just by entertaining the view that elections provide popular legitimacy but without thinking about impermanence of such legitimacy. This is the perceptual gap that has continued to haunt state-society relations. There is therefore a serious need of confidence building between state and society.

Political stability is essential to create enabling environment and implement development programmes without hindrances contributing to reduce poverty. Instability clung stubbornly with incompatible goals has led to anarchic situation and extortion have caused even joint ventures and big industries to close and encourage capital flights, discouraging investment, complicating economic productivity and denying employment opportunities impinging on the thrusts of poverty reduction and human development. This should be stopped without delay with stringent measures against unlawful activities conducted with political protection. Trade Union movements encouraged by the Maoist party need to be curbed. Otherwise, all the plans and policies would be futile when investment and the law enforcement would be retarding.

Constitution is the foundation for anchoring the legitimacy of the government. With the lapse of the CA's two years' term on 28 May 2010 as stipulated by the Interim Constitution 2007, the legitimate authority of the government elected by the CA's legislative-parliament was *in desideratum* despite the term of the CA was renewed and extended subsequently (that was certainly an explicit violation of constitutionalism), and governments formed on the majority basis. Electoral politics has provided the semblance of credibility to the governments formed despite the erosion of popular legitimacy after the lapse of the CA mandate constitutionally determined for two year's tenure is all pervasive. The 'principle of necessity' on the basis of which the tenure of the CA was extended and the government has continued was simply a political expediency. Though people's participation was meant to elect the CA for drafting constitution not to elect parties in parliament, the practice however is disposed towards the latter. Thus what counts is the majority. Exclusion of consultation with 29 minor parties (caused by the breakup of political parties) present in the CA to drive consensus was an indication of how political power works in Nepal. The CA was totally ignored and practically used as rubber stamp when necessary by the leaders in the hierarchy of political parties and their patronized 'influential' members. This situation is the reflection of the characteristics of political instability which should be overcome.

Articulate Performance Legitimacy

Grandiose plans are not the substitute for legitimacy. Performance legitimacy of the government depends on its capacity to deliver. The government needs a clear sense of direction to attend its set goals and mobilization of agencies to achieve the target. Thus, social inclusion as a political project cannot be implemented successfully without a functional government with institutional order reducing uncertainty and seeking to achieve desired objective with democratic governance. Governance implies the pluralistic and transparent nature of government that attains consensus in policy formulation and settles problems contributing to increasing self-government capacity of the society; governance means a representative and responsive government catering to public interests, in return, deriving popular legitimacy for authority building. Social inclusion presently is taking the forms of manipulative and cooptive inclusion through nomination and patronization to buy legitimacy which endangers the process.

Poverty reduction is all encompassing strategy adopted for engagement by the government which remains an enduring goal, particularly becoming a crucial objective in post-conflict Nepal. The PRPS is currently integrated with the peace building strategies, thus, demanding appropriate response from the government through an inclusive framework. The MDGs have committed to halving poverty by 2015. The NPC 2010 report claims this is achievable. It has therefore set the goal of reducing poverty to 21 per cent within the next three years. Though political space has been broadened with assertion of rights, the inherent weakness of government remains its perceptive indifference even towards policy decisions made on social issues.

Poverty alleviation programme is noted as a success; poverty is said to have reduced from 42 per cent to 25 per cent, by 17 per cent point between 1996 and 2009. But such irrefutable data source of the government which cannot generally be contested has also implied that the reduction in poverty has deferred social equity by increasing income inequality. Economic inequalities accompanying poverty reduction complicates the priorities with changing dimension of social relationships of the people living in a community impacting on their behavioural pattern. Inequality, not poverty, is a powerful social divider; it is the marker of status difference. The ever increasing and widening inequalities, as reported by Nepal Rastra Bank Survey 2008, would definitely make Nepali society prone to more violence and disorder vindicating arguments for class struggle and forcing state to spend more on punitive system than to invest on productive system. Inequality begets status inconsistency and unequal opportunities.

Ensure Local Authority and Encourage Investment

An intrinsic unit of the government is the elected representatives at the local level who are the legitimate drivers of socio-political and economic development activities. Almost a decade after the terms of the local bodies expired, Nepal has no local government at the grassroots level since 2002. This absence has not only defeated the development aspirations of the people but also weakened the political organizations and the prospects of enhanced participation to build legitimacy through good and effective governance. Elections to local bodies should be held without delay and participation and empowerment from the grassroots level encouraged.

Actually, local bodies are the main entry points for the citizenry irrespective of their caste, creed and sex both to participate in decision making process and making access to decision makers. In the absence of the elected local government, local leaders and cadres of influential political parties are ruling the roost by forming "all party mechanism" to unauthorized use of budgets meant for development activities sanctioned by the Local Development Ministry. Their illegitimate but domineering presence with political influence and control over the legitimate authority of civil servants like the Local Development Officer (LDO) have manipulated and massively misused the state fund. Despite the yearly increase in national budget for development, fiscal indiscipline and "rampant corruption" has adversely affected development activities in the districts and villages. "Keeping this reality in view troubling the headless local bodies, major political parties [had made up their mind to] start preparation to hold local elections in November-December 2012" (Bhattarai 2011), but in vain.

Table 7.1: Local Development Budget

Fiscal Year	Amount Allocated (rounded figure)
2007/08	13.08 billion
2008/09	25.40 billion
2009/10	35.70 billion
2010/11	41. 84 billion
2011/12	(Breakdown figures) DDCs – 4 billion; Municipalities – 5 billion; 41 New Municipalities- 1 billion (proposed); VDCs – 9 billion; Self fund through internal revenue – 3 to 5 billion; Social Security Stipend expenses from VDCs/ municipalities – 9 billion.

Source: Local Development Ministry, Government of Nepal, various years.

Similarly, people's accessibility to public institutions should be made easy. The area in which poor people regardless of their caste/ethnicity/gender/geography/religion feel most excluded is access to formal justice. This goes beyond the problems of discriminatory laws or weak law enforcement to a more profound sense of lack of awareness and lack of confidence that poor people would be able to access legal redress. Politician-criminal nexus has caused police even refusing to file first information report (FIR) from the victims/families in many cases; hesitating or avoiding to arrest alleged criminals under the wanted list even after issuance of warrant and let them scot free; such practice has adversely reflected on the credibility of government. Internal accountability and responsibility should, thus, be stringently maintained. Social justice is still a major issue in Nepal's development. Inequality in accessibility to the state still remains widespread. Articulating and translating commitments for social security, social justice including social inclusion of marginalized in development process essentially require.

Service delivery is the challenge facing the nation. Water, for example, is the sustenance for livelihood about which the providers remain unaccountable. Water supply situation in Kathmandu, the Metro capital city, is fast depleting and even wells are drying up. Provision of water supply remains a development project in Nepal. Energy is another facet for domestic use as well as for powering industrial growth. Failure in meeting drinking water and electrical energy needs of the people exemplify the weak state capacity. Underutilization of available resources also reflects on the condition of institutional inefficacy of the state. And every developmental agenda, particularly the infrastructural ones, becomes the means of extraction for the ruling elites. Illicit financial transactions and monetary transfer beset the dynamics of development profiting the elites resulting into the rise in project implementation cost and delayed completion as well. Bureaucracy is co-opted and turned as pawn in the political games of political leadership. Thus transparency and accountability are the twin task that civil service mostly lacks; corruption and misuse of authority have led to high public distrust.

Reform is an imperative to make national bureaucracy alert to the need of anticipated federal administrative system with a decentralized public service commission and police service commission coordinating with the central service systems to facilitate a cooperative and consensual centre-state relation under federalism. A need of rethinking on both vertical and horizontal accountability of the public officials has occurred to bridge the persistent unequal relations between the state and society. In the absence of accountability both decentralized and federalized polity may become unrewarding to the local/ regional population.

The motive behind the targeted development programmes should also be satisfactorily communicated to the people in the community where the programme is about to be launched. The local people should be informed about the eligibility criteria for their participation to minimize the sense of resentment of the people who feel they are being excluded from development programmes largely targeted to women, Dalits and Janajatis. High caste people with livelihood problems in remote villages in the Mid-West and Far-Western Nepal and even in some Tarai districts have a perception of being discriminated against by the government. This should be resolved satisfactorily. The local bodies are appropriate means to equip people with convincing information on the type of programmes to be introduced and investment to be made in the concerned areas.

Investment in agricultural and irrigation sectors could absorb considerable level of rural and semi-urban manpower in productive activities provided energy sector could also be improved. Nepal celebrated a hundred year of hydro-power generation at Pharping, Kathmandu on 23 May 2010, yet the installed electricity capacity is a mere 620 MW and reality of supply situation is 16-18 hours of load shedding throughout the year defeating the consumers' demands and failing to sustain even the Sustainable Development Agenda of the government that was introduced in 2003. The government has decided to transform the Pharping Power Station into a museum. Ironically, it did not realize that it is celebrating the failure of nation building.

As educational certificate is correlated with poverty, so is energy with industry and business linked to employment the absence of which could lead to income poverty and lag in human development. It is pathetic, however, to record the country's ability to generate just 2 MW more electricity in the fiscal year 2010/11 in this core area of national priority. This is another example of the stark failure of service delivery by the government to meet the basic need of the people and gain performance legitimacy. Hydro-power could substantially reduce the country's dependency on imports of petroleum products that amounted to over Rs. 70 billion in 2010/11 and would certainly increase as per the need coupled with the rise in the US dollar rate. Hydro-power, if properly used, could help make national economy self-reliant. A robust infrastructure attracts investors and helps development. Alternatively, chronic power shortage has become one of the crucial reasons for 0.3 per cent growth rate of manufacturing industries since over last five years. Such a situation distracts than attracts investment.

Therefore, the need is to create environment for investment and employment opportunities in private sector through power generation. A healthy private sector is the engine of sustainable recovery from the armed conflict and enduring growth that spurs investment, creates job opportunities and mobilizes productive activities meeting local needs in various forms. Private sector generates wealth and capital becoming one of the fundamental sources of revenue to the government. The endemic energy crunch has discouraged investors baring the flow of productive cycle helping the growth of the state.

Ensure best use of Education and Health Programmes

Investment in education and health should not go waste. Manpower should be trained to better integrate with the professional needs of market places; quality improvement should be fundamentals of education and health sector (It has been observed that even school teachers in rural areas are compulsorily given physical training for their use by the Maoists in *bandha* and strikes). The use of teachers/students and their affiliation with unions aligned with various political parties and political interference should be stopped if money spent on education is expected to bear positive results; teachers and student unions are not meant for muscle flexing jobs supporting political positions. Educational environment in Nepal however is thoroughly politicized from primary to tertiary levels.

It should be recollected that citizens of Finland are opening their personal purse with losing weight to aid literacy campaigns in Nepal spending over 16 million euro; they are giving 30 euro per 1 kilo weight loss of a citizen; school children of Japan have saved their Tiffin (lunch) expenses to send donation to village school children in Nepal and South Korean students visit Nepal to whitewash school buildings. Public schools are the largest employers of educated and trained manpower. Unfortunately, politicization of teaching institutions has cost the state degenerate in capacity in discharging the duty assigned to its employees. Despite tremendous investment on education the problems related to teachers' training, their appointment along with school infrastructure to improve teaching-learning situation remain inadequate. An educated population is of critical importance to nation building as a competent workforce in administering the state by cogently facing the developmental challenges. Education for poor and vulnerable needs this sector to ensure job security of the teachers. Still there are thousands of temporary teachers waiting for their tenure. For example, delay in the appointment of the Chairperson of the Teachers' Service Commission (TSC) has blocked the promotion of 40,000 teachers many of whom will retire without being promoted due to age bar (Kantipur, 9 October 2011). The vacant posts of 23,000 teachers are yet to be filled as TSC has not advertised the seats since 1996 (Sayapatri 2011). Uncertainty of the service as well as career among the teachers has direct bearing on the quality of teaching and students' performance.

As in the case of health service (discussed below) education system has been thoroughly commercialized in Nepal resulting into the worsening of public school system as compared with the private schools and university affiliated colleges. Public schools and community schools subsidized by the government are faring badly against the private schools. Although the private schools and campuses are mostly expensive, parents are compelled to pick up the bills as they wish their children to receive proper education and perform well in the society. Though the education is a public good, the cost for a good education for the children is becoming unbearable for the households with limited resources. On the other hand, public schools and state run universities are cheap and affordable, but the quality of teaching and evaluation system is ancient in most of the cases along with the curriculum.

Thirst for a good, quality education has also become one of the reasons for the national youths for their exodus to foreign universities on self-financed studies along with the draining of multi-billion rupees expenses. Such an expenses does not involve only the cases of the rich families; it also involves the families of those people becoming more sensible to the future of their children, who manage to send their offspring for better education abroad by either mortgaging their residential home or parental property, selling land etc., or drawing education loan from the commercial banks paying high interest rate. Such practice however has created a distressing situation in the country where a large number of students are still confined to the public schooling and outmoded educational system in comparison to their fortunate brethrens with advanced foreign degrees.

The situation in the public health sector is also not different despite the tall claims of improvement in service delivery. The numbers of regional and district hospitals have increased along with health posts and health service centres.

Hospitals are built and doctors appointed. But there are hospitals without practicing doctors or medical officers appointed by the government in districts, not to talk about village health posts. But phoney doctors and fake medicine are available. Even x-ray machine remains defunct in need of repair. For example, the Health Minister Rajendra Mahato has found the service situations in the hospitals he visited on inspection tour from the oldest Bir Hospital located at the centre of state capital to a 15-bed hospital pathetic. In his own words, as the roof of a 15-bed hospital is leaking, one needs umbrella to protect the patient while undergoing treatment. "This is absurd", he says, adding "a healthy person visiting hospital will turn sick."(Kantipur, 24 September 2011). The national paradox is that the Trauma Centre adjunct to the Bir Hospital built with the Indian aid by spending billions of rupees is yet not in operation just because of some bizarre political reasons. On the other hand, the experience of a famous medical practitioner and a former Royal physician, Dr. Mrigendra Raj Pandey, is the excessive commercialization of health service, which is beyond the affordability of common citizens. Discrimination continues even in the health service. For example, if a poor woman of low caste requires maternity service, she would be treated differently by the high caste midwives implicitly expressing their caste consciousness even on the issue of health care. Societal taboos persist in human relations.

In sum, the current health situation in Nepal, as per the data obtained from the Ministry of Health and Population, is concerned is pathetic despite the claim of significant improve in health service. The medical doctor versus the population ratio is 0.04 doctors per 1,000 people; with 0.23 nurses and midwives, which is far below the World Health Organization's (WHO) stipulation of at least 2.23 professional health workers needed per 1,000 people. There are only 1,092 posts of medical doctors under the Ministry of Health for 28 million people in Nepal (Kathmandu Post, 11 December 2011; The 2011 Census data record 26.4 million people). Despite tremendous increase in budget for Health sector, the situation is obviously not that promising. Evidently, the National Health Survey conducted by the Ministry of Health recently has found that 70 per cent of children below five years of age are suffering from anaemia of which 41 per cent are chronically malnourished (Ghimire 2012). Nutrient deficiency is the primary cause of stunted growth of children in the country. In 2004, "[a]bout half of the children [were] stunted and underweight in Nepal and 47 per cent of the total under five children [were] malnourished to some degree (HMG/MOH 2004:63). However, the official data show a 6 per cent reduction of the under 5 malnourished children in the country within a period of 8 years.

The above narrative hints much is warranted on the performance side which indeed is central to the legitimacy ensuring strength and stability to the government.

Facilitate State Restructuring Process

The crux of nation building is the process of state restructuring from unitary to federal state. Planning for the future under federalism, however, remains, and the sense of the republic is still to be enthused. Ethnocracy rather than democracy has become pertinent to discourse on federalism. Identity politics is meshed with the minority rights long admonished by the centralized unitary state. However, identity has become essentialism in the course of state restructuring process in creating the federal state structure. Dissenting voices and criticism, debates and denunciations on the assertion of single identity province have continued to disturb both the state and constitution making processes. Along with uncertainty around the basic issues, weak implementation could also lead to disruption of broad human development agenda as federal units will be closer to the people and more concerned with advancing their respective social inclusion agenda.

Such a choice should be integrated with and inspired by a coherent national strategy. Interdepartmental cooperation and coordination between and among the concerned ministries at the centre and broader consultation with the similar units at the state level would be a prerequisite for developing strategies encompassing development projects. State restructuring with federalism and provincial autonomy is, however, a complex and long-term process and political transition will be enduring as well. There is no short cut to political stability. Within the complex interactive process that will be developed in the centre-state relationship power sharing and devolution should be genuinely bestowed on the local bodies to make democracy both inclusive and truly participatory. A well intentioned administrative capacity, nevertheless, is a clear reflection of ideal institution on which the permanence of governance depends.

Discouraging corruption by abolishing the culture of impunity and permitting law to take its own course is the first step towards confidence building and good governance. Thus, prevalence of rule of law is indispensible for consolidating democracy based in defence of human rights with preference for human security; any infringement on the independence of judiciary, thus, should never be tolerated. Weakening of judiciary means adding fragility to the state structure with instability unabated. Corruption is all pervasive in Nepal where the rule of law is of value to only those who cannot corrupt it. High level of corruption naturally robs the investment meant for uplifting the grievous situation of the poor and needy. Corruption therefore undercuts the political legitimacy of governments.

Nepal has thus to change primarily its corrupt and tarnished image: the country has pathetically slide down to 146 positions in 2010 from143 position in 2009 and from 121 ranking in 2008 out of 180 countries on the corruption perception index (CPI) developed by the Transparency International. Nepal has become more corrupt than before falling from 2.7 to 2.3 point in a measuring scale of 10 indicted soberly with a large and growing corruption problem in democracy, particularly, in the post-monarchical period under the Communist-led governments. The worst of which is the Baburam Bhattarai led UCPN (Maoist)-Madheshi Morcha coalition government so far. A country measuring below 3 point is considered rampantly corrupt; therefore, a rethinking on the issue is urgently required. Rebuilding lost confidence also requires winning donors' trust.

It has been reported that altogether 423 corruption cases are pending at the Supreme Court (SC) for the past four years. "Major corruption cases involving high profile political leaders should be settled through the three members Special Bench without a day's gap," says a recommendation of a report by the High Level Taskforce led by the SC Justice Prakash Wasti to the Chief Justice Khil Raj Regmi (Gautam 2011). Corruption and governance are intermeshing in a situation of political disorder. Government's inability to enforce law and order opens up multifaceted problems along with corruption making it difficult to streamline the challenges in post-conflict situation. There is however the possibility of imperiling the efforts to create a stable, well functioning state with popular legitimacy if corruption is allowed to fester without restraint.

Ensure Donors' Commitment, Cooperation and Coordination

States in post-conflict situation need foreign aid and assistance to make governance functional. Weak and fragile state that task itself for economic recovery to provide relief and meet the minimum demand of the people for their sustenance needs development assistance. State building or "building of a state" (Fukuyama 2004) implies enhancing "state capability by reinvigorating public institutions" (World Bank 1997). State building as a term has become fashionable in use by international development community describing their involvement in development activities (Zaum 2007) in the post-conflict state like Nepal. State or nation building as a term is used interchangeably despite semantically being a different process. State building as a process is inclined to establishing institutions of government whereas nation building implies addressing issues related to identity of the people rather than government.

Foreign aid without any string attached, however, is a rarity. It has been so now with the increasing international concern for state building in fragile, failing and failed states. The central objective of donors is state building with aid conditionality focused on internal governance mechanisms in building capacity of the weak and fragile states in preventing state collapse. For sustaining this need the donor community, for example, had aided the country with more than USD 900 million in 2010. On the donors' typologies of the fragile states, Nepal perhaps falls in the category of the post-conflict state in transition. The flow of financial resources in 'aid' of the post-conflict Nepal has, however, remained unaccounted for. As a recent report suggests, altogether Rs.64 billion is spent by the Government of Nepal on peace process with financial assistance from bilateral and multilateral donors along with INGOs support (Rawal 2011:32-35).

Donors' support to state restructuring process (as reflected in their investment crossing over Rs. 9 billion for constitution making) and actualizing federal system of governance, institutional building and electoral processes at the highest level are crucially felt. Institution building under federalism would be highly complex task that should be aided by donors in future on the condition of transparency and mutual accountability with the government of Nepal. Such a task ranges from managing public finance, monitoring service provisions, establishing federal civil service, raising security (police) forces independent of needless political infringement, establishing public relations and cultural centres with data bank for providing social justice to deprived communities. Information should be imparted for improving knowledge in accessing legal rights through judiciary in settling disputes mostly concerned with land rights and resources use etc.

Retrospectively, Nepal has a history of foreign aid used comprehensively by the political elites as an instrument of state building enterprise in the 1960s in particular with the expansion of administrative and military reach of the authoritarian government by King Mahendra (Mihaly 1965). Driven by elitism state building was pursued through command, control, coercion and compliance for regulating the political order. The dominant discourse of the period, as of now, was political stability and development undermining the democratic aspirations of the people. The monarchical rule drew donors' reluctant support necessitated by their Cold War bipolarity. Experience thus suggests that aid served to distort national economy, did not help reduce poverty, encouraged corruption and help consolidate the power of the few by distributing patronage. Aid money has also led Nepal to become the 6th prominent country for the export of illicit financial flow among the top 10 countries in the world. The capital flight has caused it to lose USD 9.1 billion between 1990 and 2008 (Bhattarai 2011). Aid has also allegedly aided to open Swiss Bank accounts for privileged and powerful, which is yet unaccounted for.

Besides this, allegation is ripe from different quarters on the gross misuse of funds by the donors themselves working through different NGOs to incite ethnic tensions in Nepal. International agencies are accused of privileging themselves with the support of Nepali nationals, especially opportunist academics and professionals, by paying lavishly to push their agendas at the national policymaking fronts through their consultancy services. Donors are also indicted of creating a coterie of people whose mission remains serving masters' interests irrespective of national interests. The Scandinavian governments are marked for their overindulgence in ethnic domain. The British development partner, DFID is on record to have vowed not to aid NGOs pursuing ethnic agendas anymore. And Janajati groups had retorted that they are not surviving on donors' doles.

Ironic, however, is the case as noted by the report on foreign aid prepared by the Ministry of Finance, "Development Assistance Report 2010-2011", that donors spend over one-third of the aid money as technical assistance or directly through NGOs and INGOs without any knowledge of the government. Such expenses are not incorporated in the national budget and the Red Book. In addition to this, it was also noted that if the amount of aid allocated in the budget on which government cannot maintain any control is included; the government will have no say in the expenses of nearly 46 per cent of total foreign assistance (Awasthi 2012). Continuation of this unpleasant practice has a clear lesson to the donor community or the international aid regime on their overindulgence. Their liberal streak in assisting a country with generous aid package and proliferation of agencies with bread baskets and 'brain' may not work for democracy attaining the need of the hapless people. This may be so in the course of complex transition that the state is faced with.

Presently, peace, stability and development are crucial factors leading donors to script their roles for state builders in Nepal. Notwithstanding their failing, political parties are the principle actors in the process of state building in the country. Political situation, however, is not yet assuring. The UCPN (Maoist) has yet to discard its political objective of establishing a communist regime. Their propaganda of state seizure has continued to raise the fear of a powerful sense of threat. The donors have invested fortunes in anticipation of normalizing the post-conflict situation after the elections to the CA as an epitome of democracy. Their optimism had been belied. Yet their anticipation that the drafting of the constitution by the CA perhaps will raise the final curtain for a stable political order under a federal democratic republic in Nepal had vindicated.

Federal government moreover thrives on the support of the local bodies that may also influence the pattern of centre-state relations. Centre-state relations should be clearly defined to make their functional interactions conducive. Donors should focus on local governance capacity development programmes to strengthen the participation of community. Decision making power in federal democratic state is moreover autonomous and self-rule prevails under constitutional dispensation, which also implies the rights to natural resources spread within the defined territory of the federal unit. But the question on prerogative needs to be settled as the indigenous people have claimed their privilege over the natural resources' use interpreting the rights inherent in the ILO-169. This has led to a general misunderstanding in the community comprising the settlement of multicultural people.

Arguments are building up for and against 'prior-rights' reflecting on the agenda of State Restructuring Process. If prerogative right is provided to the indigenous people, as argued, it would be reinforcing discrimination and exclusion rather than inclusion in the community concerned. There is therefore a serious need to communicate the implications of such anomalous situation clearly to avert social tensions in the future. The CA Committee on Natural Resources, Economic Rights and Revenue Distribution has sensitively indicated about the rights of the local community over the natural resources on the equity basis which is more practical and palatable. The donors should facilitate dialogue and negotiations on such issues.

Disbursement and monitoring should go hand in hand while implementing the project in cooperation and coordination of local bodies and local NGOs. It has been seriously felt that disbursement of budget according to the priority of line agencies in the centre and LDO at the district level is lopsided. Power politics has led to discriminatory practices in the districts and villages in disbursement and implementation of development projects. Aid, power and relationships are critical to understanding interactions between key characters on the stages of development, a study based on the participatory observation says. The power relationships between bilateral/multilateral donors, an international NGO, partner organizations like local NGOs, their commitments and government are crucial in determining aid effectiveness. "Far from being mechanisms for embracing the voices of the poor, they have used a form of communication that has excluded the very people whom they claim to serve" (Marsden 2006). One another study concludes that "only 25 per cent of foreign aid disbursement goes at the grassroots level, which includes large volume of technical assistance". It noted several intermediaries lie between the donors and recipients blocking the flow of resources to directly reach the needy at the grassroots level. Much of the intended aid resources either go to the expatriates in many forms or lines the pockets of corrupt politicians, bureaucrats or oligarchic establishment in the country (IIDS 2004: 89). Hence the gap.

Shift in development paradigm and policy choices has led donors to no longer recognize the state as the sole representative of the citizenry. Donors' preference to work with and through INGOs and NGOs (the so called civil society organizations) has made them partners in policymaking for development even for mega institutions like the World Bank and Asian Development Bank with large amount of funding for result oriented investment. Both bilateral and multilateral donors have become more aware and concerned with the Tarai region in the aftermath of the Madheshi movement in 2007. Some 20 donors and INGOs are involved in the Nepal Tarai region presently bypassing the government and the law of the land along with helping to raise local NGOs.

However, NGOs are no longer viewed as an alternative to dysfunctional, corrupt and unscrupulous governments; they are equally non-transparent, unaccountable and corrupt and have largely become a sink for donors' funds. NGOs are largely considered dubious functionaries in the guise of social and development workers (Dahal 1997; Malena 2000; Harsh et al. 2010). NGOs have mostly become the 'new comprador bourgeoisies' versed in trading domestic poverty for individual perks. Donors' dependence on NGOs as vehicles for selfless development should thus be cautiously treated and allocated funds accounted for. The mushrooming growth of NGOs in Nepal in itself is an interesting phenomenon under democracy.

Prior to democracy in 1990, there were just 17 NGOs functioning in Nepal the number of which reached 144 in 1991-92. Presently there are 34,000 NGOs along with 202 INGOs registered in the Social Welfare Council. Besides this, there are numerous non-registered NGOs functioning making a total of 50,000 NGOs in Nepal. Most of these NGOs are Kathmandu based and thrive on networking with concerned donor agencies working as their local agents. INGOs are mostly interested in elite capture by coopting NGOs run either by the wives or close relatives of influential bureaucrats, lawyers or powerful politicians. On the average nearly Rs.6 billion is spent by NGOs in association with the INGOs per annum, says the Social Welfare Council. In most of the cases it was found that the programmes of international agencies are not linked either with PRSP or MDGs goals and objectives; so had not helped to improve the situation of the target groups (Pokharel 2004: 7). Earlier, the World Bank has noted that donor agencies and INGOs have spent USD100 million per annum in Nepal for 'capacity building' activities, albeit with very disappointing outcomes (World Bank 2004: 35). The case of over Rs.10 billion (approx USD 150 million) expenses of donors' amount for constitution making can also be taken as futile exercises administered through various I/NGOs within the past two years.

Budgetary commitment and allocation are not enough as round about two-third of development budget is funded by donors. ODA to Nepal has amounted to USD 4,733 million between 2001 and 2010. However, aid effectiveness is noted as far below satisfactory level; the gap between aid commitment and actual realization remains wide. In 2007 less than 60 per cent of aid committed was disbursed; donors' preference prevailed; much bilateral aid was/is 'tied' to procuring donor countries' goods and services; programme based support make up 32 per cent of total ODA (NPC 2010: 162). This requires rethinking and improvement on the part of donors. The allocation of aid resources in productive and enabling sectors has decreased, in relative sense, over the period and it would be detrimental to the objective of reducing income poverty. Therefore, there is added need for resource allocation in agriculture and infrastructure sectors. Similarly, resources should be allocated to different geographical areas in a balanced manner.

Donors' support to labour intensive infrastructure building projects will provide employment opportunities to semiskilled and unskilled manpower; funding agronomy and horticulture, irrigational channels, landslide prevention, reforestation works, inter-district road building, school construction, building embankments and providing skill/vocational training would be meaningful involvement and contribution. Affirmative action should prevail in such endeavour. These are certain measures with positive impact in reducing absolute poverty. Despite poverty has been a priority concern since the introduction of the US PL480 programme and foreign aid remains one of the vital components of poverty alleviation through economic development, the presence of 62 per cent of the communist political ideologues as popular representation in the Constituent Assembly of Nepal is an irrefutable illustration of the failure of foreign aid (Mellor 1999). A need to rethinking on the aid programme therefore is inevitable within the context of state restructuring in Nepal.

Besides this, it has also been growingly felt that donors have hijacked the sovereign rights of weak and fragile states like Nepal in development practices by imposing their will and choices of INGOs and NGOs as development partners. Donors have recast their role undertaking the agenda of nation or state building by merging development and security through poverty reduction measures in rebuilding the failed state and preventing state collapse. The Millennium Development Goals (MDGs) that the United Nations sets for the year 2015 is an exemplary case of donors' intervention on the basis of which perspectives on economic development are cast under the PRSP framework. PRSP, guided by the expert advice of the IMF and the World Bank, is a precondition for every weak and conflict-torn state to become credit worthy. In the case of Nepal, it was drafted and adopted as a crucial agenda of the Tenth Five Year Plan, 2002-2007.

Weak states, particularly in the post-conflict transition, suffer from institutional and functional infirmities and instabilities. They are structurally fragile and thus insecure. Such a situation provides opportunities for donors to push their 'capacity building' agenda under the pretext of guidance to the recipient state and 'share sovereignty' (Krasner 2005:69-83). This process, however, is baptized as "partnership for empowerment" of the people, thereby the state through capacity building for governance. Donors' presence and their involvement in different development works have legitimized the political process in Nepal. Although an inclusive constitutional order is yet to emerge, negotiation towards this end is moving steadily despite frustrating interludes.

Similarly, aid effectiveness is under scrutiny. The donors should, however, push for more responsive and accountable polity in which political parties genuinely become representative of popular choice and demand. State-society relationship naturally thrives on the wellbeing of the citizenry who make their representation through the electoral process. All these involve donors' interests for peace, development and stability. For a state like Nepal being swamped by the donors' financial and technical support the only way out is to rope in their unwavering commitment and draw their cooperation for coordinating efforts for development in social, political and economic spheres following the donors' preference. It does not help to be pretentious. Despite the looming question being can Nepal survive without aid, the nation is also confronted with more crucial and pertinent question: Does aid work in poverty alleviation? Both the donors and recipient are answerable. The dilemma however is that the imperative of foreign aid and assistance has also drawn critical assessments on their proper use (e.g. Bhattachan 1997; Panday 1999).

Instances of donors' dissatisfaction with the process of development works in Nepal are many. Some cases in point reproduced here are evidence based on policymaking. Some stalled development activities like the Melamchi Water Supply project had led Nepal's prominent donors to directly express their dissatisfaction. For example, the then Japanese Ambassador to Nepal, Tomohiko Yanasa, was of the view that Japanese cooperation is aimed at expanding the pace of development making Nepal self-reliant. Now Japan has made 10 percent cut in its international development cooperation. For Nepal, the cut may be bigger if problems such as poor management and inadequate budget allocations persist. He also noted that the frequent changes of government and high-level officials are additional problems in implementing development projects properly (Gorkhapatra, 16 May 1998). On 15 May 1998 the then UNDP Representative, Ms. Carroll Long had also handed over a memorandum to Prime Minister Girija P. Koirala in person on behalf of several donor agencies involved in Nepal pointing out about the economic misfortune facing Nepal.

Likewise, the Asian Development Bank (ADB) Director of Programme (where as everybody knows that Japan has more than 50 percent of shares) Greet Van Der Linden had reiterated that Nepal will have to increase its efficiency in the utilization of loans if it is to maintain a constant level of future assistance.... ADB would accord priority to countries, which can use funds most effectively, and with the highest development impact. A total of 24 development projects were underway in Nepal with ADB loans assistance totaling 822 million dollars. Only 30 percent of such projects are implemented on time.... "(Rising Nepal, 24 July 1998). This was followed by the criticism laid by the British Overseas Development Minister of State, Clare Short, who bluntly asserted that corruption and incompetence had adversely affected the progress of the last Eight Five Years Plan (Kathmandu Post, 18 November 1998).

This, however, is only one side of the story of the donor-donee relations. In the 1990s, the Nepali people had become increasingly aware of the donors' manipulation and exploitation of the aid money through imposing severe conditionality on the recipient country like Nepal. A fresh example relates to the Melamchi Water Supply Project for the Kathmandu Valley, which is now delayed further by a year leading to the increase in the total project cost by US $ 96 million. The ADB, as the main investor on the project, has been appointing several consultants for designing and completing the project one of whom was paid a salary of US $ 27,000 per months for 18 months and another one was paid US $ 22,000 per month to run a project in a country where the per capita income of the people then was around USD 200 (Sharma 2000). The delay in tunneling of the project has lead to controversy and the withdrawal of the Chinese construction company from the project recently. Discrepancy in project handling and terms of contract had contributed to raising project cost than helping project completion. Therefore, Melamchi Water Supply Project is yet a mirage for the people of Kathmandu Valley in 2012.

Ensure Gender and Sustainable Development

It is usually argued that women who benefit from affirmative action are already elites who need no 'assistance'. This is reflected in the 32 per cent representation of high caste women as against 2 Dalit women in the CA and some 70 per cent women belonging to the high caste in civil service, though mostly in the non-Gazetted positions. Such a pattern of high caste women's representation can also be discerned in numerous user groups in the rural areas (one estimate suggests there are 400,000 user groups in Nepal), which is fundamentally an elite capture of resources and use. Hardly are there any Dalits represented in the decision making position; if any, they are symbolic and showcasing of social inclusion. The representative case to this is the *Dalit Sewa Sangha* (Dalit Service Organization)an NGO in Surkhet district in which 8 male and 6 female Dalits were employed to work under three male employees from the high caste group (Kumar 2009: 199).

Gender imbalance is the common indicator of discrimination both in discourse and practice. But the concern is continued discrimination amongst the women of different social groups themselves; high and low caste; urban and rural; educated and uneducated as well as high circle ladies and village girls. The demand for proportional representation and participation of women from marginalized and excluded groups in accordance with Article 21 of the Interim Constitution is therefore getting strong. Gender politics is commonly thought as a campaign for emancipation of oppressed groups as sustained by the UN Security Council Resolution 1325 adopted in the year 2000. Gender equality is a need of a peaceful society. In a country like Nepal where Census 2011 data present female outnumbering the male population by 1.5 per cent (CBS 2012), continued discrimination against women is no longer possible if development is to achieve in essence with their participation.

There is also a need of drastic change in policy thrust and pattern of government spending so far the regions like Karnali Zone are concerned. Governments in Nepal have been sustaining survival of the people living in five hazardous districts of Karnali Zone since over last 50 years by airlifting food along with 'food for work' programme with multibillion rupees expenses exclusive of the donor funded World Food Programme failing to make them self-reliant but further dependent on aid and food supplies. Government regularly spends, at least, Rs. 400 to Rs. 500 million for airlifting food supplies per annum exclusive of the expenses of the World Food Programme. In the fiscal year 2009/10 over Rs. 350 million for food transportation was disbursed. The Food Corporation had demanded Rs. 880 million for transporting food as the government had spent nearly Rs. 620 million for the purpose in the FY 2008/09 (Nagarik, 14 April 2010). Karnali Zone draws the government's unflinching commitment for its development every year in its fiscal budget statement. But it is still remote and inaccessible by road despite construction of the highly accident prone 232 km Surkhet-Karnali Highway was started long back. However, the road has become a north-south link both for commuters and supplies.

So where has the planning gone? And, what has the money spent on food aid done? Has expense on food aid supplies made the people's plight palatable and reduced hunger? Dirt-poor poverty correlates with Karnali Zone. Thus the result: all these exercises have led to further food crisis, deepened dependency with evident failure of government policy. This cycle of unproductive aid, unsustainable investment and dependency should be changed by changing the habits of the people and even generously relocating people from sparsely populated areas to relatively accessible places to ease their livelihood problems. Though relocating of population now would not be feasible in view of the shaping up of federal structure in the state restructuring process, it is observed that such relocating strategy has also not worked in the past when people from Humla and Jumla districts were rehabilitated in Chishapani of Bardia district.[2]

Recently, a Government Committee formed to study the problems facing the Karnali Zone has proposed to (i) end the investment on food transportation within five years by changing the food habits of the region making them self-reliant on the local products; (ii) invest on integrating all the five districts by improving the road networks to ease the movement of people and goods and services; and (iii) plan to provide an integrated package for improving the productive situation of paddy crop in Sinja valley of the Jumla district inclusive of irrigation and other necessary facilities and commercialize the agricultural product (reported in Nagarik, 14 April 2010). In addition to this, the "One family, one employment" programme launched since the fiscal year 2006/07 has anticipated making life sustainable to the people in the Karnali Zone (MoF 2010b: 235).

Karnali Zone, where every kind of social anomaly persists, has long been portrayed as a case of denial by the state. With the presence of I/NGOs it is no longer so. Hundreds of I/NGOs are involved in various development projects in all the five districts with multimillion rupees worth aid packages. Karnali Zone thus is no longer neglected. Nor is it remote from the gaze of governmental and nongovernmental development practitioners. For example, the total government budget in the Kalikot district is Rs.1.51 billion. Some 19 INGOs and 355 registered NGOs spend around Rs.560.187 million, which is 36 per cent of the total. If the annual budget in the district is distributed proportionately to all the 22,927 households, each household will receive around Rs. 66,000. In Jumla, there are 200 registered NGOs. Their annual budget is over Rs.350 million. In Humla, some 21 INGOs and 140 NGOs contribute about 14 per cent of the total budget of Rs. 1.69 billion in development works amounting to Rs. 178.485 million. Similarly, in Mugu district the NGO activities in development works have provided employment, thereby discouraging people to migrate to India for labour works. NGOs spend around Rs.190 million per annum in Mugu. In Dolpa, some 97 registered NGOs spend Rs.500 million per annum as it is the largest district in the biggest zone of the country. Despite massive investments as such by the nontransparent I/NGOs on development works, the result, however, is like the adage "pouring of water on the sand" (Pandey et al. 2011). The beneficiaries are not the local people but the missionaries of development.

Given the pathetic situation in the Karnali Zone, government has undertaken a 100-day employment programme for the people living in the five districts since the fiscal year 2006/07. Beginning with 22-days employment at first, the programme slides down to 18 days, 14 days and 11 days work in the fiscal year 2011/12. Allocation for the programme was Rs. 240 million in 2010/11 and Rs. 250 million in 2011/12. Of the 77,000 households in five districts 71,000 households are unemployed (Bista 2011). The social security net requires expansion even to meet government target of 100-days employment. Otherwise such flimsy programme would create annoyance rather than assimilation of the people in the national mainstream.

The NPC's Three-Year Plan should be concerned with the measures to design and implement poverty reduction and development policy initiatives with substantial inputs from village/district level. The plan should reflect the voices of the poor and needy and identify with their acute needs like land reform, irrigation, livelihood opportunities, connectivity, etc. Land is tied to livelihood security for a majority of Nepalis, and Dalits in particular are landless. This may need assistance for capacity building for local government human resources coordinated by the line agency at the centre with donors' fund. In the districts and villages, the efforts of the government, donors and local NGOs need to be better coordinated to implement programmes tailored to the specific situation at the location.

Nepal is indeed a showcase of bilateral and multilateral donors contributing to secure development. Donors should help the government to ensure collect appropriate disaggregated data on gender, caste, ethnicity, religion and region by Poverty Monitoring and Analysis System to be abreast with the accurate records of efforts on social inclusion and service delivery systems. Inclusive access to services like education for excluded children and support through the sector-wise approaches (SWAp) to gender sensitive issues should be made to facilitate inclusion in remote districts. A serious review of the specific situation in all the 75 districts should be initiated and information collected before prioritizing project investment with local specificity and people in mind. Such recommendation also features in Collier's prescription, "policies for rural development must be adapted to local circumstances and so require a much larger investment in local knowledge" perhaps to overcome external constraints. Discussing how to make development possible by a landlocked country like Nepal, Collier has advised that the country should try to be 'as attractive as possible to donors' (2007: 62).

Ensure Public Security

Provision for public security is the first among equally important services in a fragile situation for establishing a relatively safe and secure environment. Well-meaning security plan has remained defunct due basically to the needless political interferences.

Political preferences indeed have led to breakdown in crime control measures encouraging impunity with repercussion on public trust of police as the law enforcing agency. People have very low opinion on government's ability to maintain law and order. Despite police are the first choice to report on any crime, one public opinion survey has noted police are either not "very reliable or not at all reliable in bringing criminals to justice" (IDA 2010: 12-13, 37). Police temperament and attitude towards general public are also not that sanguine. They are power-addict and subservient to their political masters. They treat poor and people without political contacts very unfairly (IDA 2010: 49). Encounter with the police, particularly in the rural areas, is unpleasant for many poor people. Their presence in most cases has been found insensitive to preservation of social justice. It reveals two crucial deficiencies from which the government is suffering. First, the Nepali state lapses in security assurance to the people in exchange for which it buys their loyalty. Second, security is unevenly distributed between rich and poor people as discrimination remains on accessibility to power and justice based on social class, gender and minority. Groups without having access to or protection of Nepal Police are impoverished people (88.7%), women (52.6%), Dalits (34.0%), Disables (16.6%) and LGBT (12.4%), a study suggests (USIP 2011:45).

Police reform has been one of the crucial agendas of state building under the adage of 'capacity building' in which donors' involvement ranges from training of police officials at home and abroad to the protection of human rights. The experience of the Maoist insurgency throughout the decade between 1996 and 2006 sadly did not help police as an institution in Nepal to assert its independence from excessive political interference inculcating the view that a strong and impartial police is an imperative for maintaining internal security. Police forces in Nepal, however, are easily amenable to political use and are motivated to work for meeting the political ends of their master, i.e., the Home Minister or the ruling political party. Political loyalty is a precondition for a police official to rise to the higher or highest rank that was evident by the transfer/sacking of the NC-friendly IGP and appointment of the CPN (UML)-friendly one as replacement and vice versa. The Intelligence Department is almost always filled with the police and the favourites of the Home Minister drawn from the party workers and mostly from related constituency. It has been observed that until and unless criminalization of police with excessive political interference is resisted with "ethical stand" by police officers, nothing will substantially change as "political parties [are] seen second only to criminals in bearing responsibilities for other illegal activities..." (USIP 2011: 7-8).

Daylight killings of business persons and leaders of civil society in busy thoroughfare of Kathmandu have become a common feature; gunshots within the premise of the visiting room of a heavily guarded prison in the national capital become possible due to negligence and lethargy; even deadly attack against a CPN (UML) leader hours after being appointed as a cabinet minister are all causes for consternation. Businesspersons are afraid of kidnapping, huge ransom, extortion and killings under political protection (Chaudhary 2009). The daylight killing of Feisal Ahmad, the General-Secretary of the Islamic Federation on 26 September 2011 at Central Kathmandu has been admitted as the serious security lapse by the Council of Ministers with decision to strengthen the security system. This has been the case even when the TV tycoon Jamim Shah was killed under the glaring sun at Lazimpat, another busy thoroughfare of Kathmandu Central the previous year. The police, as always, refrain from all the responsibility to book the criminals with their statement that the murders are the international assassins who might already have crossed the national border. Prime Minister Baburam Bhattarai also hinted at sharing this view to the BBC Nepali Service broadcaster, but did not say who the culprits are. He has also expressed the "government's inability to arrest the murders because of the pressure from abroad" to the members of the Muslim community who met the prime minister demanding justice. Presumptuous statements are made for the denial of responsibility of a sovereign executive. The slaying of the Supreme Court Justice Rana Bahadur Bam, while on the way to office on 31 May 2012 is another proof of the glaring evidence of the moribund public security situation in the national capital. The assassins escaped with ease; yet without a trace.

These incidents are some of the conspicuous examples of the policing gap. The emasculation of 62,000-strong police institution that has expanded from 32,000 prior to 1990 along with the Intelligence Service is woeful for public security. The Police claim the assassins are all contract killers sent to complete mission in Nepal from India. They are thus helpless. And, the nature of the crime committed in Kathmandu and elsewhere in Nepal is homicide and the choice of victims is Nepali Muslims, except Justice Bam. But never had the Nepal police alert the Interpol about the crime committed in Nepal. Contrarily, the incumbent Home Minister Bijay Kumar Ghachhedar thinks that the policing gap is also caused by the small size of police force and, therefore, claims for the need of the recruitment of 42,000 more police personnel in Nepal. He has proposed for the allocation of Rs. 22 billion to strengthening the internal security through "Grihaprashashan Sudhridhikaran Yojana" at a press briefing on 5 January 2012. Such measures were also taken previously to meet challenges arising out of the criminal activities in the Tarai. Hence the government of every dispensation feels that the way out of the security lapses is to increase the coercive power of the state; a mediaeval and bogus thinking on crime control. However, security provision is not making people feel more secure.

Political parties have their own militant groups that create havoc in the society; some like the youth organization of the CPN (UML) have directly challenged the authority over the case of severely beating a journalist for reporting against the murderous assault of their associates at a court hearing in Biratnagar. Others, like the Tarun Dal of the Nepali Congress Party are in killing spree under the slightest pretext of differences with other party stalwarts, like in Chitwan district. The more fearful Youth Communist League (YCL) of the UCPN (Maoist) are maintaining low profile although they have not refrained from their extortion activities. The YCL, which is drawn from the ablebodied Maoist guerrillas, constitute as a shield to the Maoist leadership in public. Although point 3 of the 6 point agenda agreed by the High-Level Political Committee has decided to disband the YCL, the UCPN (Maoist) has raised a Special Task Force and trained them to remain in high alert round the clock (Annapurna Post, 15 April 2010b; Khadka 2010).

These paramilitary forces are, indeed, challenging the civilian order. The absence of the legal order has encouraged such groups to abuse state power under the protection of the ruling or influential political parties. Factionalism within the political party is so strong that the then prime minister of the CPN (UML) Jhala Nath Khanal was overruled by the defiance of the leader of the Youth Force he himself had established as the Chairman of the party in the case of the beating of the journalist. In addition to this, political parties are safeguarding all the known gangsters with their affiliation to the party organizations in return for servicing personal or party funding and electoral politics (Himal Khabarpatrika, 1-17 August 2011: 30-37).

Reforming Security Sector

Security sector remains one of the crucial areas requiring institutional change according priority to internal peace and for the defence of the federal democratic state. It is an important part of the peace process and essential in the post-conflict situation. Security sector reform (SSR), although encompasses several agencies of the government like police and paramilitary forces, intelligence and penal systems, is specific with the armed institution like the military. Army is the most sensitive security sector that has long been viewed as a coercive force monopolized by the government for defending the state, waging war and maintaining peace with integrity. Restructuring the national armed forces along with the integration of the Maoist guerrillas into the military institution is long overdue despite its stipulation in the Comprehensive Peace Agreement for 'democratization' of the armed forces (Article 4.7). Article 144 (4 and 4A) of the Interim Constitution of Nepal 2063 (2007) has further detailed on the inclusive measures to be taken for democratization, a report on which was submitted to the prime minister by the Committee formed under the convenorship of Defence Minister in July 2010 (MoD 2010). Political consensus on this report and on its implementation is yet to be reached. Reform in the security sector is felt necessary both from the military and political dispensation for congeniality in civil-military relations under democracy.

The controversy over the process of integration of the Maoist guerrillas along with the formation of the Directorate General, the rank of the armed personnel heading the Directorate and the rank and file of the Maoist guerrillas opting for integration has persisted. Nearly 1,400 guerrillas selected for integration in the army are still undecided to join the military service on account of uncertainty of allocation of ranks to them. Similarly, the recruitment of the 10,000 Madheshi citizens in the national army as a commitment of the government for making the army inclusive has become a bone of contention in the process of democratizing the armed forces. Along with this a host of problems facing the armed forces in Nepal for making it a truly professional institution are yet to be addressed (Kumar 2010: 111-64). Inclusive and impartial recruitment is the thrust for democratization of the armed forces with stringent pursuit for maintaining civilian supremacy through objective practice of civil-military relations.

Modernizing the military along the vision proposed by the Army Headquarters to the Defence Ministry in its 10-year plan could begin with formal Defence Review and publication of White Paper by correspondingly formulating the national security policy. This requires activating the National Security

Council Secretariat to conceive and concretize a broad based national security policy against the appreciation of both possible and plausible threats. Though the National Security Council (NSC) is constitutionally endowed with providing an advisory role to the government on the mobilization and use of the armed forces by anticipating challenges to national security, it remains duplicitous in decision making structure, therefore, neglected. Its institutional presence remains cosmetic failing to make any impression behind the objectives of its formation. Even its advice solicited by the government was not honoured, for example, in the case of the establishment of 24 District Soldiers Board by India in Nepal during the period of Interim Government led by the Nepali Congress President Girija P. Koirala as the prime minister.

Deliberations on security are prone to relate to external threats that have historically dominated policymaking on defence. Despite the threat perception is presumably built on challenges coming from the south that is India, it is the closest neighbour with whom Nepal interacts pervasively and maintains unparallel military-to-military relations depicted as "brother armies". The COAS of both the countries are the honorary Generals of each other's armed forces. War between the two is unimaginable. National security based on the defence of the realm, therefore, is not the envisionable external threats. In the case of Nepal, the threats are internal, not external. National security sensitivities of the country can be tampered with societal challenges and breakdown in social cohesion. Countering the violent internal disturbances would perhaps make the armed reprisal of the military obvious. But threat to security is elusive not only as a concept but also as a fact when civil war occurs. The Maoist insurgency and counterinsurgency has proven it to be true even when the governments of the period tried to buy security through military build up. Heavily armed military is not a panacea to societal conflicts. It only reflects the government's menacing posture. This may become counterproductive in a country where the livelihood problem of the people is pernicious. In the event of any decision making on the SSR, it is advisable that policymakers should consider this grievous national reality. Guns do not confer security; guns can rather contribute to insecurity.

The erstwhile Royal Nepal Army that was one half of the size of its present force structure of nearly 95,000, when the Maoist insurgents engaged the army for the first time with brutish force in 2001, has continued its plan to expand, not shrink as the peace time demands. The government is required to maintain the military structure with additional force, first, not to alienate the military and risk retribution; second, fearing the country relapsing again into internal conflict and violence; and, third, as a symbol of statehood. There is no peace dividend.

On the other hand, despite the number of the Armed Police Force is being doubled since the day of its formation in 2001, its role in the ambiance of security has not been determined yet. Besides the occasional display of the riot police function, guarding the border checkpoints and border custom offices, its performances remain indistinct from the Nepal Police. But its demand for more sophisticated weapons and better facilities has made its existence a burden than an asset to the government with an undefined role. The APF is also under the Ministry of Home Affairs and headed by the Inspector General. Stipulated to function as (a) to control an armed struggle occurring or likely to occur in any part of Nepal; (b) to control armed rebellion or separatist activities occurring or likely to occur in any part of Nepal; and (c) to control terrorist activities occurring or likely to occur in any part of Nepal, the APF had experienced counterterrorism operation under the command of the then Royal Nepal Army during the Maoist insurgency. The 33,500-strong APF is organized into five combat brigades, one in each development region and headquartered at Halchowk, Swoyambhu in Kathmandu. Their role and responsibility require to be clarified for their meaningful use in the context of a restructured federal state.

The open border with India which was left unguarded till recently has been transformed suitably for transnational criminal activities with mounting security challenges to either country. Border security curbing the criminal as well as terrorist activities has sensitized the 1,747 kilometer long Nepal-India border symbolizing their unique relations unfortunately turning it into a headache to the policymakers in both countries. Increasing deployment of security forces in checkpoints in either side of the porous border has been thought of no help despite the APF in Nepali side is working stringently to discourage illegal activities. The SSB (Sima Surachya Bal) on the Indian side has been deployed densely since 1999 to rigorously control undesirable movements across the border. The problem however is that transnational criminal activity commences more often with the connivance of the security authorities and the nexus they form with the local crime syndicates. The challenges facing Nepal from criminal activities are also burgeoning from its northern border with Tibet in China. Smuggling of contraband goods are a major challenge that should be curbed to prevent the country falling into a disastrous consequences in the future.

Notably, police service is actually in humiliating situation in Nepal. Most of the former IGPs are serving jail terms on corruption charges. The incumbent IGP Kuber Singh Rana is accused of enforced disappearances and extrajudicial killings of five youths in Dhanusha district in October 2003. Police-criminal nexus is proven in various cases. This is freshly evident by the case of SSP Ravi Raj Shrestha's involvement in the foreign currency smuggling racket at the Tribhuvan International Airport on 7 October 2012. Police thus have a tinted image. As well the police have utterly failed to book the culprits in heinous cases of murder and assassinations. Excessive politicization has virtually paralyzed the institution of police force as a law enforcing agency and public-friendly organization.

The demand and recommendation for establishing the Police Service Commission has tarried too long. As in other institutions police service also has a price tag both in recruitment, transfer to lucrative stations and promotional processes. This has compromised their credibility and destroyed the public trust. The agency thus has lost its sway in governance for public security. This is not because of the inadequacy or incompetency or understrength of the police personnel as the reason that the Home Minister thinks proposing more recruitment. But such a proposition would merely be crowding the police structure in the absence of proper training and incentives, useable equipment and logistic support, and family welfare of the serving, retiring and deceased personnel. Effective policing requires staunch government support which unfortunately is lacking. It would thus be immature to think of a police force in Nepal that could function independently. Criminalization of politics and politicization of crime has rendered police service out of the law and order contingency despite being the law enforcing agency.

The open question therefore is that how would the Nepal Police institution function under the federal structure of the republican state? Is there any sense imparted by the police on their trustworthiness? Under federalism the function of the policing would be divided into central and state services with their respective loyalties. The state police organization will have its own jurisdiction within the state in support of the provincial government for maintaining public order. However, as the states function under the federal directives, the police will have to comply with the constitutional stipulations in the service of preserving internal security.

On the other hand, the National Intelligence Department has largely been converted into the recruitment ground for the cadres of the ruling party or specifically the Home Minister, the most powerful person primarily responsible for internal security of the state endowed with the control of civil as well as security administrations. Unfortunately, this system has paralyzed the intelligence service in the state losing its relevance in making any substantial inputs of information for national security decision making. The serious loss of credibility of the security agencies is not making people comfortable with the new security provisions.

Ensure Rule of Law

Democracy thrives only in the case of the rule of law and governance practice coheres. Law, in reality, is the lifeblood of democratic polity. Politics, in other words, is a practice of legal order in the absence of which state becomes criminalized with corruption and condemnation of law. Abuse of state power either by elected or non-elected authority destroys public confidence leading ultimately to anarchy undermining the three core functional values of the state – security, welfare and representation in essence. Rule of law therefore is the key to political stability and state building. The true test of democratic credentials is an independent judiciary. This is not the ideals of the Maoists' game plan. They are not comfortable with the judiciary functioning under the rubric of the separation of power. They prefer a judiciary kowtowing to their party's diktat. The assertion of independence by the judiciary, however, has continued to make the Maoists irksome.

Patronage and impunity that the political leadership ensures have crucified the capacity of judiciary and penal system. Criminals with homicide record and even implicated by the apex court are elected to the CA, appointed with ministerial portfolios, protected by the political parties and left scot free to public discontent. Although the donor community has been simultaneously involved in the task of building justice and law-enforcement systems with basic training for improving intelligence system and human rights situation in the country along with development works, bad governance has, however, created unbridgeable gaps in regulating the law of the land. Despite the implementation of the *Five-Year Strategic Plan* for the Nepali judiciary the weak judicial process and limited access to legal counsel and legal aid along with the government's reluctance to work in conjunction to the law of the land, including enforcing the Supreme Court decisions continue to weaken the justice system. As a matter of fact, the rights based approach remains desirable to furnish justice as vulnerable section of society and victims of crime have continued to suffer from injustice. Decay in the criminal justice system has weakened the police morale.

Dispute resolution remains highly desirable through capacity building by establishing basic courts and tribunal systems considering indigenous culture, customary law and legal traditions. But these features should not impinge on the modern legal tradition, meaning equality before the law. Improving internal security system requires impartiality on the part of qualified judges and advocates institutionalizing a fair penal system with competent police force.

Though the post-conflict challenges are many including the successful conclusion of the peace process and drafting of a constitution for the republic based on federal structure for power sharing making the state inclusive, the immediate priority however is the credibility of the political leadership by accelerating the process of economic development and poverty reduction, if Nepal has to stabilize the political system by peacefully effect the change. To make the change credible in the process of state building the government must monopolize the coercive function and the means of violence. This requires an end to "two armies, one state" situation to avoid the potentiality of violent eruption of social conflict. The threat therefore is inherent.

The challenge facing Nepal is central to legitimacy of authority in the absence of its willingness to ensure public security and ability to mobilize and redistribute resources and services. Insecurity and poverty create social inequality and instability breeding violence. The story behind state building has been violence unending and the "key to violence and instability... has to be found in ongoing dynamics of 'ethnic conflict', 'economic volatility' and 'empires in decline' (Ferguson 2006). Phenomena like these have created both 'state in crisis' and 'development in crisis' situations connected integrally spreading insecurity pervasively with deepening poverty, economic vulnerability and unabated violence. A rethinking is needed in managing both 'state in crisis' and 'development in crisis' for endurance of national polity.

One meaningful measure to ensure the rule of law is to return the looted property to its rightful owners. Articles 5.2.8 and 5.2.9 of the Comprehensive Peace Agreement concluded between the Government of Nepal and the Communist Party of Nepal (Maoist) on 21 November 2006 clearly state,

> Both sides express their commitment to allow the persons displaced due to the armed conflict to return back voluntarily to their respective ancestral or previous places of residence without any political prejudice, to reconstruct the infrastructure destroyed as a result of the conflict and to rehabilitate and socialize the displaced persons with due respect.... Both sides express their commitment to not to discriminate against and give any kind of pressure on other members of the family by the reason of associating a member of the family with one or the other side (CPA 2006).

Article 19 of the Interim Constitution of Nepal 2007 thus has endorsed the 'right to property' as undeniable citizens' right. This has been the context within which the people forcibly displaced and dislocated in the course of the Maoist "people's war" by the insurgents and the militants are claiming their rights to return to their domiciles and restoration of their properties looted by the Maoists. The return of the property has become one of the crucial issues in contentions between the Maoists and other major political parties. This has also become an example of struggle for ensuring the rule of law in the country flaunted as a norm by the strong party. Although nobody (even the Peace and Reconstruction Ministry of the Government of Nepal) is sure till date about the actual figure of displaced and dislocated people in Nepal as a consequence of the violent conflict, these people are actually the community of survivors most of whom were extremely vulnerable and had lived in trauma. They deserve an honourable treatment by the state; their human rights restored; their loss compensated and rehabilitated satisfactorily.

The principle of governance under the new political dispensation should at least be based on the rule of law to gain public support and endorsement. The political system requires being sensitive to longstanding issues involving caste-based and gender-based discrimination, 'witch-hunting' and violence, for progressive social change. The crucial dimension of the rule of law is accountability in relations to public security, access to justice by the poor and vulnerable and respect for human rights. Institutional reforms requiring policing, criminal justice and penal system should be addressed with urgency with the law enforcing agencies allowed to function without political interferences.

Broadening Participation and Giving People a Voice

Central to the democratic policymaking should be the voices of the poor and needs of the marginalized groups. Accessibility of the common people to the corridors of power has been as low as it was the case before. Under the democratic dispensation, party politics required political affiliation of the people for mending the bureaucratic maze and get their personal or collective works done, even getting employment or transfer to the plump positions and placement to a beneficial station. The political parties in government have been found least bothered about public criticism while protecting and promoting their interests undermining rules and regulations even to the extent of causing damage to national interests. This situation persists in the absence of transparency and accountability and the flow of appropriate information to the public or at the local level to generate inquisitiveness of the people on public policymaking process.

The situation in Nepal for public participation and filtering the voices of the people is further complicated and compromised by the absence of the local elected bodies since a decade after the term of the local government expired in 2002. Thus when participation of the people at the grassroots level is denied the efforts towards community development for the actual benefits of potential users at the local level, the ownership of such efforts and their sustainability become questionable and in some cases disappear with the money invested based on top-down approach policy projects. Nepal, at present, is a burning case of denial of democracy and development. Elections to local bodies have not been held over the last 15 years. Hence access of the people to the government at the grassroots level is denied. Their local needs are not responded despite the furnishing of the local development budget annually. Evidently, the Auditor General's Office has found excessive financial indiscipline in the Local Development Ministry's bureaucracy and rampant financial anarchy at the political level leading to insolvency of the arrears (Gyawali 2012).

The National Development Council used to hold cosmetic meetings for priority setting through the select participation of the people from different walk of life even during the Panchayat System. Such conclaves usually turn into jamboree. Priorities become politicized to promote partisan interests of the Royal regime and prospective resource mobilization never seriously undertaken. Such a tendency is reflected presently in the exploitation of hydropower potentialities, agricultural expansion, use of raw labour forces through training and infrastructure building with an eye on planned development of tourism and internal trade.

With every change of government under the leadership of a particular political party, the head of the National Planning Commission also changes leading to change in the policy priority and thrust. This makes the national policy to wear political hat further complicating development programmes as per the demands of the needy people. Nepal has long practiced a unique system of elite circulation in every conceivable agencies of the government related to public welfare. But the Nepali syndrome produces disillusioned, frustrated, poor and unemployed people with corrupt, greedy and criminal political and power elites as a consequence.

Need of Democratic Consolidation

Last, but not the least, is the context of democratic consolidation with upholding the legitimacy of the political system governed by the democratic norms and values. The task of democratic consolidation, though difficult to ensue, should begin with political will and determination of the national leadership at the earnest during the transitional period. Transition should be understood as a crucial interlude from the past to the future for which the political leadership should sensitively use the present towards attaining stability and order by promoting the rule of law. Transition is actually a most sensitive and challenging period of political management of state ordering process. Changing the course of instability to stability is the crucial context that confronts the efficacy of political leadership.

It should be recognized that democracy is not a top-down process. The need of the local bodies is a necessity for the consolidation of democracy. Local bodies are the entry-point both for popular participation and democratic representation. Absence of local bodies erodes the legitimacy and effectiveness of democratic practices as witnessed in the case of Nepal since 2002. The implication of this has thoroughly been negative in the political process. Gradual withdrawal of the people from the political space has weakened the thrust for democratization providing the opportunity hoarders the chances to profit from the democratic inertia. The local bodies are the grassroots organizational units of democratic institutions in which citizens play crucial role through organized political parties. These grassroots organizations are privileged with the exercise of political rights of the citizenry. These rights are the basis for the exercise of freedom and choice.

As democracy is fundamentally redistributive, its consolidation requires the grassroots institutions. Disenfranchising people for long would be antagonizing the citizenry and oscillating the political process between nondemocratic and democratic conundrum. Elections to local bodies therefore should not be delayed. Democracy cannot be sustained in the absence of local government. The testimony to this is obviously provided by the present political process that tends to undermine democratic practices. Though putting political opposition at bay is the norm of the government, the measure requires to be democratic not dictatorial. A relapse to violence needs to be avoided cautiously if political parties functioning in the country are serious for institutionalizing democracy.

Notes

1. Social capital is defined in terms of relationships that are based, in structures of voluntary association, norms of reciprocity and cooperation (Brown and Ashman 1996: 1470; Shucksmith 2000: 3-5).

2. Kailash N. Pyakuryal in his written 'comment' on the study report.

VIII
Points to Ponder

Political instability is at the heart of the problem. Transition has further prolonged the instability. This needs to be reversed and stability attend. Unless political parties achieve this primary goal for governing the state the proponents of good governance would always face stiff challenges in managing the political process amid democratic competition. It has been observed that political parties have yet to transcend the social segments. Despite the need to create all-inclusive national identity with all-party consensus they have only nibbled with the idea but making no firm commitment on it. The monopolistic urge, in other words, the traits of authoritarianism, has continued as a model of governance, whether monarchy or republic. During monarchy or ranarchy[1] power elites made great fortunes while the rest were excluded. The historical past has reminded us about the "Thatched Huts and Stucco Palaces."[2] Land as property was allocated to the courtier, the politically powerful persons, and military personnel as *Birta* as well as *Jagir* to buy loyalty.

The republican elites, as the bosses of political parties, have also concentrated power and wealth in the clique closer to themselves enduring corruption with their commitment to social change abandoned. Patrimonialism is entrenched that has contaminated every aspect of policymaking in the government by sharing the spoils of Jana Andolan-II. Political parties are functioning as the racketeers/gangsters profiting from the national woe by severely affecting the governing process. Groupism has influenced factionalism and breakdown of the political parties. As a result, party politics has become more fragmented from within and discredited from without.

The distrust among the political parties has widened further, particularly, after the abrupt dismissal of the CA by the prime minister. Controversies ensued over the formation of a national consensus government to hold elections announced first for 22 November 2012; failing which, rescheduled tentatively for June 2013. But elections remain only a proposition. Consensus has yet to arrive to conduct elections. Likewise, any fundamental shift towards federalism has become just an aspiration as democracy itself is bogged-down with ideological mist. Agreement on federal structure is crucial to the development of a functional polity in the future departing from the excessively centralized unitary state. Ethnic discourse has sensitized the political process leading to national predicament by problematizing the state restructuring agenda. Federalization of state structure thus has become intractable with the consequent dispute over single identity or multiple identity federal units. There is also no consensus on the organizing ideology of the state. Divergence in values and attitudes has led to institutional drift. Promised reforms stay undelivered. The imperative of policymaking on national future thus hangs on uncertainty.

Similarly, the question of accountability remains. The Nepali state is yet to function with the interests of the common people. The popular aspirations have been belied by the political leadership despite political upheavals have occurred in the name of the people even leading to the extent of unceremoniously abolishing monarchy by the first meeting of the Constituent Assembly. The crisis that Nepal faces is the case of deliberate dysfunctionality of the governance masqueraded by the politicians with their criminal intents. The CA election that was a fresh start towards the new initiatives for nation building has become meaningless in relation to the popular mandate of drafting constitution to frame Nepal's future. The assembly died after four years of political bickering.

CA was assurdly a peaceful process for democratic consoliodation which unfortunately failed. Popular enthusiasm on constitution making for framing the national future resulted into the greatest disappointment. Constitutional void made governance lose democracy and legitimacy. Democracy in reverse trend thus needs to be arrested. Transition therefore has no end in sight. Vote decides representation but cannot determine accountability, which, in reality, is the defining characteristic of democracy. Democracy does not mean unlimited power to the winner and intimidating rules for personal rulership. Rather it is a system based on the culture of accommodation, sharing, equity, freedom and social justice. The formidable challenge Nepal faces is that of establishing a functioning democracy. Then only the image of the country in despair could change to one of hope.

Economic growth has stagnated in the post-conflict period. Particularly with sagging agricultural and industrial sectors unemployment has increased. Agriculture as an occupation is suffering because the farmers are not the beneficiaries of government policies. Subsidies in agriculture have long vanished; inputs like seeds and fertilizers are scarce, irrigation is beyond reach and monsoon rain unpredictable. And, with the drive of the Nepali youths for foreign employment, farmland is deserted and farming has become an unproductive sector.

Though decrease in the manpower dependency ratio on agriculture is thought to be a significant sign of modernizing economy, Nepal needs a productive agriculture sector to avoid food insecurity and hunger in the course of poverty alleviation programme. The national economy comprises of 35 per cent contribution from agriculture sector on which some 65 per cent people still depend. The 20-years Agriculture Policy formulated and adopted in 1995 is reaching its dead end. The effect however is dwindling of food production and escalating grain imports. The national scenario has changed from Nepal being a grain exporting to a grain importing country. This way, Nepal is financing agriculture development in another country by selling hard earned foreign currency.

On the other hand, enduring political instability and trade union movements have discouraged investment affecting industrial growth and employment opportunities. The intimidating policies of the government and extortionist behaviour of the UCPN (Maoist) have led to closure of several businesses and industries. This is reflected in the fall of the contribution of the industrial sector from 11 to 6 per cent in the national GDP. Economic incentives and infrastructural facility for the entrepreneur are lacking conspicuously. Chronic power shortage destroys the productive capacity of the existing industries. Energy security has not been dealt with sincerely. Already a high cost economy, widening trade imbalance is making Nepal purely an import regime. Though the essence of globalization is actually the export of goods/services and an import of finance/investment, Nepal is oddly at deficit in both aspects of national economy. Nepal has failed in arresting the opportunities provided by the globalization process in utilizing its cheap labour forces domestically by attracting investment capital in productive sectors. This has dented the chance and affected livelihood of people making lives stressful by aggravating social tension. Hence the youth exodus. Hardly are the youths optimistic about their future in the country.

Nepal, thus, has become a deeply troubled state. Despite reported improvements, its social indicators are also not satisfactory; mostly falling behind the South Asian neighbourhood. Economy is plummeting with crumbling infrastructure and with misplaced political priorities the country has dipped into the unprecedented cycle of instability. Economic slump has added further to the fragility of democracy and vulnerability of the people who are poor and numerous in numbers. Pessimism is entrenched in the public psyche. The feeling of betrayal by the political leadership has loosened the faith and depreciated the trust. This makes Nepal a "flailing state" – described as a situation in which indifference, incompetence, and rampant corruption prevails.

The urgency therefore is to strive for changing this bleak national scenario posing crucial challenge to political economy. Maintaining political system needs managing national economy. Expanding productive base to generate employment is a necessity. Reliance on remittance has its own folly. Pouring of foreign aid in the post-conflict situation has done little to improve life of the commoners. Multimillion dollars have been wasted in maintaining and servicing the aid community itself and consultancy services along with phoney projects subcontracted to INGOs and NGOs. Foreign aid has failed in Nepal to help develop inclusive institutions with governments committed to public service and capable of maintaining systemic order. As noted before, foreign aid has encouraged corruption and trivialized the development process in the name of combating poverty in Nepal. Hence, excessive dependence on foreign aid too has its own drawbacks. The problem related to extractive institutions remains, therefore, the scrambling of political parties' for grabbing state power has continued to create political instability.

But economy cannot thrive in the absence of political stability. Central to the problem is the primacy of politics. The risk of social conflict increases without the presence of political order. A rethinking on the adverse situation facing the country is seriously required against the background of the imprints of globalization with market expansion and the movement and mobility of capital in a "borderless world". The poor are the serious casualty of the globalization trend. They are not benefitting from the most liberal economic process and are virtually excluded from equitable distribution of resources by exacerbating poverty and inequality thus aggravating social vulnerability and human insecurity. Human security is the state obligation. This is tied particularly to economic security with welfare provisions. Rising inflation, particularly on uncontrollable food price, has beleaguered the fixed income group and the poor. Fundamental to poverty alleviation, therefore, is the concern for economic development and security. The livelihood problems can no longer be ignored. This can only be made possible or achieved through post-conflict socioeconomic rebuilding along with the state and nation building simultaneously with the market forces. Central to this phenomenon is the state capacity building without which polity cannot be stabilized and policy implemented.

The state capacity has obviously been weakened by its preoccupation on bringing the destabilizing forces to peaceful resolution of conflict. This has been done by appeasing the violent forces at the expense of perusal of strategies crucial to consolidation of peace by addressing humanitarian needs, by delivering public good, restoring rule of law and public security, and confidence building requiring political consensus to address and implement the state restructuring process.

Social inclusion being the real thrust of broaching reform in nation building process raised the need for ingenuous commitment of the national leadership. High expectation on leadership commitment has eventually faltered and distrust and tension replaced the momentum for reform with the result of Constituent Assembly elections. The governments formed after the CA mostly disoriented from functioning as mandated. The coalition governments even lacked intra-party cohesion and functioned as independent authority in ministerial portfolio. The coalition partners are highly motivated by their survival stakes pursued with strategies to strengthen one's powerbase. This has defeated all the fateful strategies of social inclusion, state restructuring and reconstruction processes. The concern therefore is the question: would Nepal stumble further?

There is thus a dismal record of failures of political leadership in the task of delivering even a semblance of hope to the people. Social problems multiplied and intensified with different ethnics holding their fort. Identity assertion in a multicultural society has complicated the national priority setting process leading to indecision and unpredictability in political trajectory. Tearing of social fabric has led to the situation of political anomie. This is the consequence of the popular rejection of the traditional state structure by the people previously denied their rightful role in the bodypolitik.

Demands for the equitable allocation of socioeconomic and political space by the hitherto deprived and marginalized social groups have become the most critical agenda to resolve satisfactorily in order to avert any potential social conflict. The degenerating social cohesion has to be arrested before addressing social inclusion. There is therefore a need to rekindle hope in the minds of people at least with fresh efforts of political leadership by reinforcing their commitment to nation building. The leadership should learn from the past experiences what deserves the policy decision and what makes them click. The leadership should understand that the period of transition is also the period of transformation. Extractive practice and rent seeking would never make a state inclusive.

The changing reality today is that the politics of denial is no more acceptable to those who had previously been exploited and suffered under discriminatory social customs, laws and regulations. The nightmare is now over. They are now agitated and becoming the forces of change. They deserve their rightful place in the society and the state. No more should they be neglected. Without seriously taking the claims of these politically and economically marginalized people societal tensions cannot durably be resolved. The road ahead should be built with their perseverance and craft. Hence the political leadership needs to transcend the petty self-regarding to encompass and integrate hitherto excluded people into the national mainstream by investing a fortune in human capital to save Nepal from catastrophe.

Notes

1. A system of family rule introduced by Jang Bahadur Kunwar Rana after the successful *Kot* massacre in 1846 by snatching *de facto* power from the Nepali Crown. It lasted till 1951. For history see (Adhikari 1984).

2. This is the title of one of the most valuable contributions on Nepalese political economic history by late Mahesh Chandra Regmi's book (Regmi 1978).

Appendix I
Nepal at a glance

Population 2008	29 million	Agriculture Growth	2.3 per cent
Average annual percentage of growth 2000-2008	2 per cent	Population Growth per annum	2.24%
Density of population per sq.km.	200	HDI	0.553
Population age composition 1-14 years (2008)	37 per cent	HPI	32.1 %
Gross National Product (GNP) 2008	11.5 billion (USD)		
GNP per capita 2008	400 USD		
Purchasing Power Parity Gross National Income	32.1 billion (USD)		
PPP per capita 2008	1,120 (USD)		
GDP per capita percentage growth 2007-08	3.6 per cent		
Life expectancy at birth			
Male:	63 (2007)		
Female:	64 (2007)		
Adult Literacy Rate, ages 15 and above	57 per cent (2007)		
Source: "Table 1: Key Indicators of Development," The World Bank, *World Development Report 2010: Development and Climate Change*, Washington DC: World Bank, 2010: 379.		UNDP, *Human Development Report 2009*, New York; Oxford University Press, 2009.	

Variation of estimates from three sources: compare The World Bank, UNDP and NPC, Nepal. The preliminary report of the National Census 2011 conducted by the Central Bureau of Statistics has put the population figure of 26.6 million. If the population growth continues at 2.25 per cent, it will double by at least 48.5 million within next 20 years, the government says.

Appendix II

Human Development by caste and ethnicity with regional divisions, Nepal, 2006

Country/caste/ethnicity	Life expectancy at birth	Adult literacy	Mean years of schooling	Per capita income in PPP US$	Life expectancy index	Educational attainment	Income index	HDI	Ratio to National HDI	Rank
All Nepal	**63.69**	**52.42**	**3.21**	**1597**	**0.645**	**0.421**	**0.4624**	**0.509**	**100.0**	
Caste/Ethnicity										
All Brahman/Chhetri	**62.95**	**63.65**	**4.40**	**2027**	**0.633**	**0.522**	**0.5022**	**0.552**	**108.4**	**5**
Hill Brahman	68.10	69.93	5.40	2395	0.718	0.586	0.5301	0.612	120.1	3
Hill Chhetri	60.61	58.40	3.69	1736	0.594	0.471	0.4763	0.514	100.8	9
Tarai Madhesi Brahman Chhetri	63.89	83.80	6.40	2333	0.648	0.701	0.5257	0.625	122.7	1
Tarai Madhesi Other Caste	**61.94**	**41.85**	**2.30**	**1119**	**0.616**	**0.330**	**0.4031**	**0.450**	**88.3**	**15**
All Dalits	**61.03**	**38.02**	**1.73**	**977**	**0.601**	**0.292**	**0.3804**	**0.424**	**83.3**	**18**
Hill Dalits	60.89	45.50	2.07	1099	0.598	0.349	0.4001	0.449	88.2	16
Tarai/Madhesi Dalits	61.26	27.32	1.21	743	0.604	0.209	0.3348	0.383	75.1	20
Newar	**68.00**	**68.20**	**4.66**	**3097**	**0.717**	**0.558**	**0.5730**	**0.616**	**120.9**	**2**
All Janajati except Newar	**62.91**	**51.67**	**2.96**	**1404**	**0.632**	**0.410**	**0.4410**	**0.494**	**97.1**	**12**
Hill/Mountain Janajati	63.61	53.81	3.05	1490	0.644	0.427	0.4509	0.507	99.5	11
Tarai Janajati	61.55	48.11	2.81	1224	0.609	0.383	0.4180	0.470	92.3	13
Muslim	**60.99**	**30.32**	**1.60**	**890**	**0.600**	**0.238**	**0.3648**	**0.401**	**78.7**	**19**
All Janajati plus Newar	63.33	53.52	3.14	1697	0.693	0.427	0.4726	0.513	100.7	10
All Hill Janajati plus Newar	64.15	56.23	3.31	1869	0.652	0.448	0.4887	0.530	104.0	7
All Hill/Mountain Groups with Newar	63.12	58.47	3.67	1846	0.635	0.471	0.4866	0.531	104.3	6
All Hill/Mountain groups without Newar	62.86	57.75	3.60	1699	0.631	0.465	0.4728	0.523	102.7	8
All Tarai/Madhesi groups with Muslim	61.59	42.34	2.37	1094	0.610	0.335	0.3993	0.448	88.0	17
All Tarai/Madhesi groups without Muslim	61.69	43.74	2.47	1143	0.612	0.346	0.4066	0.455	89.3	14
Others	66.35	57.97	3.70	2227	0.689	0.469	0.5180	0.559	109.7	4

Source: Nepal Human Development Report 2009: 156.

Appendix III

Key Development and MDG Indicators and Their Values of Nepal

Indicator	Value	Year
Population size (in millions)	28.5	2009
Population growth rate (%) (average)	1.28	2009
Life expectancy at birth (years)	63.5	2006
GNI per capita (US$)	476	2007/08P
Real GDP growth rate (%) (average)	5.56	2007/08P
Inflation (%)	6.4	2007/08
Human development index (value) & (rank)	0.534 (142)	2007/8
Percentage of population below national poverty line	25	2009
Percentage of underweight children under five	38.6	2006
Literacy rate (15–24 age) (%)	86.5	2008 from NLFS
Net enrolment rate in primary education (%)	93.7	2009 from MoE
Mortality rate under-fives (per1000 live birth)	50	2009. CHD/DHS
Maternal mortality ratio (per 100,000 live births)	229	2006
Prevalence of HJIV/AIDS in age group 15-49 yrs	0.24	
Proportion of people using wood as their main fuel (%)	68.4	2007
Commercial Energy/GDP (TOE/mRs)	3.7	2007
Area under forest coverage (%)	39.6	2009
Proportion of population with sustainable access to an improved water source, both rural and urban (%)	84.1	2008
Proportion of population with sustainable access to an improved sanitation (toilet), both rural and urban (%)	49.2	2008

Source: Nepal MDG Progress Report 2010, Kathmandu: NPC 2010: 9. Note: CBS Population Census 2011 data put the total population at 26.6 million.

Appendix IV

Ranked according to the overall composite index and poverty and Deprivation index*

Most Developed		Intermediate		Least Developed	
District	Rank	District	Rank	District	Rank
Kathmandu	1 (9)	Makawanpur	26 (26)	Ramechhap	51 (53)
Chitwan	2 (3)	Gulmi	27 (38)	Parsa	52 (43)
Jhapa	3 (1)	Surkhet	28 (24)	Rasuwa	53 (62)
Bhaktapur	4 (12)	Solukhumbu	29 (28)	Kapilbastu	54 (48)
Lalitpur	5 (21)	Banke	30 (16)	Bara	55 (42)
Kaski	6 (4)	Bhojpur	31 (15)	Dadeldhura	56 (52)
Dhankuta	7 (2)	Gorkha	32 (34)	Darchula	57 (59)
Palpa	8 (14)	Taplejung	33 (27)	Siraha	58 (49)
Syngjha	9 (22)	Bardiya	34 (20)	Jajarkot	59 (58)
Manang	10 (25)	Kanchanpur	35 (19)	Rukum	60 (55)
Morang	11 (5)	Nuwakot	36 (29)	Sarlahi	61 (57)
Ilam	12 (6)	Nawalparasi	37 (36)	Baitadi	62 (63)
Rupendehi	13 (11)	Khotang	38 (30)	Dailekh	63 (64)
Sunsari	14 (10)	Okhaldhunga	39 (32)	Rolpa	64 (65)
Kavrepalanchok	15 (18)	Kailali	40 (31)	Mahottari	65 (61)
Tanahu	16 (23)	Dolakha	41 (47)	Doti	66 (66)
Terhathum	17 (13)	Arghakhanchi	42 (50)	Dolpa	67 (69)
Sankhuwasabha	18 (7)	Udayapur	43 (41)	Rautahat	68 (68)
Mustang	19 (33)	Dhading	44 (51)	Jumla	69 (67)
Parbat	20 (39)	Salyan	45 (40)	Kalikot	70 (71)
Dang	21 (8)	Dhanusa	46 (46)	Bajura	71 (72)
Lamjung	22 (35)	Saptari	47 (37)	Achham	72 (74)
Panchthar	23 (17)	Sindhupalchok	48 (60)	Baihang	73 (70)
Baglung	24 (45)	Sindhuli	49 (56)	Humla	74 (73)
Myagdi	25 (44)	Pyuthan	50 (54)	Mugu	75 (75)

Source: *Districts of Nepal: Indicators of Development*, Kathmandu: CBS/ICIMOD/SNV, 2003: 22-24.

* The figure in parenthesis denotes poverty and deprivation ranking.

Appendix V

Joint Statement

KANTIPUR DAILY, 9 JUNE 2010

संयुक्त प्रेस विज्ञप्ती

नेपाल सरकारद्वारा प्राविधिक शिक्षा तथा व्यावसायिक तालिम परिषद् (CTEVT) सञ्चालित, नक्कलसमेतका तराई मधेस भाड जिल्लाका दलित तथा विभिन्न मुसलमान परिवारका छात्रहरूका लागि प्रदान गरिने विशेष सुविधानि कर्णेलम अन्तर्गत मिटएक प्रवेश परीक्षामा उत्तीर्ण छात्रहरूलाई पठनपाठनका लागि बन्दोबस्ती, मिरहा स्थित PQ योग्य प्राविधिक शिक्षालयहरूमा २५ प्रतिशत अ.न.सी. कोटामा भर्ना गर्न पाउने जानकारी प्राप्त भएकोप्रति हाम्रो तीनै संस्थाहरूको गम्भीर ध्यानाकर्षण भएको छ। CTEVT अन्तर्गत क्षेत्रमा राजदेवी टेक्निकल इन्स्टिच्युट रजबिराज र हा घोरेल्स ठाकुर एजुकेशन एकेडेमी लहान मात्र PQ योग्य ठहन्याइको थियो। यिनै इन्स्टिच्युटहरूमा तरीका लागि सम्बन्ध गर्दा प्राविधिक शिक्षा तथा व्यावसायिक तालिम परिषद् चानौठीमी नक्कलपरको मिति २०६७ २६ १९ गते च.न. १४५ को पत्र अनुसार २५ प्रतिशत अ.न.सी. कोटामा भर्ना गर्न नसक्ने भनी उक्त दुवै इन्स्टिच्युटहरूले जानकारी गराएपछि शान्तिपूर्ण कार्य गरेका हौं।

तराई मधेसका दलित तथा विभिन्न मुसलमान समुदायको शैक्षिक तथा व्यावसायिक प्रगतिका लागि सरकारले ल्याएको यस्तो नीति सराहनीय छ। उक्त कार्यक्रम अन्तर्गत भर्ना का लागि सिरहाको प्रवेश परीक्षामा हम्सरी, सिरहा, प्रचुनजालवाच्च धनुषनसिका जिल्लाबाट भएको परीक्षार्थीहरू भाग लिएका थिए। कठिन परिश्रमले समग्रमा एक सत ६२ जना छात्रहरू भर्नाका लागि छनौट समेत भइसकेका छन्। यी विभिन्न तथा भौगोलिक क्षेत्रहरूलाई २५ प्रतिशत अ.न.सी. कोटामा भर्नामा गतिरोध हुनुका लागि CTEVT बाट PQ योग्य ठहन्याइएका यसै क्षेत्रका टेक्निकल इन्स्टिच्युटहरूमा भर्ना र पढनपाठनको व्यवस्था मिल्न हामी भने हाम्री माग गरेका छ।

उक्त २५ प्रतिशत अ.न.सी. कोटाका लागि PQ योग्य घमरी ठहन्याइएका टेक्निकल इन्स्टिच्युटहरू यसै धरामा उल्लेख रहेको अवस्थामा यस क्षेत्रका छात्रहरूलाई असहज वातावरण मध्या हाला का इन्स्टिच्युटहरूमा पढन प्रयास नागाएका हो। नेपाल सरकार शिक्षा मन्त्रालय अन्तर्गत पर्ने CTEVT को मधेसी समुदायलाई सुनिश्ची अवसरबाट वञ्चित गराउने षडयन्त्रको रूपमा लिएका हौं।

सहर सामाजिक परिवेश र आचारणके जिल्लाग PQ एएका टेक्निकल इन्स्टिच्युटहरू उपलब्ध रहेहरूले स्थेसी मूलक रहेका जसा विभिन्न अनुसन्धान समुदायका छात्राहरूलाई कामीजाती जस्तक सामाजिक परिवेश र शहरका इन्स्टिच्युटहरूमा गराहरू उनीहरूलाई भा आर्थिक भार गरी अवसरबाट वञ्चित हुने अवस्था उत्पन्न हुन लागेको छ। गम्भीरतावलेन शिल्त सम्बन्धित पक्षको गम्भीर ध्यानकर्षण गराउन चाहन्छौं। सरक समाई सम्पूर्ण पक्ष तथ्यलाई गम्भीरतापूर्वक लिन आग्रह सम्मत गर्दछौं। हाम्रा माग बेवास्ता गरिए हामी अन्दोलन गर्न बाध्य हुने चेतावनी दिन चाहन्छौं।

दिग्गम्बर रजक   मो. इस्माक   मो. हासिम अन्सारी
(मधेसी दलित विकास महासंघ) (नेपाल मुस्लिम समाज राष्ट्रिय मञ्च) (राष्ट्रिय मुस्लिम मञ्च नेपाल)

(Published in Kantipur Daily, 9 June 2010)

Appendix VI

School: Dhuloma Phool

(Courtesy: Kantipur Daily, 2011)

References

Aasland, Aadne and Marit Haug, 2008. "Social Exclusion in Nepal: Stronger or Weaker?," NIRB *Working Paper 2008:115*, Oslo: Norwegian Institute for Urban and Regional Research.

Acharya, Usha D., 2002. *Primary Education in Nepal: Problems and Prospects*, Kathmandu: Ekta Books.

ADB, 2011. *The Revised Social Protection Index: Methodology and Handbook*, Manila: Asian Development Bank.

ADB, 2010. *The Rise of Asia's Middle Class* (A report prepared by the Asian Development Bank based on the study of 22 developing countries in the Asia Pacific), Manila: Asian Development Bank.

ADDCN, 2001. *Decentralization in Nepal: Prospects and Challenges*, Kathmandu: Association of District Development Committees of Nepal.

Adhikari, Deepak, 2004. "Nepal's Budgetary Exercise During the Nineties: An Assessment," *Economic Review*, No.16, April, (Occasional paper, Nepal Rastra Bank).

Adhikari, Krishna Kant, 1984. *Nepal Under Kang Bahadur, 1846-1877*, vol.1, Kathmandu: BUKU.

Adhikari, Roshan, 2012. "Khana Basnai Dhau Dhau," *Kantipur* Daily, 31 August.

Anderson, Benedict, 1983. *Imagined Communities: Reflections on the Origins and Spread of Nationalism*, London: Verso.

Annapurna Post, 2010a. "Garibi nibaran karyakramprati bishwa bank santushta," 3 June.

Annapurna Post, 2010b. "Uchhastariya rajnitik sanyantrale taya gareko 6 bunde agenda," 15 April.

Ansari, Gani, 2012. "Muslims win battle for identity," *Republica*, 21 May.

Awasthi, Gokarna, 2012. "Sarkarsangha ektihai sahaysatako lekhajokha chhhgaina," *Kantipur* Daily, 29 April.

Awasthi, Gokarna, 2010. "Bikas kharcha nirashajanak," *Kantipur* Daily, 10 June.

Baniya, Balram, 2011. "Thekedarko laparawahile Melamchi surung nirman dhilai," *Kantipur* Daily, 27 September.

Baniya, Balram, 2010. "Khadya dhuwani garna 20 karor maag," *Kantipur* Daily, 12 May.

Baniya, Balram and Abdullah Miya, 2011. "Pahunchawalalai 29 karor bandiyo." *Kantipur* Daily, 10 August.

Bashir, Bashir and Will Kymlicka, 2009. "Introduction: Struggle for Inclusion and Reconciliation in Modern Democracies," in Will Kymlicka and Bashir Bashir, eds., *The Politics of Reconciliation in Multicultural Societies*, Oxford: Oxford University Press.

Bendix, Reinhard, 1964. *Nationbuilding and Citizenship*, New York: John Wiley.

Berger, Mark T., 2006. "From Nationbuilding to Statebuilding," *Third World Quarterly*, 27 (1).

Beteille, Andre, 1999. "Empowerment," *Economic and Political Weekly*, 6-13 March.

Bhalla, Ajit and Frederic Lapeyre, 1997. "Social Exclusion: Towards an Analytical and Operational Framework," *Development and Change*, July.

Bhandari, Kiran, 2011. "Mantri lai jema pani kamishan," *Nagarik* Daily, 28 November.

Bhattachan, Krishna B., 2009. "Discourse on Social Exclusion and Inclusion in Nepal: Old Wine in a New Bottle," in SIRF, *Identity and Society: Social Inclusion and Exclusion in Nepal*, Kathmandu: Mandala Book Point in association with Social Inclusion Research Fund.

Bhattachan, Krishna B., 1997. "Nepalese Perceptions of European Donors' Approaches to Poverty Reduction in Nepal" (Final Report on Comparative Study of European Aid for Poverty Reduction: Collaborative European Research Project, Country Study Nepal, July 31).

Bhattachan, Krishna, Tej Sunar and Yashokanti Bhattachan, 2008. *Nepalma Jatiya Vedbhav* (Caste Discrimination in Nepal), Kathmandu: DNF/NNDSWO/IIDS/IDSN.

Bhattachan, Krishna B. and Sarah Webster, 2005. *Indigenous Peoples, Poverty Reduction and Conflict in Nepal*, (Pro 169), Geneva: International Labour Organization.

Bhattachan, Krishna B., Tek Tamrakar, Yam Bahadur Kisan et.al. 2004. *Dalits' Empowerment and Inclusion for Integration in the National Mainstream: Strategy for Influencing Policy and Institutions*, Kathmandu: Dalit Empowerment and Inclusion Project.

Bhattachan, Krishna B., Kamala Hemchuri, Yogendra Gurung and Chakraman Biswakarma, 2003. *Existing Practices of Caste based Untouchability in Nepal and Strategy for a Campaign for its Elimination*, Kathmandu: ActionAid Nepal.

Bhattachan, Krishna B., and Kailash N. Pyakuryal, 1996. "The Issue of National Integration in Nepal," *Occasional Papers in Sociology and Anthropology*, Kathmandu: Central Department of Sociology and Anthropology, Tribhuvan University.

Bhattarai, Pravat, 2012. "Deshle thegna nasakne bhar," *Himal Khabarpatrika*, 16-30 November.

Bhattarai, Kamal Dev, 2011. "Parties agree to hold local polls late next year," *Kathmandu Post*, 5 December.

Bhattarai, Nimisha and Meena Bhattarai, 2012? "Nepal's Ageing Population: Are we prepared for elderly care?", Nepalnews. com

Bhattarai, Pranav, 2011. "Illicit Financial Flows," *Republica*, 19 June.

Bishankhe, Anjana, 2007. "Naya Sambidhanle Sametanuparne Dalit Mahilaka Sawal," (A paper read at a two-day seminar on Naya Nepalma Dalit Nagrik Sammelan, June 16-17).

Bista, Dor Bahadur, 1991. *Fatalism and Development: Nepal's Struggle for Modernization*, Hyderabad: Orient Longman.

Bista, Dor Bahadur, 1989. "The Structure of Nepali Society," in Kamal P. Malla, ed., *Nepal: Perspective on Continuity and Change*, Kirtipur: Centre for Nepal and Asian Studies.

Bista, Dipendra, 2011. "Karnalibasilai barshama 11din matra rojgari," *Kantipur* Daily, 19 August.

Blaikie, Piers, John Cameron and David Seddon, 1980. *Nepal in Crisis: Growth and Stagnation in the Periphery*, Delhi: Oxford University Press.

Bohara, Rameshowar, 2011. "Nirlajja Loot," *Himal Khabarpatrika*, 18 September-2 October.

Brahimi, Lakhdar, 2007. "State Building in Crisis and Post–Conflict Countries," paper prepared for the 7th Global Forum on Reinventing Government, Vienna, Austria (June 26–29). Available at http://unpan1.un.org/intradoc/groups/public/documents/UN/UNPAN026305.pdf

Brainard, Lael and Derek Chollet, eds. 2007. *Too Poor for Peace? Global Poverty, Conflict, and Security in the 21st Century*, Washington DC: Brookings Institution Press.

Brown, D. and D. Ashman, 1996. "Participation, Social Capital and Intersectoral Problem Solving: African and Asian Cases," *World Development*, 24 (9).

Byman, Daniel, 2000. *Keeping the Peace: Lasting Solutions to Ethnic Conflicts*, Baltimore: Johns Hopkins University Press.

Byrne, David, 2009. *Social Exclusion*, Jaipur: Rawat Publications.

Caplan, Patricia, 1972. *Priests and Cobblers: A Study of Social Change in a Hindu Village in Western Nepal*, Aylesbury: Chandler Publishing Company.

Caplan, Lionel, 1970. *Land and Social Change in East Nepal: A Study of Hindu -Tribal Relation*, Berkeley, CA: University of California Press.

Carothers, Thomas. 2002. "The End of the Transition Paradigm." *Journal of Democracy, 13:1.*

CBS, 2012. *Statistical Year Book Nepal – 2011*, Kathmandu: Central Bureau of Statistics.

CBS, 2011. *Nepal Living Standard Survey 2010/11: Final Report*, Kathmandu: Central Bureau of Statistics.

CBS, et.al 2006. *Resilience Amidst Conflict: An Assessment of Poverty in Nepal 1995-96 and 2003-04*, Kathmandu: CBS/The World Bank/ DFID/ ADB.

Charkavarti, Uma, 2008. "Beyond the Mantra of Empowerment: Time to Return to Poverty, Violence and Struggle," *IDS Bulletin*, 39 (6), December.

Chambers, Robert, 1989. "Vulnerability: How the Poor Cope?," *IDS Bulletin*, 20 (2), April.

Chaudhary, Binod Kumar, 2009. "Aparadh vadhanuma rajyako udasinta," *Kantipur* Daily, 13 July.

Collier, Paul, 2007. *The Bottom Billion: Why the poorest countries are failing and what can be done about it*, Oxford: Oxford University Press.

Collier, David and Steven Levitsky, 1997. "Democracy with Adjectives: Conceptual Innovation in Comparative Research," *World Politics*, 49 (3), April.

Conner, Walker, 1972. "Nation-Building or Nation-Destroying?", *World Politics*, 24 (3), April.

CPA, 2006. "Bistrit Shanti Samjhouta" *Kantipur* Daily, 22 November.

Dahal, Dilli Ram, 2009. "Social Exclusion and Group Mobilization: A Case Study of Yadavs and Tarai Dalits in Dhanusa District," in Social Exclusion and Group Mobilization in Nepal, *Contributions to Nepalese Studies*, Vol. 36, Special Issue.

Dahal, Dilli Ram, 1997. "Is there anything as "Good Governance" in Nepal?" (Paper presented at a Seminar on "Local Self-Government in Nepal" organized by the Political Science Association of Nepal, July).

Dahal, Dilli Ram, 2005. "Democracy and Regionalism: Perspectives from Nepal Tarai," *Nepali Journal of Contemporary Studies*, 5(1).

Dahal, Dilli Ram, 2002. "Madhese Regionalism and National Integration: A Case of the Nepal Tarai," *Nepali Journal of Contemporary Studies*, 2 (1), March.

Dahal, Dilli Ram and Dhruba Kumar, eds., 2009. *Social Exclusion and Group Mobilization*, Kathmandu: Centre for Nepal and Asian Studies (Contributions to Nepalese Studies, Vol.36, Special Issue).

Dahal, Dilli Ram and Bidhan Acharya, 2008. "Socio-Economic and Demographic Perspective: An Analysis of Selected Variables of NDHS 2006 Data by Caste/Ethnicity," *Contributions to Nepalese Studies*, 35(1), January.

Dahal, Dilli Ram, et.al, 2002. *National Dalit Strategy Report*, Kathmandu: Action Aid-Nepal, CARE Nepal, Save the Children.

Dahal, Rajendra, Aychut Adhikari and Kiran Nepal, 2000, "Paisa Ta Chha, Tara Ke Garne?."*Himal Khabarpatrika*, 1-16 September.

Dahl, Robert A., 1971. *Polyarchy: Participation and Opposition*, New Haven, It: Yale University Press.

De Haan, Arjan, 2010. *Towards a New Poverty Agenda in Asia: Social Policies and Economic Transformation*, Los Angeles: SAGE.

De Haan, Aryan, 1998. "Social Exclusion: An Alternative Concept for the Study of Deprivation?," *IDS Bulletin*, 29 (1), January.

DFID, 2004. *Nepal: Country Assistance Plan 2004-2008*, Kathmandu: Department for International Development.

Delanty, Gerard, 2000. *Citizenship in a Global Age: Society, Culture, Politics*, Buckingham: Open University Press.

Deshantar Weekly, 2007. "Sarkar ra Madheshi Janaadhikar Forumbich bhayeko samjhouta," 2 September (Document).

EIU, 2011. *Nepal: Country Report*, London: Economic Intelligence Unit, May.

EIU 2010a. *Democracy Index 2010: Democracy in Retreat*, (A Report from the Economic Intelligence Unit), London: Economist Intelligence Unit. www.eiu.com/democracyindex (accessed 17 January 2011).

EIU, 2010b. *Nepal: Country Report*, London: Economic Intelligence Unit, May.

Ferguson, Niall, 2006. *The War of the World: Twentieth Century Conflict and the Descent of the West*, New York: Penguin Books.

Fukuyama, Francis, 2004. *Statebuilding: Governance and World Order in the 21st Century*, Ithaca, NY: Cornell University Press.

FWLD, 2000. *Discriminatory Laws in Nepal and their Impact on Women: A review of the current situation and proposals for change*, Kathmandu: Forum for Women, Law and Development (FWLD), August.

Gaige, Frederick H., 1975. *Regionalism and National Unity in Nepal*, Berkeley, CA: University of California Press.

Galtung, Johan, 1969. "Violence, Peace and Peace Research," *Journal of Peace Research*, 6 (3), August.

Gautam, Bimal, 2011. "Taskforce urges daily hearings to clear graft case backlog," *Republica*, 29 September.

Ghimire, Kalpana, 2012. "70 pratishat Balbalikama kuposhan," *Kantipur* Daily, 26 September.

GON 2011. "Budget Speech, Fiscal Year 2011-2012," (Presented by Hon'ble Finance Minister Bharat Mohan Adhikari at the legislative parliament of the Constituent Assembly on 15 July).

GON, 2010. *Statement Delivered by Finance Minister Mr. Surendra Pandey in the Legislature-Parliament of the Constituent Assembly on 12 July 2010 Regarding the Special Arrangement for Revenue and Expenditure for the Fiscal Year 2010-11*, Singha Darbar: Ministry of Finance.

GON, 2009a. "Budget Speech, Fiscal Year 2009-2010," (Presented by the Hon'ble Finance Minister Surendra Pandey at the legislative parliament of the Constituent Assembly on 13 July).

GON, 2009b. "Policy and Programme of the Government of Nepal," (Presented by Rt. Hon'ble President Dr. Ram Baran Yadav at the legislative-parliament of the Constituent Assembly on 9 July).

GON, 2009c. *Progress Report of Sector Ministries, Fiscal Year 2008/09*, Kathmandu: Government of Nepal, Ministry of Finance.

GON, 2008. "Budget Speech, Fiscal Year 2008/09," (Presented by Hon'ble Finance Minister Dr. Baburam Bhattarai at the legislative-parliament of the Constituent assembly on 19 September).

GON, 2007. "Budget Speech, Fiscal Year 2007/08," (Presented by Hon'ble Finance Minister Dr. Ram Saran Mahat to the legislative-parliament formed in accordance to the Interim Constitution 2007)

GON, 2006. "Budget Speech, Fiscal Year 2006/07," (Presented by Hon'ble Finance Minister Dr. Ram Saran Mahat to the parliament restored after the success of the Jana Andolan-II).

Gorkhapatra, 1998. 16 May.

Gurung, Harka, 2007. "From Exclusion to Inclusion," in SIRF, 2007. *From Exclusion to Inclusion: Socio-Political Agenda for Nepal*, Lalitpur: Social Inclusion Research Fund.

Gurung, Harka, 2006. "Social Inclusion and Nation Building in Nepal," (Paper presented at the Civil Society Forum Workshop for Research Programme on "Social Inclusion and Nation Building in Nepal" organized by Social Inclusion research fund/ SNV in Kathmandu on 13 February).

Gurung, Harka, 2003. *Trident and Thunderbolt: Cultural Dynamics in Nepali Politics*, (The Mahesh Chandra Regmi Lecture -2003), Lalitpur: Social Science Baha.

Gurung, Harka, Malla K. Sundar, Krishna B. Bhattachan and Om Gurung, 2004. *Development of Nationalities – A Strategy Paper*,

Kathmandu: Nationalities Development and Coordination Centre.

Gyawali, Balkrishna, 2012. "Daliamilomatoma ek arba bandidai," *Nagarik*, 22 April.

Gyawali, Krishna, 2012. "Kaha pokhindaichha sthaniya budget?" *Kantipur* Daily, 2 June.

Gyawali, Krishna, 2012b. "Saptarima pani 30 karod aniyamitata." *Kantipur* Daily, 29 November.

Gyawali, Krishna, 2010. "Badhyo atmahatya," *Kantipur* Daily, 11 September.

Hachhethu, Krishna, 2009. "Social Exclusion and Nepali Muslim: A Case Study of Banke District," in Social Exclusion and Group Mobilization in Nepal, *Contributions to Nepalese Studies*, Vol.36, (Special Issue).

Hancock, Graham, 1989. *Lords of Poverty: The Power, Prestige and Corruption of the International Aid Business*, New York: The Atlantic Monthly Press.

Harsh, Matthew, Paul Mbatia and Wesley Shrum, 2010. "Accountability and Inaction: NGOs and Resource Lodging in Development," *Development and Change*, 41 (2), March.

Haq, Mahbub ul, 1996. *Reflections on Human Development*, Delhi: Oxford University Press.

Haug, Marit, Aadne Aasland, 2009. "A review of the Academic and Policy Debate on "Social Exclusion" in Europe and Its relevance to Nepal," in Social Exclusion and Group Mobilization in Nepal, *Contributions to Nepalese Studies*, Vol. 36, Special Issue.

Haug, Marit, Aadne Aasland and Dilli Ram Dahal, 2009. "Patterns of Socio-Political Participation in Nepal and Implications for Social Inclusion," *Forum for Development Studies*, 36 (1).

Himal Khabarpatrika, 2011. "Gundatantra." 1-17 August.

Hippler, J., ed., 2005. *Nation-Building: A Key Concept of Peaceful Conflict Transformation?*, London: Pluto Press.

HMG/UNDP, 2005. *Nepal Millennium Development Goals: Progress Report*, Kathmandu: National Planning Commission and United Nations.

HMG/MOH, 2004. Nepal Health Sector Programme – Implementation Plan 2004- 2009, Kathmandu: Ministry of Health, October.

HMG/NPC/MOPE, 2003. *Sustainable Development Agenda for Nepal*, Kathmandu: National Planning Commission and Ministry of Population and Environment.

HMG/NPC, 2001. *Report on the Situation of Women, Children and Households: Between Census Household Information, Monitoring and Evaluation System (BCHIMES), March-May 2000*, Kathmandu: National Planning Commission Secretarial.

Huntington, Samuel P., 1996. *The Clash of Civilizations and Remaking of the World Order*, New York: Simon & Schuster.

Huntington, Samuel P., 1993. "The Clash of Civilizations?," *Foreign Affairs*, 72 (3), Summer.

ICIMOD, 2003. *Districts of Nepal: Indicators of Development*, Kathmandu: International Centre for Integrated Mountain Development/ Central Bureau of Statistics/ SNV-Nepal.

IC, 2009. *Nepalko Antarim Sambidhan 2063 (2007)*, Kathmandu: Jana-Pragatishil Prakashan.

IDA, 2010. *Treading Water? Security and Justice in Nepal in 2009*, Kathmandu: Interdisciplinary Analysts and Saferworld.

IIDS, 2004. *Foreign Aid Utilization at the Grassroots Level*, (A Draft report submitted to the South Asia Network of Economic Research Institute), Kathmandu: Institute for Integrated Development Studies (IIDS).

Ka. Mukunda et al, 2005. Naya Chetna: Jana Sachhayarata Pustak, Rolpa: Chetriya Janashichhya Bivag, Kendriya Adhar Ilaka, CPN (Maoist).

Kabeer, Naila, 2006. "Poverty, Social Exclusion and the MDGs: The Challenge of 'Durable inequalities' in the Asian Context," *IDS Bulletin*, 37 (3), May.

Kaini, Prabha Devi, 2009. "Reserved Seats for Women in Politics: Right Way for Inclusion," (Paper presented at a seminar on "Social Inclusion Policies in South Asian States" organized by CNAS/SIRF/SNV-Nepal in Kathmandu, 25-27 June).

Kanbur, Ravi and Andy Sumner, 2011. "Poor Countries or Poor People? Development Assistance and the New Geography of Global Poverty," February 3, kanbur.dyson.cornell.edu/... (accessed on 31 August 2011).

Kantipur, 2012a. "72 lakh gariblai parichayapatra diyinea," 12 September.

Kantipur, 2012b. "Garibi nivaran kosh ka upadhachhya ko rajinama," 28 December.

Kantipur, 2011. "Shichhyakko padonnati rokiyo," 9 October.

Kantipur, 2011. "Aspatal pugne sadhya pani birami hunchan: Mahato," 24 September.

Kantipur, 2011. "Ajhai 61 pratisata nirachhyar," 8 September, (International Literacy Day).

Kantipur, 2011. "Aarthasachibko rajinamale hulchal," 31 March.

Kantipur, 2011. "Rojgarko pramukh gantabya Qatar," 23 February.

Kantipur, 2010. "Dui ghantama ek Nepalidwara atmahatya,", 7 July.

Kantipur, 2010. "Garibi nibaranma hune kharcha sadupayog bhayena," 27 January.

Karelis, Charles, 2007. *the Persistence of Poverty: Why the Economics of the Well-Off Can't Help the Poor*, New Delhi: Oxford University Press.

Kathmandu Post, 2011. "Four Doctors per 100,000 people," 11 December.

Kathmandu Post, 2010. "Women still subject to torture," 5 December.

Kathmandu Post, 2010. "Stop health aid, CIIA tells govt.," 1 June.

Kathmandu Post, 2008. "Nepal's average monthly household income Rs 27, 391," 20 August.

Kathmandu Post, Edit. 1998. "Blame it on corruption," 18 November.

KC, Durga Lal, 2010. "Hinshapidit mahila nyayabata banchit," *Kantipur* Daily, 9 June.

Khanal, Rameshore Prasad, 2009. "Transformation of Nepal's Economy: Agenda for Growth and Social Equity," (A Draft for Discussion at the Nepal Development Forum Stakeholders' Consultation Meeting, 16 April).

Khadka, Amar, 2010. "Maobadiko kamando toli," 15 April.

Krasner, Stephen, 2005. "The Case for Shared Sovereignty," *Journal of Democracy*, 16 (1).

Kumar, Dhruba, 2011. "At Peace but Insecure: The Nepali State in Quandary," (Paper presented at the International Conference on *Changing Dynamics in Nepali Society and Politics*, jointly organized by Alliance for Social Dialogue, Association for Nepal and Himalayan Studies, and Social Science *Baha* at Hotel Shankar, Kathmandu, 17-19 August 2011).

Kumar, Dhruba, 2010. "Challenges to Democratic Control of Armed Forces in Nepal," in Rajan Bhattarai and Geja Sharma Wagle, eds. *Emerging Security Challenges of Nepal*, Kathmandu: Nepal Institute for Policy Studies.

Kumar, Dhruba, 2009. "Encountering Marginality: Social Exclusion of Hill Dalits in Surkhet District," *Contributions to Nepalese Studies*, 36 (Special Issue).

Kumar, Dhruba, 2008a. *Nepali State, Society and Human Security: An Infinite Discourse*, Dhaka: University Press Ltd.

Kumar, Dhruba, 2008b. "Obstacles to Local Leadership and Democracy in Nepal," in David N. Gellner and Krishna Hachhethu, eds. *Local Democracy in South Asia: Microprocesses of Democratization in Nepal and Its Neighbours*, New Delhi: Sage Publications.

Kumar, Dhruba, 2007. "Politics of Contempt, Casualty and Culpability," (A paper presented at an International Seminar on "Constitutionalism and Diversity in Nepal" Organized by Centre for Nepal and Asian Studies, Tribhuvan University in collaboration with MIDEA Project and ESP-Nepal 22-24 August).

Kunwar, Sunjuli, 2011. "Confronting realities in Jumla," *Republica*, 9 November.

Kymlicka, Will and Bashir Bashir, eds., 2009. *The Politics of Reconciliation in Multicultural Societies*, Oxford: Oxford University Press.

LDM, 1995. *Afno Gaun Afai Banau Karyakram Karyawayan Nirdeshika 2051* (The Directives for Implementing Build Your Village Yourself Programme): HMG/Local Development Ministry.

Lemay-Hebert, Nicolas, 2009. "Statebuilding without Nationbuilding? Legitimacy, State Failure and the Limits of Institutionalist Approach," *Journal of Intervention and Statebuilding*, 30 (1).

LFP, 2005. *Pro-Poor and Social Inclusion Strategy*, Kathmandu: Livelihoods and Forestry Programme, December.

Lohani, Prakash Chandra, 2011. "Rajya punrasanrachanama utheka kehi prashna," *Kantipur* Daily, 8 April.

Lohani, Prakash Chandra and Bal Gopal Vaidya, 2009. "Samabeshikaran garinuparne samudayako pahichan" *Kantipur* Daily, 11 August.

Lohani, Gunaraj, et al., 2005. *Hamro Kitab, Kachhya-1*, Rolpa: Janashichhya Bivag, Kendriya Adhar Ilaka ra Bheri-Karnali Chhetra, CPN (Maoist).

MacLaughlin, Jim, 2001. *Reimagining the Nation-State: The Contested Terrains of Nation-Building*, London: Pluto Press.

Mahat, Sujeet, 2011. "Aarthalai cholera swathabata sahayata," *Kantipur* Daily, 31 August.

Majorano, Francesca, 2007. "An Evaluation of the Rural Microfinance Development Centre as a Wholesale Lending Institution in Nepal," (Asian Development Bank Working Paper Series No.8, online version: http://www.adb.org/Documents/Papers/NRM/wp8.pdf).

Malena, Carmen, 2000. "Beneficiaries, Mercenaries, Missionaries and Revolutionaries," *IDS Bulletin*, July.

Malla, K. Sundar, Keshav Man Shakya and Arjun Limbu, 2005. *Rajyako Pursanrachana: Adibashi Janajati Dristikon* (Presented as political proposal at a National Conference organized by the Janajati Empowerment Project, National Federation for Indigenous Nationalities, 28-29 August).

Manandhar, Rajendra, 2010 "Allowance doled out to fictional persons," *Kathmandu Post*, 5 December.

Marsden, Ruth, 2006. "Exploring Power and Relationships: A Perspective from Nepal," in Leslie Groves and Rachel Hinton, eds., *Inclusive aid: Changing Power and Relationships in International Development*, London: Earthscan.

Mellor, John W., 1999. "Why has Foreign Aid been So Ineffective in Reducing Poverty," *Policy Dialogue*, Kathmandu: HMG/Ministry of Agriculture/Winrock International.

Micklethwait, John, 2011. "Taming Leviathan," *The Economist*, 19-25 March.

Mihaly, Eugene B., 1965. *Foreign Aid and Politics in Nepal: A Case Study*, Oxford: Oxford University Press.

Miya, Abdullah, 2011. "Sabhasadle Kurshi Phyke," *Kantipur* Daily, 2 April.

MoD, 2010. "Report of the Taskforce on Democratization of the Army and Security Sector Reform Recommendation Committee", (Submitted to the Prime Minister Madhav Kumar Nepal by the Defence Minister Ms Vidhya Bhandari as a

Convenor of the six-member Taskforce on BS 2067-4-17-2 [31 July 2010AD]).

MoF, 2012. *Economic Survey: Fiscal Year 2011/12, Vol. I*, Kathmandu: Ministry of Finance, July.

MoF, 2010a. *Budget Speech, Fiscal Year 2010/11* (Red Book), Kathmandu: Ministry of Finance.

MoF, 2010b. *Economic Survey: Fiscal Year 2009/10, Vol. I*, Kathmandu: Ministry of Finance, July.

MoF, 2007. *Economic Survey: Fiscal Year 2006/07*, Kathmandu: Ministry of Finance, July.

MoF, 2003. *Public Statement on Income and Expenditure of the Fiscal Year 2003-2004*, Kathmandu: Ministry of Finance.

Nepal, Kiran, 2011. "Report, Arthasachibko rajinama: Jiuda muktinath," *Himal Khabarpatrika*, 14-28 April.

NESAC, 1998. *Nepal: Human Development Report 1998*, Kathmandu: Nepal South Asia Centre.

Neupane, Govinda, 2000. *Nepalko Jatiya Prashna: Samajik Banote ra Sajhedariko Sambhavana*, Kathmandu: Centre for Development Studies.

NPC, 2010a. *Nepal Millennium Development Goals: Progress Report*, Kathmandu: National Planning Commission, Government of Nepal, Singha Darbar. January.

NPC, 2010b. *Three Year Plan Approach Paper 2010/11-2012/13*. Kathmandu: National Planning Commission, Government of Nepal.

NPC, 2007. *Three Years Interim Plan 2007/08-2009/10*, Kathmandu: National Planning Commission, Government of Nepal, Singha Darbar.

NPC, 2005. *An Assessment of the Implementation of the Tenth Plan (PRSP)*, (Second Progress Report: On the Road to Freedom from Poverty), Kathmandu: HMG/National Planning Commission Secretariat, Singha Darbar.

NPC, 2003. *The Tenth Plan: Poverty Reduction Strategy Paper, 2002-2007*, Kathmandu: HMG/ National Planning Commission Secretariat, Singha Barbar.

NPC, 2002. *The Tenth Five Year Plan 2002-2007*, Kathmandu: HMG/ National Planning Commission Secretariat, Singha Barbar.

NPC, 1998. *The Ninth Plan 1997-2002*, Kathmandu: HMG/National Planning Commission Secretariat, Singha Darbar.

OECD, 2010. *Do No Harm: International Support for Statebuilding*, Paris: Organization for Economic Cooperation and Development.

Onta, Pratyoush, 1996a. "Creating a Brave Nepali Nation in British India: The Rhetoric of *Jati* Improvement, Rediscovery of Bhanubhakta and the Writing of *Bir* History," *Studies in Nepali History and Society*, 1 (1).

Onta, Pratyoush, 1996b. "Ambivalence Denied: The Making of *Rastriya Itihas* in Panchayat Era Textbooks," *Contributions to Nepalese Studies*, 23 (1).

Onta, Pratyoush, 1994. "Rich Possibilities: Notes on Social History in Nepal," *Contributions to Nepalese Studies*, 21 (1).

OPHI, 2010. *Country Briefing: Multidimensional Poverty Index (MPI) At a Glance*, Oxford: Oxford Department of International Development, Queen Elizabeth House, University of Oxford, July. http://ophi.qeh.ox.ac.uk www.ophi.org.uk

Oxford, 2005. *Advanced Learner's Dictionary*, Oxford: Oxford University Press.

PAF, 2009. *Poverty Alleviation Fund Nepal, Annual Report 2007/08*, Kathmandu: Poverty Alleviation Fund, Nepal.

Panday, Devendra Raj, 1999. *Nepal's Failed Development: Reflections on the Missions and the Maladies*, Kathmandu: Nepal South Asia Centre.

Pande, Sriram Raj, Shawna Tropp, Bikas Sharma and Yuba Raj Khatiwada, eds. 2006. *Nepal: Readings in Human Development*, Kathmandu: United Nations Development Programme.

Pandey, Binda, 2012. " Naya pustale chyama dine chhaina," *Kantipur Daily*, 15 May.

Pandey, Tula Ram, Jaya Bahadur Rokaya, Raj Bahadur Shahi and Bishnu Lal Budha, 2011. "Karnalima Gaisasa: Dherai lagani, thorai pratifal," *Kantipur* Daily, 25 June.

Pandey, Dipak, 2009. "Jandajaandai Arabouko Durupayog," *Dristi* Weekly, 20 May.

Pant, 2011, "Dinhu mahila hinsaka ujuri," *Kantipur* Daily, 3 August.

Petras, James, 1999. "NGOs in the Service of Imperialism," *Journal of Contemporary Asia*, 29 (4).

Pokharel, Santosh, 2010. "Bhoko petma Karnaliko shichhaya," *Nagarik* Daily, 5 December.

Pokharel, Hem Sharma, 2004. "Overall Perspective of His Majesty's Government of Nepal for Mainstreaming Dalit," (Paper presented at the International Consultation on Caste-based Discrimination, 29 November – 1 December 2004, Kathmandu, Nepal, jointly organized by DNF/Nepal and IDSN).

Pokharel, Jagadish Chandra, 2004. "International Assistance and Inclusion of Dalits," (Paper presented at the International Consultation on Caste-based Discrimination, 29 November – 1 December 2004, Kathmandu, Nepal, jointly organized by DNF/ Nepal and IDSN).

Poudel, Anmolmani, 2011a. "Vidhyalaya hastantran niti trutipurna," *Kantipur* Daily, 2 August.

Poudel, Anmolmani, 2011b. "School pathyapustakma 73 caror hinamina," *Kantipur* Daily, 5 July.

Pradhan, Bina, 2006. "Gender and Human Development," in Sriram Raj Pande, et al. eds., *Nepal: Readings in Human Development*, Kathmandu: United Nations Development Programme.

Pradhan, Rajendra and Ava Shrestha, 2005. *Ethnic and Caste Diversity: Implications for Development,* (Working Paper Series No.4, Nepal Resident Mission), Kathmandu: Asian Development Bank.

Pyakuryal, Bishwambher, 2010. "Nepalese Economy: Structure, Trend, Constraints and Prospects," (Power Point presentation at the CIG Consultant's Seminar, Adam Smith International, Hotel Raddison, Kathmandu, 13 June).

Pyakuryal, Bishwambher, 2009. "Economic and Social Impact of Financial Crisis on Households," (Prepared for Asian Development Bank/Pakistan Institute of Development Economics, Karachi, 25 October).

Pyakuryal, Bishwambher, et al. 2009. *Fiscal Management and Revenue sharing in the Federal State of Nepal,* Kathmandu: Nepal Economic Association.

Rai, Usha Kala, 2012. "Aitihasik kathgharama neta,", *Kantipur* Daily, 8 May.

Rawal, Ram Bahadur, "64 arba swaha!," *Nepal* Weekly, 28 August.

Regmi, Mahesh C, 1995. *Kings and Political Leaders of Gorkhali Empire 1768-1814,* Hyderabad: Orient Longman.

Regmi, Mahesh C., 1978. . *Thatched Huts and Stucco Palaces: Peasants and Landlords in 19th Century Nepal*, New Delhi: Vikas Publishing House.

Republica, 2010. "Huge leakage in anti-poverty program: PM", 25 January.

Rising Nepal, 1998. 24 July.

Rubio-Marin, Ruth, 2009. "Gender and Collective Reparation in the Aftermath of Conflict and Political Repression," in Will Kymlicka and Bashir Bashir, eds., *The Politics of Reconciliation in Multicultural Societies*, Oxford: Oxford University Press.

Sachs, Jeffrey, 2006. *The End of Poverty: How We Can Make It Happen in Our Lifetime*, London: Penguin Books.

Sah, Tulanarayan, 2010. "Vikas bujet neta ra karmacharibich baandchund," *Kantipur* Daily, 5 September.

Sayapatri, Madhav, 2011. " Samudayik vidhyalayako sankat," *Nagarik* Daily, 9 November.

Seddon, David, 1987. *Nepal: A State of Poverty*, New Delhi: Vikas Publishing House.

Sen, Amartya, 2006. *Identity and Violence: The Illusion of Destiny*, New York: W.W. Norton.

Sen, Amartya, 2000a, *Development as Freedom*, New Delhi: Oxford University Press.

Sen, Amartya, 2000b. "Social Exclusion: Concept, Application and Scrutiny," (Social Development Paper No. 1., Office of Environment and Social Development), Manila: Asian development Bank.

Shah, Shree Govind, 2006. "Social Inclusion of Madheshi Community in Nation Building," (Paper presented at the Civil Society Forum Workshop for Research Programme on "Social Inclusion and Nation Building in Nepal" organized by Social Inclusion Research Fund/SNV in Kathmandu on 13 February).

Sharma, Rajan 2000. "Melamchiko Lagat Pheri Badhyo, Ayojana Ekbarsha Dhilai," *Deshantar* Weekly, 6 August.

Sharma, Pitamber, 2006. "Introduction to Human Development," in Sriram Raj Pande, Shawna Tropp, Bikas Sharma and Yuba Raj Khatiwada, eds. 2006. *Nepal: Readings in Human Development*, Kathmandu: United Nations Development Programme.

Shetty, Salil, 2005. "Can a Rights-based Approach Help in Achieving the Millennium Development Goals?," *IDS Bulletin*, 36 (1), January.

Shrestha, Damber Krishna, 2010. "Pahichan ra Pratistha Chumdai," *Himal Khabarpatrika*, 14-23 March.

Shrestha, Nanda R., 1990. *Landlessness and Migration in Nepal*, Boulder, CO: Westview Press.

Shrestha, Sangeeta, 2008. "Bajhangko Serophero," *Kantipur Daily*, 1 July.

Shucksmith, Mark, 2000. "Endogenous development, social capital and social inclusion: perspective from LEADER in the UK," *Sociologica Ruralis 2000* – huss.ex.ac.uk (accessed on 11 April 2010).

Sigdel, Kamal Raj, 2009. "Laws riddle with errors," *Kathmandu Post*, 18 September.

Singh, Bhim Bahadur, 2011. "Mahila hinsa badhyo," *Kantipur Daily*, 8 August.

SIRF, 2009. *Identity and Society: Social Inclusion and Exclusion in Nepal*, Kathmandu: Mandala Book Point in association with Social Inclusion Research Fund.

SIRF, 2007. *From Exclusion to Inclusion: Socio-Political Agenda for Nepal*, Lalitpur: Social Inclusion Research Fund.

Stiller, Ludwig F., 1975. *The Rise of the House of Gorkha*, Kathmandu: Ratna Pustak Bhandar.

Subba, Chaitanya, 2008. "Samajik Nyaya ra Samabeshikaran" (A paper presented at a Seminar Organized by NCCS at Hotel Himalaya, Kupandol, on 20 December).

Sumner, Andy, 2012. "Where Do The world's Poor Live?: A New Update," *IDS Working Paper* 393, Sussex: Institute of Development Studies, June.

Sumner, Andy, 2010. "Global Poverty and the New Bottom Billion: What if Three-Quarters of the World's Poor live in Middle-Income Countries?." *Working Paper No.74*, Sussex: Institute of Development Studies/International Policy Centre for Inclusive Growth, November.

Takahatake, Takashi and Keshav Lal Maharjan, 2002. "An Examination of the Socio-Economic Implications of Microfinance Programs: An Alternative Approach in Nepal," *Contributions to Nepalese Studies*, January.

Text of Memorandum presented to Prime Minister Girija P. Koirala by a Group of Donors representing an overwhelming majority of donor agencies working in Nepal as Nepal's Development Partners, 1998, 15 May.

Thapa, Kamal, 2010. "Thahai napai vidhayala bharna abhiyan sakiyo," *Nagarik* Daily, 21 May.

The Economist, 2011. "Inequality: Unbottled Gini," 22 January.

Tiwari, Madhu Nidhi, 2009. "Sabai lai sametne, rastriya ekata baliyo parne" (All encompassing for strengthening national unity), *Himal Khabarpatrika*, 15-29 May.

Tiwari, Bishwa Nath, 2006. *Readings in the Millennium Development Goals: Challenges for Attaining MDGs in Nepal*, Kathmandu: Department of Economics, Tribhuvan University.

Toba, Sueyoshi, 1992. *Language Issue in Nepal*, Kathmandu: Samdan Books.

UNDP 2010. *Human Development Report 2010, The Real Wealth of Nations: Pathways to Human Development 2010*, New York: Palgrave Macmillan for United Nations Development Programme.

UNDP, 2009. *Nepal: Human Development Report 2009: State Transformation and Human Development*, Kathmandu: United Nations Development Programme.

UNDP, 2004. *Nepal: Human Development Report 2004: Empowerment and Poverty Reduction*, Kathmandu: United Nations Development Programme.

UNDP, 2004. *Human Development Report 2004: Cultural Liberty in Today's Diverse World*, New Delhi: Oxford University Press.

UNDP, 2002. *Nepal Human Development Report 2001: Poverty Reduction and Governance*, Kathmandu: United Nations Development Programme.

UNDP, 1994. *Human Development Report 1994*, New Delhi: Oxford University Press for United Nations Development Programme.

USIP, 2011. *Calling for Security and Justice in Nepal: Citizens' Perspective on the Rule of Law and the Role of Nepal Police*, Kathmandu: United States Institute of Peace.

Vera-Sanso, Penny, 2008. "Whose Money Is It? On Misconceiving Female Autonomy and Economic Empowerment in Low-Income Households," *IDS Bulletin*, 39 (6), December.

Wagle, Mana Prasad, 2011. "Gundpak, Mantralaya ra Shichhaya," *Kantipur* Daily, 12 September.

Wetherell, Margaret, Michelynn Lafleche and Robert Berkeley, eds. 2007. *Identity, Ethnic Diversity and Community Cohesion*, Los Angeles: SAGE Publications.

Wetherell, Margaret, 2007. "Introduction: Community Cohesion and Identity Dynamics: Dilemmas and Challenges," in Margaret Wetherell et al, eds. 2007. *Identity, Ethnic Diversity and Community Cohesion*, Los Angeles: SAGE Publications.

WHO, 1995. *Bridging the Gaps*, Geneva: World Health Organization.

Wolfensohn, James, 2000. "Address to the United Nations Security Council on HIV/AIDs in Africa", 10 January, World Bank News release 2000/172/8.

World Bank, 2012. *World Development Report, 2012: Gender Equality and Development*, Washington DC: The World Bank.

World Bank, 2011. *World Development Report, 2011: Conflict, Security and Development*, Washington DC: The World Bank.

World Bank, 2005. *World Development Report 2006: Equity and Development*, New York: Oxford University Press for the World Bank.

World Bank, 2004. *Nepal: Country Assistance Strategy, 2004-2007*, Kathmandu: The World Bank.

World Bank, 2000. *World Development Report 2000/2001: Attacking Poverty*, Washintgton DC: The World Bank.

World Bank, 1997. *World Development Report 1997: The State in a Changing World*, Washington DC: The World Bank.

World Bank, 1991. *Assistance Strategies to Reduce Poverty*, Washington DC: The World Bank.

World Bank, 1990. *World Development Report 1990*, Washington DC: The World Bank.

World Bank Group, 2008. *Aid Architecture: An Overview of the Main Trends in Official Development Assistance Flows*, Washington DC: World Bank Group, 2008: 19. http://siteresources. worldbank.org/IDA/Resources/Aid_Architecture-May2008. pdf. (Retrieve 27 September 2010).

World Bank/DFID, 2006. *Unequal Citizens: Gender, Caste and Ethnic Exclusion in Nepal*, (Summary), Kathmandu: World Bank/ DFID.

Yadav, Ram Prakash. 2006. "Madeshi: A Disadvantaged Social Group," *The Organisation Quarterly*, Vol. 9 (2), April-June.

Yadav. Ram Prakash, 2005. *Caste /Ethnic Representation at Policy Making Level in Nepal*, Lalitpur: Nepal Centre for Contemporary Studies.

Yadav, Yogendra P. 2009. "Linguistic Diversities in Nepal: Situation and Policy Planning," in SIRF, *Identity and Society: Social Inclusion and Exclusion in Nepal*, Kathmandu: Mandala Book Point in association with Social Inclusion Research Fund.

Zaum, Dominik, 2007. *The Sovereignty Paradox: The Norms and Politics of International Statebuilding*, Oxford: Oxford University Press.

Index